AR11³⁵ QCB

7⁵⁰

Palestinians
and Israel

Y. Harkabi

Palestinians and Israel

A HALSTED PRESS BOOK

JOHN WILEY & SONS, New York • Toronto
ISRAEL UNIVERSITIES PRESS, Jerusalem

ISRAEL UNIVERSITIES PRESS
is a publishing division of
KETER PUBLISHING HOUSE JERUSALEM LTD.
P.O. Box 7145, Jerusalem, Israel

Published in the Western Hemisphere by
HALSTED PRESS, a division of
JOHN WILEY & SONS, INC., NEW YORK

Library of Congress Cataloging in Publication Data

Harkabi, Yehoshafat, 1921–
    Palestinians and Israel.

    "A Halsted Press book."
    Consists of a selection of the author's articles,
mostly translated from Hebrew, published 1967–1974.
    1. Jewish-Arab relations—Addresses, essays, lec-
tures.   2. Fedayeen—Addresses, essays, lectures.
I. Title.
DS119.7.H37544 1975   327.5694′017′4927   74–23800
ISBN 0–470–35211–6

Distributors for Japan, Southeast Asia and India
TOPPAN COMPANY LTD., TOKYO AND SINGAPORE

Distributed in the rest of the world by
KETER PUBLISHING HOUSE JERUSALEM LTD.
IUP cat. no. 26002
ISBN 0 7065 1423 8

Set, printed and bound by Keterpress Enterprises, Jerusalem
PRINTED IN ISRAEL

Contents

Italicized dates in parentheses indicate dates of first publication

v

Preface

Professor Yehoshafat Harkabi, of the Departments of International Relations and Middle Eastern Studies at the Hebrew University of Jerusalem, is an internationally known expert on the Arab-Israel conflict and has published several books and articles on the subject. He is one of the first Israeli academics whose research has been devoted mainly to the study of this conflict.

Born in Haifa, he graduated (M.A.) from the Hebrew University in Philosophy and Arabic Literature in 1947. In 1949 he was sent as an Israeli delegate to the Rhodes Armistice Negotiations. He later served as deputy-chief (1950–55) and then chief (1955–59) of Army Intelligence of the Israel Defense Forces. He continued his studies at Harvard University, where he took a master's degree in Public Administration.

Palestinians and Israel is a selection of articles, mostly translated from Hebrew, on the general nature of the Arab-Israel conflict, and in particular on the role of the Palestinians. These articles were written at different times and should be viewed against their historical background. In writing them the author was chiefly concerned with an Israeli audience, convinced as he is of the importance of Israelis learning to understand the nature of the conflict, and especially the Arab position in it, as a prerequisite for their own rational behavior and adequate response to its ordeals. The author's individual approach to his subject does not in any way detract from the interest of his material to a wider audience. On the contrary, it perhaps adds another dimension, and the book thus provides the outsider with an insight into Israel's dilemmas in confronting the conflict.

The articles fall into several categories.

The first, serving as a *general introduction,* discusses the main features of the conflict. Articles 12 and 13 also deal with general aspects, explaining the obduracy of this conflict and the obstacles to its solution.

The bulk of the work (Articles 2, 3, 8 and 9) deals with the *Palestinian problem.* Articles 6 and 7 are more technical and provide an analysis of the Agreement of May 6, 1970 and the Resolutions of the Eighth Palestinian National Council. To this group belongs also the lengthy analysis (Article 4) of the "Democratic State" as the declared main objective and slogan of the Palestinians, including its significance and implications. Article 5 gives an evaluation of guerrilla warfare against Israel. Article 17 surveys the grand debate taking place in the PLO after the October 1973 War.

Israeli problems and policies are surveyed in Articles 10, 11 and 14, the last two being mainly the author's personal, subjective reflections.

Developments *subsequent to the October War* and their implications for Israel are covered in Articles 15 and 16.

* * *

The reader's attention is drawn to the following inconsistencies in the English translation of key terms. These inconsistencies stem from variance in the official translations of PLO documents.

1) The supreme legislature of the Palestine Liberation Organization (PLO) is rendered either as "Council," "Assembly" or "Congress." For the sake of brevity its sessions

are referred to as "the Second Council," etc., and not in full as "the Second Session of the Palestinian National Council," etc.

2) "Covenant" and "Charter" are used synonymously as translations of *Mithaq*, the basic document of the PLO.

* * *

The following is a brief outline of the publishing history of the articles appearing in this book:

1. "The Arab-Israel Conflict"—first published in *Time Bomb in the Middle East*, Friendship Press, New York 1969, pp. 17–43; included in Prof. Michael Curtis (ed.), *People and Politics in the M.E.*, Transaction Books, Rutgers University 1971.

2, 3. "The Palestinians in the Arab-Israel Conflict" and "The Palestinian National Covenant"—first given as a lecture at Tel Aviv University on May 18, 1969. Appeared in *Ma'ariv* (Hebrew evening newspaper), November 21, 1969. Translated into English by Y. Karmi. Published in: *Midstream*, March 1970, pp. 3–18; and in *New York University Journal of International Law and Politics*, Vol. 3, No. 1, Spring 1971, pp. 209–244.

4. "The Meaning of 'a Democratic Palestinian State'"—first appeared in *Ma'ariv*, April 3 and 17, 1970. Translated into English by Y. Karmi and published as pamphlet entitled "Three Articles on the Arab Slogan of the Democratic State." Revised versions appeared in: *The Weiner Library Bulletin*, London 1970, Vol. 24, pp. 1–6; and in *Transaction*, Rutgers University, Vol. 7, July–August 1970, pp. 62–67.

5. "The Weakness of the Fedayeen"—originally part of a paper presented to a study group in Chicago on March 25, 1971.

6. "Fedayeen Consensus: The Agreement of May 6, 1970"—first appeared in *Ma'ariv*, July 17, 1970. Translated into English by Y. Karmi. Published in a revised version as "Score and Limit of Fedayeen Consensus," *The Wiener Library Bulletin*, 1970/1, Vol. 24, No. 4, pp. 1–8.

7, 8. "Resolutions of the Eighth Palestinian National Council" and "The Palestinians and Egypt's Acceptance of a Political Settlement"—first appeared as a serialized article in *Ma'ariv*, April 9 and 15, 1971.

9. "The Problem of the Palestinians"—first appeared in *Ma'ariv*, June 9 and 16, 1972. Translated into English by Misha Louvish and published in a revised version in booklet form by the Israel Academic Committee on the Middle East, Jerusalem.

10. "Reflections on Israel's Policy in the Conflict"—first appeared in *Ma'ariv*, May 10, 1970. Translated into English by Y. Karmi.

11. "Prudence in Situations of Conflict"—first published as Introduction to booklet *The Indoctrination Against Israel in UAR Armed Forces*, Israel Defense Forces, Chief Education Officer, November 1967.

12. "Obstacles in the Way of a Settlement"—paper presented at a seminar held at the Van Leer Jerusalem Foundation on May 27–31, 1973.

13. "Who is to Blame for the Persistence of the Arab-Israel Conflict?"—first appeared in *Ma'ariv*, September 26, 1973. Translated into English by Haya Gallai.

14. "A Dream of Israel"—first appeared in *Ma'ariv*, November 1, 1973. Revised version translated into English by D. Dishon.

15. "Toward a National Stocktaking"—first appeared in *Ma'ariv*, April 19, 1974. Translated into English by Haya Gallai.

16. "Israel in the Face of Present Arab Policy"—first appeared in *Ma'ariv*, June 7, 1974.

17. "The Debate at the Twelfth Palestinian National Council"—first appeared in *Ma'ariv*, July 12, 1974.

THE PUBLISHER

1

The Arab-Israel Conflict

In the fortnight before the Six-Day War, Arab leaders gave
great prominence to the Arab objective of destroying the
State of Israel. Today, realizing how damaging to their cause
such rabid declarations have been, Arab spokesmen excuse
themselves on the ground that they had only been carried
away by their own exuberance. Examination of recent Arab
declarations, however, indicates that their basic position
has not changed. For instance, Hasanein Heikal, editor of
al-Ahram, considered to be President Nasser's spokesman,
stated recently:

> . . . . There is no room in the Middle East for Arab nation-
> alism and Zionist nationalism. The struggle between them
> may be protracted without arriving at an accommodation.
> Let me make it clear, in the Middle East there is room
> for the Arab nation and any Jews who desire to live in
> its midst, however in the Middle East there is no room for
> the Arab nation and Israel, with its aggressive and ex-
> pansionist ambition (*al-Ahram,* February 21, 1969).

Many Arabs say now that they denounce Shukeiry,
former head of the Palestine Liberation Organization, for
his extreme pronouncements. Yet the difference between
what Heikal says today and what Shukeiry has said in the
past is merely in elegance of style and not at all in substance.
Both advocated the liquidation of Israel as a state. In the
Middle East Heikal says there is room only for Arab states

1

and Arab nationalism, but not for Jewish nationalism and a Jewish state, which he declares must always be aggressive and expansionist.

History is full of cases of conflict, but in most of them the bone of contention was generally limited to competition for superiority or quarrels over a certain region; the sheer existence of the two adversaries as political entities was outside the conflict. So rare has been the objective of abolishing the opponent's political entity that there was even no term for it. Several years ago I proposed to name it "politicide."

Zionism

Arabs usually justify their program of politicide by enumerating the historical evils of Zionism. Zionism certainly aimed to establish a Jewish state. Zionism was not, however, as Arabs are fond of describing it to be, a plot to expel them. Once Theodor Herzl failed to get an international charter allotting Palestine to the Jews, Zionism had no clear program for achieving the miracle of bringing a Jewish state into being. Thus Zionism concentrated its efforts on buying land, cultivating it and bringing in Jews. Land was not confiscated but sold by the Arabs themselves at high prices. Arab apologists, for whom this fact is disturbing, explain that only about six percent of the land in Palestine was sold. Yet in a country where more than half the territory is uncultivable desert and mountainous terrain, it was a considerable part of the arable private area.

The Zionist's idea of the possibility of buying out the Arabs *cannot* be blamed on them alone. Arab nationalism as a popular movement hardly existed. Some Arab leaders expressed their readiness to recognize the special interests of Jews in Palestine and its transformation into a Jewish entity, as long as they were to be compensated politically elsewhere, and the Zionist leaders were willing to have a

Jewish state as a member in an Arab federation. The Palestinian Arabs gave little evidence of being particularly attached to the country, and many of their leaders themselves sold land, even while to the outside protesting against it. Of course these Arab leaders are now branded as traitors, but in those days they represented the Arabs and were their spokesmen.

On many occasions the British and the Jews suggested compromise solutions, though none that satisfied the more extremist Arab demands. Had the Arabs accepted the Legislative Council offered in the 1920s, Israel would not have existed. Instead, they launched riots against the Jewish immigrants and Zionism became an imperative for the Jewish community in Palestine, as it already was for the Jews abroad. The Jewish community had to organize and set up a defense organization, not because of inherent militarism or plans to seize the country by force, but for the purpose of sheer self-defense.

Arab intransigence forced partition and Jewish statehood. It is an irony of history that the Arabs should deservedly be counted among the founding fathers of the Jewish state.

This long tradition of intransigence reached a climax when the Arabs attempted to prevent, by force, the execution of the United Nations Partition Resolution. This effort to subvert a UN decision has been described by them as just, and they do not see any inconsistency in their demands that Israel adhere to all UN decisions. The plan of the Arab armies to converge on Tel Aviv and Haifa is described by them as only a defensive action, while all the efforts of the Jews are described as offensive.

If the Palestinians were displaced, they mostly displaced themselves. The atomization of their society, the weakness of its social links, their lack of confidence in one another (the same reasons that are at the root of the debacle in the Six-Day War) caused Palestinian society to disintegrate.

Each man felt deserted, and consequently they all dispersed. Some acknowledged this truth. A nationalist like Walid al-Qamhāwi, in his magnum opus *Disaster and Construction in the Arab Fatherland* (Vol. 1, pp. 69–70), has written:

> Four months passed . . . while most of the rich families and those of the leaders were quitting the country for tranquility in Egypt, Syria and Lebanon, leaving the burden of struggle and sacrifice to the workers, villagers and middle class. . . . These factors, the collective fear, moral disintegration and chaos in every domain, were what displaced the Arabs from Tiberias, Haifa, Jaffa and scores of cities and villages.

Arabs now explain that their exodus came from the impact of one case of atrocity by the Jewish side: Dir Yasin. Interestingly, at the time (April 1948) Dir Yasin was little spoken about or mentioned in the press. At the time of its occurrence it was intertwined with the hundreds of cases of Arabs attacking Jewish villages and disrupting Jewish traffic. Victory did not come easily. The Israeli army was an extraordinary improvisation, and unlike the Arabs, the Jews did not then possess a government, with all its instruments. Knowledge of what awaited us in case of defeat was at the base of our victories in 1948 and 1967, and victory was achieved through endless cases of heroism and sacrifice. Our dead in that short war in 1948 amounted to 6,000 (about one percent of the population—the total U.S. casualties in World War II were a quarter percent of the population). The war was initiated by the Arabs' rejection, by force, of the Partition Resolution. They failed, but by continued adherence to an uncompromising position they vitiated, even in the eyes of many foreigners, their subsidiary demand that Israel withdraw to the 1947 lines. Had the Arabs succeeded in converging on Tel Aviv and Haifa, would they have been ready to restore the prewar situation?

As Professor W. C. Smith has explained: "The Árab writing of history has been functioning . . . less as genuine inquiry than as a psychological defense."[1] Thus, the usual Arab version of the history of the Arab-Israel conflict and its origins in Zionism seems motivated by a need to describe the present reality as if it had been imposed on the Arabs, so that they can revolt against it. Actually, it is to a great extent their own handiwork.

The Growth of Arab Intransigence

For the Arabs to admit their share of responsibility for the situation that has developed would be to undermine their cause. How much easier it is to shirk all responsibility and to externalize all blame. As Dr. S. Hamadi, a Lebanese herself, has explained in her book, *Temperament and Character of the Arabs* (Twayne Publishers, New York 1960, p. 43):

> The Arab is reluctant to assume responsibility for his personal or national misfortune and he is inclined to put the entire blame upon the shoulders of others.

Dr. Hamadi quoted the authority of Professor Fayez Sayegh, who in his pamphlet, *Understanding the Arab Mind*, generalized:

> The Arab is fascinated by criticism of foreigners, of fellow countrymen, of followers, always of 'the other,' seldom of oneself . . . which accordingly serves to thwart collective and personal accomplishment rather than to stimulate creative efforts and bold enterprises.

Thus, instead of constructive efforts to remedy the situation, such as letting the refugees settle where they could, a public stigma was placed on their settlement in order to perpetuate their cause and their misery, while their leaders and intellectuals indulged in descriptions of self-victimization and dreams of vengeance.

Arab nationalism and Zionism came into being at more or less the same time. Both tried, in those days, to enlist the support of the Western powers. Arab nationalism developed along political-nationalistic lines. Consequently many of the Arab states came under authoritarian military regimes. Zionism, on the other hand, gave a social content to its message, striving to build a democratic society based on social justice. Thus Israel, despite all prophecies that it would become a garrison state, retains its democracy, and its social organizations are a model for many developing countries.

Hidden among Arab detractions of Zionism and Israel are many ambivalences and expressions of admiration. The easiest escape from this dissonance is in identifying Zionism with colonialism. Colonialism means living by exploiting others. But what could be further from colonialism than the idealism of city-dwelling Jews who strive to become farmers and laborers and to live by their own work? Reviving a language and developing a culture require the creation of a community, but that does not mean simply exclusivity. On the other hand, the contention that Jews should have become assimilated into Arab society only implies a domineering Arab stance.

The Zionists were not fiends, as the Arabs often describe them to be. They were driven to the Land of Israel by deep and powerful bonds, together with the pressure of the terrible sufferings of the Jewish people, culminating in the European Holocaust. They had no intention of harming Arabs. They hoped to settle *among* them, and to contribute to the progress of the Middle East as a whole. Faced with the horrors of the Holocaust in Europe and the pressure of the need for a haven for the remnant of European Jewry, they found Arab resistance to immigration the less important problem.

Zionism did not, and perhaps could not, have a solution for the Arab problem it created. This fact is a heavy burden, which Zionism will have to carry on its conscience. Members of the young Israeli generation in particular are aware of it. The Arabs do have a case, though not as they themselves describe it. Acknowledging that the Arabs have a case does not mean that we are ready to restore the situation as it existed before, nor does it justify the barbarity of calling for the destruction of the State of Israel. The assertion that the coming of the Jews to Palestine and the establishment of Israel are the causes of the conflict is correct. The inference that, therefore, the destruction of the state, and still worse, the eviction of the Jews, is the only solution is mere casuistry. The Arabs are unwilling to admit that their demand that Israel disappear borders on the absurd. No state can be expected to commit suicide. The tragedy of the Arab case is that their grievance cannot be redressed to their satisfaction without perpetrating an even greater evil. Human destiny decrees that many misfortunes cannot be rectified. The Arabs' ruminating endlessly on past events and on the vices of Zionism will get them nowhere. Israel's problem is that with the best will in the world it cannot meet the Arabs' demand, because it is *unlimited* and cannot be satisfied so long as Israel exists. Their vision is not peace *with* Israel but peace *without* Israel.

Firstly they explain that the very existence of Israel is, as a matter of principle, not acceptable to them. This is only a euphemistic way of calling for Israel's liquidation. They then proceed to enumerate subsidiary items of accusation against Israel: Israel would not let the refugees return, it retaliated against the acts of infiltrators and it launched attacks; it is expansionist, aggressive, callous and so on. The Arabs are not aware that these accusations, whether real or fanciful, are the outcome of their basic position, which is that Israel as a Jewish state should be destroyed, and do not realize the threat that this implies. The ethics of the responsibility to defend its people sometimes impels Israel to take measures that run counter to other values. The Arabs describe the conflict as a battle for survival, and they make it so for Israel. But they then expect Israel to behave as if the conflict was a genial game.

Furthermore, these accusations are basically somewhat irrelevant. Even if Israel behaved impeccably, the Arabs' principle of its unacceptability would still remain. Some even spell this out, asserting that if the refugee problem did not exist and even if Israel shrank to the size of Tel Aviv, its existence would still be unacceptable. Whatever its size, they condemn it as a "cancerous foreign body" that must be excised. Thus the Arab position, centering on the principle of the rejection of Israel's statehood, becomes inelastic and impervious to any policy that might be adopted by Israel.

Some Arabs philosophize that Jewishness is a matter of religion, not nationalism. Therefore the Jews, as a matter of principle, do not deserve to have a state. Some would go on to assert that a Jewish state is a hybrid creature, doomed to collapse. It is true that some Jews sense their Jewishness as only a religion, but some feel otherwise. The Arabs need not pontificate to us on the nature of Jewishness. Finding "contradictions" in Israel and its society has become a pastime for Arab intellectuals. True, there are problems, both within Israel and in its relation to the position of Jews abroad, yet no societies—including those of the Arab states—are free from internal difficulties and "contradictions." Arab nationalism abounds in ambiguities, such as for example, its relationship to Islam, or the great gap between the ideology of Arab unity and the reality of Arab disunity.

Arab Anti-Semitism

The volume of anti-Semitic literature published in the Arab world has had no parallel in modern history since the demise of Nazi Germany. What makes this literature even more significant is that it has been put out by official government publishing houses—not from the fringes of Arab society but from its very center. Let any Arab, disclaiming Arab anti-Semitism, account for this flood of publications. The *Protocols of the Elders of Zion* (a forgery by the Russian Czarist secret police, which "describes" a meeting of Jewish leaders conspiring to achieve world domination by odious means, and the basic writ of modern anti-Semitism) has been published by the UAR Ministry of Orientation.[2] President Nasser's brother has reissued it. The UAR government has gone to the extreme of publishing books like *Human Sacrifices in the Talmud*, in which Jews are accused of the ritual murder of Gentile children.[3] The Jordanian prime minister, Sa'ad Jum'a, has published a book that explains Israel's victory as based on the *Protocols*.[4] An Arab newspaper has published a "Letter to Eichmann" pledging to avenge his death and to follow his example in destroying all Jews still left alive.[5] Rabid anti-Semitic themes, including excerpts from the *Protocols*, are found in textbooks for schools and in the indoctrination literature for the armed forces.

These are only a few random examples. No intellectual acrobatics can brush them aside. The argument that the Arabs, being Semites themselves, cannot be anti-Semitic is only specious, for anti-Semitism means hatred of Jews and not of Semites. The fact that Arabs could view the moral havoc wrought by anti-Semitism in Germany without feeling inhibited, indicates the vehemence of their anti-Semitism. True, the Germans destroyed millions of Jews, but after reading what Arabs write about Israel, I cannot escape the impression that many Arabs also harbor just such a dream. It may even be possible that such desires are more prevalent and central in Arab society than they were in German society. The Arabs have gone far in their vilification of Israel and Jews, and the road back is not a short one.

There is now a tendency in some Arab quarters to give an Islamic form to Arab anti-Semitism. Many such examples are found in the monthly magazine of al-Azhar, which is the oldest and principal Islamic university in Cairo. In the magazine's October 1968 issue, a religious dignitary evokes a tradition (*hadith*) according to which Muhammed was said to have declared that a Muslim slaughter of Jews will precede the Day of Resurrection. The learned sheik asserts the authenticity of this tradition and its importance as gospel. He explained that the slaughter of the Jewish minorities, whose position in the Arab countries was low, was unbecoming (thus illustrating the basic Arab attitude toward Jews—the Quran decreed (II, 58, III, 108) that they should be "in a low and miserable position"). Therefore, God ordained that the Jews would develop an aggressive state and attain power, so that the *hadith* might be realized: thus the hidden meaning of this tradition, he argues, will henceforth unfold. A theological justification is, thus, given to politicide-genocide and a comforting explanation to Arab defeats. Had a similar article appeared in a Christian publication, it would have created an uproar of protest.

Professor R. I. al-Fruki has delivered a series of lectures to the Arab League's Institute of High Arabic Studies, entitled "The Origins of Zionism Are in the Jewish Religion," in which he furnished a disparaging analysis of Judaism. Arab efforts to differentiate between Judaism and Zionism usually flounder. Both are too frequently described in Arab writings as identical (*sinwān*), or else Zionism is said to be only "the executive mechanism" of Judaism. "World Zionism" and "World Jewry" are treated as identical. Thus it is no wonder that anti-Zionist Jews are stigmatized as hypocritical and fraudulent.

I do not argue that Arab anti-Semitism has social or religious roots; its origins are mainly political. Nevertheless, this is no accidental growth in the Arab stand against Israel. The need to substantiate the evil of Israel, as a state that deserves a death sentence, produced an inclination to present this evil as profound. Only evil people could give rise to such a monstrosity as Zionism, could "usurp" a country and build an inherently aggressive state such as Israel.

A Palestinian State

For a long time the Arabs kept stressing that the Palestinian problem was a pan-Arab problem. To view it in the narrow framework of Palestinians versus Israel was stigmatized as anti-nationalist. It used to be a basic doctrine of Arab nationalism that national boundaries in the Middle East were the artificial fabrications of colonialism. Thus to acknowledge the existence of a Palestinian entity, precisely because of its colonialist parenthood, was considered a heresy. With the defeat of the Arab states, the Palestinian cause has been resurrected and sanctified. The Palestinians once complained that the Arab states were using them as instruments in inter-Arab bickerings and that they were being treated as pawns. These roles have now been reversed, and the tools have become the actors. It is explained that the Palestinian aspect is the major one in the conflict. Yet this had been left to hibernate for at least sixteen years.

I do not doubt that the Palestinians share feelings of communality, for they have suffered a great deal. Their national aspirations could have been partially satisfied on the West Bank, in the Gaza Strip and even in Jordan. If they stick to their totalistic demand that their aspirations can only be fulfilled if Israel disappears, if they do not see a possibility of accommodation between Israeli nationalism and their own, they will probably lose out.

A new slogan that has recently appeared in some quarters urges that Israel be superseded by a "lay, democratic, pluralistic Palestine." It is easy, though, to show that this slogan is only politicide in a new, "humanistic" guise. Among themselves Arabs specify that this new state will be *Arab* and part of Arab nationalism, which stresses homogeneity. Fatah and the other organizations end their proclamations with the formula "Long live an *Arab*, Free Palestine."

The Fatah position toward the Jews is enunciated in an authoritative document called the Palestinian National Covenant. In its original (1964) version it read that the *Jews of Palestinian origin* (which could be interpreted as those living in the country before 1948) would be recognized as Palestinians—and permitted to stay. The Covenant was revised in July 1968, when Fatah became the prominent factor in the Palestine Liberation Organization, and the stand on the Jews has now been radicalized. Now the corresponding Article reads that only those Jews who have been living in Palestine permanently "before the beginning of the Zionist invasion" (i.e., 1917), would be considered Palestinians; the rest would be considered aliens, and expelled. The need to reduce the number of Jews in the country by all and any means is understandable, for by now they form the majority of the population, and this fact undermines the claim that the country is Arab. Yet the whole issue only shows the absurdities in which the Arab position has enmeshed itself.

Jews will only be allowed to exist as a minority in an Arab state. Unwittingly, perhaps, such a slogan implies a return to the fundamentalist Islamic stand. Islam recognizes neither independence nor equality for Jews. The Jews, like all the "People of the Book," have to be fought until they submit to the supremacy of Islam (Quran, IX, 29).

The Islamic aspects of the struggle against Israel have been accentuated, as for instance by Fatah's repeated appeals to Islamic religious leaders to declare a *jihad* (holy war), and to consider monetary contributions to Fatah as *zakat* (a religious obligation). Ironically, then, a holy war must be waged in order to establish an allegedly *lay* republic! The constitutions of all the Arab states (with the exception of Lebanon) specify Islam as the state religion or as the source of legislation. This, of course, does not restrain Arabs from branding Israel as a reactionary state based on religion. The advocacy of a democratic Palestine, too, is odd, when one considers that the general trend in most Arab countries has been away from democracy.

In the past the Zionist leaders have called for a bi-national state. Now it is too late for that. The Arabs refuse to make peace, or even to meet us face to face, as though our very presence were contaminating. They seethe with desire for vengeance; they use the most abusive invectives against Israel and resort to anti-Semitic vilification. The veritable festival of hangings of Jews in Baghdad reflects the Arab mood and attitude much more accurately than does the synthetic Arab position portrayed by Arab professors at the American University of Beirut. The direct leap made from such a hostile stance to one advocating the intimacy of a common state must give rise to a suspicion of some ulterior motive—that the Arab call for a pluralistic Palestine may be only a euphemism for the destruction of Israel. The sublimity of such a suggestion may bring self-gratification to its propagators, as proof of their own nobility of soul, but its true intent may be of a much lower order. The acid test of the Arabs' peaceful intentions is their readiness to make peace with an Israel that is alive, and not with its ruins. When the conflict has been settled and when the mood in the Middle East has changed, integration may indeed come about, and on a higher level, of a union of Middle Eastern states, of which Israel will be a member.

The Middle East is in the throes of the Age of Nationalism. To suggest at this point a solution to suit a post-nationalistic age demonstrates neither farsightedness nor idealism; it is at best irrelevant. Those who wish to suggest a political solution must have the humility to consider reality. However, the Arabs sometimes tend to downgrade reality, and give greater importance to the word: " . . . language, for Arabs, is not a means to describe reality, it is reality itself," writes H. E. Tutsch.[6]

Fancy, and words, blurring reality, cause delusions and deception. Arab writers, when analyzing their society, often point to the extraordinary frequency of deception, lies and false communiqués by governments as constituting a major social weakness. In the literature now being published in the Arab countries on the lessons to be drawn from their defeat in 1967, these flaws are described as one of the major causes of that defeat. This is a subject I feel uneasy discussing. No society can claim to be blameless of distorting facts. Still a quantitative difference may have a qualitative significance. I find it baffling that the very Arab academics who reproach their people for distorting facts, resort to such distortions themselves.

In order to understand the Arab position in the conflict one must learn their terminology. *"A peaceful settlement of the present crisis"* does not necessarily mean a peace settlement with Israel, but only the withdrawal of Israeli troops to the pre-1967 war lines. The meaning of *"crisis"* is limited to indicate the pressure put on the Arabs by the occupation; it does not mean the state of continuous tension between the two sides. *"Liberating the Occupied Territories"* may apply to the area occupied in the Six-Day War and also to the liquidation of Israel, since Israel, prior to 1967, was already referred to in Arabic as *"the occupied territory."* *"Recognition of Israel's existence"* may mean no more than an awareness that there *is* such a thing as Israel. Az-Zayat, the UAR spokesman, has reiterated to foreign journalists that Egypt had always recognized the existence of Israel. (Since Egypt has continuously called for the destruction of Israel, he apparently senses no contradiction between recognizing the existence of Israel and calling for its liquidation.) *"Nonbelligerence"* means that the Arab regular armies will not take military action against Israel, but it does not exclude support of terrorist action operating from Arab territory. Since the Arabs declare that they agree to nonbelligerence but not to peace, nonbelligerence must thus be interpreted as merely a pause in the war.

Strangely enough, the principle of Arab policy (as agreed upon at the Khartoum Conference and as pronounced in Nasser's speech of June 23, 1968) of adherence to the right of the Palestinians to regain their fatherland, is also a euphemism for politicide. For the Palestine Liberation Organization and all the fedayeen groups repeatedly declare that they reject a political solution and that their aim is the liquidation of the "Zionist entity." The support of the Arab leaders of the aims of the fedayeen organizations is a blatant contradiction of their alleged acceptance of the November 22 Security Council Resolution. Such support implies endorsement of politicide, despite the Arab leaders' and spokesmen's ambiguous expressions when addressing foreign audiences. Similarly *"a pluralistic Palestine"* may be no more than an elegant phrase for politicide.

Rejection of Coexistence

The Arab rejection of Jewish statehood and of coexistence with the State of Israel lies at the heart of the conflict. The Arabs are demanding that their national aspirations for self-determination (including those of the Palestinians) should be met while the national aspirations of the Jewish community in Israel should be rejected. The Jews, they say, notwithstanding the fact that they now form a political community, should not have the right to political self-determination. Herein lies the asymmetry that is basic to the Arab stand. Arabs may fight against Israel and do it harm, but if Israel fights back, she is aggressive. Israel must observe the ceasefire: the Arabs are exempt from its limitations.

The Arab attitude has caused an important change in the attitude toward statehood of many Israelis. It has come to acquire a great value, even to those for whom previously it meant but little. It became clear to those who (like Achad Ha'am[7]) would have been content with only a "spiritual center" for Jewry that it could not be achieved without some guardian, in the form of a state. Statehood, to Israelis, has become the defense line for survival. "Zionism" has now come to mean that Jews should possess a country and a state, as do other peoples. Thus "de-Zionization" of Israel is, too, only a euphemistic expression for the destruction of Israel.

The Arabs' acceptance of coexistence with Israel and of peace is possible and will come about one day. Yet the significance for the Arabs of such a change should not be underestimated. To the Arab states it may appear as a betrayal of the national cause and of their obligations toward the Palestinians. The United States did not have to change the Constitution in order to make peace with Japan, for the conflict with Japan was not enshrined in the American Constitution. The Arab-Israel conflict and the non-acceptability of the existence of Israel are inscribed in Arab sacred writs, as National Charters. If in the West people tend to dismiss Arab extremist declarations as stemming from exuberance, flamboyance or momentary hot-headedness,

Arab writings are free from such notions. They are the result of long deliberation: the rejection of the existence of Israel has become an important component of Arab national thought. Though Israel's existence is not the sole concern of the Arabs, they have forged their national thinking on the anvil of the conflict to a much greater extent than could have been expected.

This applies particularly to Israel's neighbors. For instance, the conflict is referred to six times in the UAR National Charter (considered the most sacred writ in Egypt's national life) and was hailed by "The National Congress of the Popular Powers" on June 30, 1962 as "the frame for our life, the path to our revolution and the guide for the future." In it, the liquidation of Israel is specified in unmistakable terms: "The insistence of our people on liquidating the Israeli aggression on a part of the Palestine land is a determination to liquidate one of the most dangerous pockets of imperialistic resistance against the struggle of peoples." Thus, the Arab position toward Israel is not only expressed in their diplomatic or political stand, but it is a basic tenet of Arab nationalism, practically ingrained in the Arab ethos. This development is extremely unfortunate, and many in Israel prefer to ignore it. Yet it is better to see reality, bitter and disheartening though it may be, than to indulge in illusions, which will only court disappointment.

Changing the Arab position on the acceptance of Israel would not involve a political or diplomatic act alone, but a national transformation. It would be a change not *in* but *of* the Arabs' national stand; not of a *norm* but of a *value*. It would entail a modification of their educational system, with its many ramifications in national life. Of course, such a change could not be accomplished overnight. A political settlement might signal the first step to a change in the national stance. Yet, any political settlement that did not entail a change in the national position would be only ephemeral. It could produce an absurd situation, comparable to that of a state making peace with its rival but continuing to sing the verse in its national anthem that calls for the destruction of the other state. Thus Israel, before foregoing the security advantages that the present borders afford, demands a manifestation of readiness on the part of the Arabs to change their national position by negotiating a peace settlement.

The Arabs reject direct negotiation, not because they prefer another procedure leading to peace but because refusal to negotiate directly has symbolized, for them, their rejection of coexistence and peace. Israel's insistence on direct negotiations does not stem from procedural pedantry, but from recognition of what such negotiations symbolize to the Arab mind. So long as the Arabs reject direct negotiations, they have not given up the intention to destroy the State of Israel. A peace that contains the provision that the parties to the conflict do not meet is a contradiction in terms. It is without precedent in human history. Recognition, peace and direct negotiations were all lumped together and proscribed at the Khartoum Conference (September 1, 1967). The Arab contention that direct negotiations imply a surrender does not so much follow from psychological sensivity about meeting with Israelis, as from the realization that negotiations imply a renunciation of politicide.

Arab diplomacy is trying to achieve an arrangement that will snatch from Israel its present means of applying pressure on the Arab states to make peace, in order that the Arabs might be in a position to renew the conflict. What they want is at most an armistice, for which Israel, pressured by the big powers, will be made to pay as if for peace. Though a contractual peace settlement negotiated between the parties is not an absolute guarantee against resumption of the conflict, it is a step in the right direction. Having learnt some bitter lessons from the Armistice Agreements concluded with its Arab neighbors in 1949, Israel is resolved not to agree to any arrangement short of peace. Because the Arabs categorically refuse to conclude such a peace agreement, the conflict becomes a test of endurance.

Prospects for Peace

Arab leaders repeatedly declare that if Israel does not withdraw to the former borders, they will force her back by renewing the war. The urge for vengeance and to wipe out the shame of defeat is strong among the Arab military. Yet memories of the Six-Day War have served as deterrents. In such a situation there is always the danger of a flare-up and war.

In the meanwhile, the fedayeen will continue their terrorist and subversive activities. Despite Arab claims, the effects of these activities have been limited. In the period from the Six-Day War to May 2, 1969, there were ten times more deaths from suicide and traffic accidents than from fedayeen actions in Israel. No society can be immune to terrorist activities. We shall have to treat them like the toll in road accidents paid by modern societies, and take them in our stride.

Fedayeen thinking is fuzzy, and no coherent action can flow from incoherent thought. They do not examine the relationship between means and aims; the suitability of guerrilla warfare to the circumstances. They claim that guerrilla warfare will bring about the liquidation of Israel, but—to use a parallel—while the FLN *could* induce the French to relinquish their rule in Algeria, no amount of terrorism could force the French to give up *France*. Yet that is precisely what the Arab fedayeen hope to do in the case of Israel.

The fedayeen organizations fill the gap between their pretensions and their accomplishments by false reporting.

The new generation of Palestinians is now reproaching its parents for their evasion of reality, illusions, self-delusion and deception. In their misrepresentations, the fedayeen communiqués surpass all description. It is not just rationalistic optimism to think that such fabrications are self-defeating. These fictitious reports create a certain problem of education in Israel. When the fedayeen claim, for example, to be responsible for the death of the late Prime Minister Levi Eshkol, it becomes difficult to expect people to have respect for an adversary who resorts to making such fantastic claims.

Educating the present Arab generation on vengeance and brutality, though it is directed outward, may rebound and take a heavy toll within the Arab states themselves. The fedayeen may well become a sect. Continued frustration on the Arab side may cause, at least for some time, greater radicalization. Latent disparities between the fedayeen organizations and the Arab states may come into the open and bring havoc to the Arab societies.

The Arab-Israel conflict is not the source of all Arab problems. The Arab states suffer from instability in political life, the militarization of their regimes, from backwardness, the alienation of their peoples from public affairs, etc. This *malaise* has much deeper roots and may outlive the conflict; however, the conflict serves to aggravate the *malaise*.

The Arabs need peace no less than Israel does. Continuation of the present conflict may be a nightmare for Israel; but it is also destructive for the Arabs. International conflict is always a calamity, yet for Israel it has had beneficial effects as well, for it has promoted national integration, construction and creativity. For the Arabs the conflict has been a national disaster and an obstacle to modernization. Many Arabs stress that only all-embracing change can overcome the structural weaknesses of their societies, which were reflected in their debacle in the Six-Day War. Presumably, such a catastrophe could be an all-powerful incentive to reforms that might usher in a national revival. It seems, however, that so far the defeat has had adverse effects, bringing greater social atomization, internal disintegration and hopelessness. The Arabs are caught in a vicious circle because their obsession with the conflict has had paralyzing effects. National reforms require collective effort, but it is precisely their failure to sustain a collective effort that thwarts them. This trend toward disintegration takes place in a parallel fashion on both the social and the state levels. The Arab states are now experiencing, not political growth but political decay. For example, Iraq today is "less a state" than was the Iraq of Nuri as-Said, and the same holds true for the other Arab states.

It is difficult to be optimistic about the settlement of the conflict in the near future, though developments not yet envisaged may emerge. One should never be too positive in predicting international events. I am most sanguine about Israel's ability to withstand the conflict, protracted though this may be. A settlement that does not entail liquidation of the conflict may mean its perpetuation. Only the parties to the conflict themselves can end it. A solution imposed from the outside may be only a palliative, producing even more harmful after-effects. Third parties can contribute as mediators, but they cannot act as substitutes for the two sides.

Arab political literature often claims that if Israel is not liquidated, Arab nationalism and the Arab states will be obliterated by Israel. On the one hand, this is an apocalyptic dramatization; on the other, it is an attempt to impose symmetry on a situation that is inherently asymmetrical. Between these two prophecies of doom there is a third possibility—much less melodramatic but more practical and humane—the coexistence of Jewish nationalism and Israel with Arab nationalism and the Arab states.

Though the conflict originated with the coming of the Jews to Palestine, its resolution rests more with the Arabs. We Israelis find ourselves in a morally awkward position, for we appear to put all the onus for a solution to the conflict on the Arabs. Yet until we are accepted as a partner in the Middle East comity of nations, we must stay put. This is our predicament. In any conflict, the side that wants to change the status quo is dominant while the side that tries to preserve the status quo is respondent and mostly reactive. Before 1948 the Zionist position was the primary factor in the conflict. Since then the roles have been reversed.

Of course, Israel must not resign itself to a waiting position. It must do its best to explore and initiate steps and policies to facilitate a change in the Arab position and in resolution of the conflict. Nevertheless, so long as the Arabs maintain that any concession by Israel that leaves its existence intact is too small, Israel's latitude to make concessions is very limited. Israel cannot compromise the principle of its statehood. A compromise could take place, on a higher level, by Israel's gradual transference of some attributes of its sovereignty to the central authority of a Middle Eastern confederation or federation. Such a union, though pluralistic in nature, would be predominantly Arab, and that may reassure the Arabs and calm their fears about Israel.

If the Arabs had been ready for a real peace settlement immediately after the Six-Day War, Israel would have withdrawn from almost all the occupied areas. The longer the wait, the stronger grew the feeling in Israel that our only course of action was to strengthen ourselves and to settle the strategic areas. If we cannot placate Arab hostility, and since they do not give up the tenet of the inevitability of war, preparation for war becomes for us an overriding imperative. The possibility of the radicalization of the Arab regimes, with all that may entail for the radicalization of their policies, even if it is, for them, self-defeating, looms on the horizon.

The contingency of war becomes real, and volunteering to forego the margin of security that the present borders give is tantamount to madness. Furthermore, Israel cannot allow ". . . every area . . . Israel will evacuate [to] serve as a firm base for fedayeen action" (as the Egyptian *Ruz al-Yusuf* May 12, 1969 explained was Arab intent and strategy).

Both sides are caught in a vicious circle. Arab hostility has driven Israel to enlarge its grip and that action is interpreted by the Arabs as expansionism and has aggravated their hostility. The only escape from such a predicament is peace.

It is to be hoped that the cumulative effect of the repeated failure of the Arab efforts to liquidate Israel will eventually induce the Arabs to resign themselves to Israel's existence and thus spell the end of the conflict. Then a period of collaboration may start. Raw wounds will heal, hostilities evaporate and problems now outstanding will be solved constructively. The day may still be far away—but it will come!

Notes

1 *Islam in Modern History*, Princeton University Press, 1957, p. 20.
2 Series of *Political Books*, No. 5, Cairo 1957.
3 *National Books*, No. 184, Cairo 1962.
4 *The Plot and the Battle of Destiny*, Dar al-Katib al-'Arabi, Beirut 1968.
5 *Jerusalem Times*, April 24, 1961.
6 *Facets of Arab Nationalism*, Wayne State University Press, 1965, p. 116.
7 The cultural Zionist essayist.

2

The Palestinians in the Arab-Israel Conflict

Aftermath of Palestinian Dispersion

These days a sharp controversy prevails in Israel concerning the place of the Palestinians in the conflict, their collective identity and the question whether they are the party with whom Israel can negotiate a peace settlement.

Their self-definition as Palestinians gives them a strong sense of common identity. The overwhelming majority of them preserved their identity and attachment to Palestine despite the passage of time, their hardships and dispersion. This is also true of the period which preceded the Six-Day War. Children who were born to Palestinian parents in other countries did not identify themselves to foreigners with the country where they were born; they said rather, "I am from Haifa" or "I am from Jaffa," thus demonstrating their Palestinianism in a specific and concrete way.

It is true that states like the UAR and Iraq evoked the idea of "the Palestinian entity" in meetings of the Arab League from 1959 on, doing so for tactical reasons within inter-Arab rivalries, and the establishment of the Palestine Liberation Organization (PLO) was initiated and materialized by decisions of the Arab rulers at their First and Second Summit Conferences. However, the call for the Palestinians to organize themselves and assume the central role in the struggle against Israel came *also* from within the ranks of the Palestinians themselves. Such ideas recur with great forcefulness in the writings of Palestinians at the beginning of the 1960s. This applies also to the fedayeen organizations. Though some of them were formed and continued to exist owing to the support of one or another Arab state, it would be a mistake to regard the Palestinian organizations as mere pawns that serve the aims of the Arab states.

A number of factors contributed to this feeling of identity and attachment to Palestine. First and foremost, the factor of a common place of origin, shared experiences, and common fate and suffering in the past and present. Another factor was the difficulty of absorption into Arab countries economically and, no less, socially. Despite the common language and cultural background, and notwithstanding Arab nationalism, the Palestinians felt like strangers in Arab countries and expressed this in their poetry. It is significant that one collection of poems was called "Hymns of the Stranger." [1] Their admission to feeling like strangers in Arab countries contradicts the basic conception of Arab nationalism, which has emphasized Arab unity, expressed in the feeling of being at home in every Arab country. The fact that a considerable segment of the Palestinians has been living *en masse* in refugee camps has also contributed to their preservation of group identity. The Zionist example may also have had some influence. A conflict is a competitive situation, and the preservation by the Jews of their attachment to Palestine served as an example to be emulated. It is as though the Palestinians said, "We are no less than the Jews, who preserved a tie to this country for a long period of time." Tibawi notes that "a new Zionism" was formed among the refugees.

Among the refugees a state of mind developed which stigmatized assimilation into Arab societies as an act of disloyalty. A mission of the Norwegian Institute for Peace Research, which investigated the situation in the Gaza Strip in 1964, was impressed by the unity of presentation and consensus in the argumentation of the refugees. They noted in this respect: "It is difficult to imagine a social group with a more homogeneous perception and definition of the past and the present than the refugees in the Gaza Strip. Regardless of age, income or educational level and the social status in general of the men we spoke with, the definition seemed to be the same—at least insofar as they wanted to present it to foreigners." Their report relates that among the refugees there was even a prevailing tendency to disparage efforts at improving living conditions in the camps, lest this imply the admission that these were permanent living places. The report notes that Palestinians tended to prefer short-term work contracts in Arab countries, again lest they be considered of little faith regarding the anticipated imminent "return." A need was generated to demonstrate a faith that, indeed, they soon would return to "the homeland." The refugees began calling themselves officially "returnees" (*'ā'idūn*) instead of "refugees," in accordance with a decision of the First Congress of the Palestine Liberation Organization. There may have been an expectation that the psychological mechanism of "self-fulfilling prophecy" would operate, that is, the very name "returnees" assures not only that the hope would not fade but more, that it would be realized. The word *'auda*, "return," or "repatriation," was made a principal slogan. In the recesses of their heart many refugees probably doubted that hope for "the return" would materialize in the near, or even distant, future. But, according to the report of the Norwegians, the mechanism of "pluralistic ignorance" operated among them; that is, each one was apprehensive that only he was of little faith, as though the others were wholly confident in an early return, and as a result no one dared make his doubts public. Ideas that are repeated, even if not believed at first, are slowly assimilated in human consciousness, for otherwise a "cognitive dissonance" is created. It is uncomfortable to live in two different conceptual frameworks, what is said and what is believed, and ultimately belief is adjusted to what is said. Because of the stigma of absorption into Arab countries it was presumably easier for a Palestinian to become assimilated before 1948 than afterwards. Nevertheless, many have in fact been absorbed within Arab and other countries.

In their preservation of group attachment there was also an element of protest and negation of their situation as refugees, which is translated into the hope that one day redemption would come and they would return to their land. The return is seen as a collective salvation and messianic vision. Tibawi speaks of "the mystique of the return."

The form of attachment to Palestine varies with the generations. In the attachment of the *older generation* to the country there was a concrete factor: longing for property they left and their former way of life. Among the older generation a process of "idylization" of the way of life before "the disaster" operated against the background of negation of life in the present. By selective memory, the shadows of Arab life in Palestine were forgotten, and the village house expanded with the passage of time and became a palace. In their stories to their children the parents probably described their life before the war in 1948 as a period of glory and a heroic struggle. It is significant that 'Arif al-'Arif entitles his book, *al-Firdaws al-Mafqūd* ("Paradise Lost").

Among the *younger generation*, which constitutes the majority of the Palestinians, the attachment is not directly experiential. The younger generation did not experience the hardships of the 1948 war and the exodus. Their quest to return did not stem from longing for some property, as in their parents' case, but from negation of their present life and from an *ideological* position: the wrong that was inflicted on the Palestinians, Israel's aggressiveness, and the requirement that justice be done and Israel liquidated. The education that the youth received brought them to the point where the village life of most of the parents ceased to enchant them. The return does not appear as a return to the village of their parents but as a political act in which the Palestinians become the sovereigns over Palestine and all their problems, as it were, are solved.

Paradoxically, the ideological attachment of the youth, though indirect, is by no means weaker than the concrete, direct attachment of the parents. The vehemence of the ideological and learned attachment can be much stronger than that of the concrete and direct attachment.

The Six-Day War, and the possibility given to many Palestinians to see Israel, and even to visit their place of origin, could impair the concrete attachment, for it became clear to the visitors that the property for which they longed, and in whose imagined existence they sought consolation, was no longer. The concrete attachment to the country is more vulnerable to the concrete reality expressed in changes that took place in the scenery and the consolidation of the State of Israel, while the ideological attachment of the younger generation is more immune to these facts.

Illusion ultimately disappoints. This applies to us Israelis also. It is best for us to acknowledge facts of reality. An acknowledgment that the Palestinians have an attachment to Palestine need not produce in us a state of anxiety. The conflict is also a contest of attachments. Our awareness that the Arabs also have an attachment to the country need not impair our own. I emphasize this because I have found that there is among us a degree of fainthearted reluctance to see some of the facts of the Arab-Israel conflict as they are. An example of this is the reaction I have found in Israeli audiences to evidences of Arab attachment to Palestine.

In lectures before an Israeli audience I sometimes read a paragraph from Nasir ad-Din an-Nashashibi's book, *Return Ticket* (Beirut, 1962). Toward the end of the book (p. 205) the author says:

Every year I shall say to my little son: "We shall return my son, and you will be with me; we shall return; we shall return to our land and walk there barefoot. We'll remove our shoes so that we may feel the holiness of the ground beneath us. We'll blend our souls with its air and earth. We'll walk till we come to the orange trees; we'll feel the sand and water; we'll kiss seed and fruit; we'll sleep in the shade of the first tree we meet; we'll pay homage to the first martyr's grave we come across. We'll turn here and there to trace our lives. Where are they? Here with this village square, with this mosque's minaret, with the beloved field, the desolate wall, with the remains of a tottering fence and a building whose traces have been erased. Here are our lives. Each grain of sand teaches us about our life. Do you not remember Jaffa and its delightful shore, Haifa and its lofty mountain, Beth Shean and the fields of crops and fruit, Nazareth and the Christians' bells, Acre and the memories of al-Jazzar, Ibrahim Pasha, Napoleon and the fortress, the streets of Jerusalem, my dear Jerusalem, Tiberias and its peaceful shore with the golden waves, Majdal and the remnant of my kin in its land?"

When one reads this paragraph, even if he be poisoned by the abundant words of abuse and calumny against Israel found in Nashashibi's book, he will admit, even if reluctantly, that there is here an expression of genuine longing and love for the country.

I found that older Israelis, upon hearing this, tend to be moved. The divulgence that an Arab too may have an emotional attachment to this country comes as an ominous surprise. In a younger audience the reaction was different. Among them the prevailing tendency was to accept the plain meaning of the words as something natural and understandable. In their reaction the youth said, in effect,

"If the author wishes to run barefoot, let him run and get himself stuck by thorns." I think that, despite its frivolousness, such a reaction is more healthy.

Whoever is moved by these manifestations of human longing for this country, and whose heart is touched by this phenomenon, should have no illusions concerning its significance for Israel. The refinement expressed in feelings of yearning does not, by any means, become refinement toward the Israelis. On the contrary, on the following page Nashashibi describes the effect his words will have on his son:

> I shall see the hatred in the eyes of my son and your sons. I shall see how they take revenge. If they do not know how to take revenge, I shall teach them. And if they agree to a truce or peace, I shall fight against them as I fight against my enemy and theirs. I want them to be callous, to be ruthless, to take revenge. I want them to wash away the disaster of 1948 with the blood of those who prevent them from entering their land. Their homeland is dear to them, but revenge is dearer. We'll enter their lairs in Tel Aviv. We'll smash Tel Aviv with axes, guns, hands, fingernails and teeth, while singing the songs of Qibiya, Dir Yasin and Nasir ad-Din.[2] We shall sing the hymns of the triumphant, avenging return. . . .

Truly, it is a tragic complication in which we are enmeshed. In the presence of the design of annihilation Israelis cannot permit themselves to become soft, for this would be a self-contradiction.

The leaders of the Palestinians have made special efforts to preserve the Palestinian attachment of the members of their flock and to nurture it by means of education, writing of history and collection of folklore, and the like. In brief, efforts were made to mold a Palestinian people although it had no territory. Also in this the Jews, as a people without territory and government, served as an example. It was easy for the Palestinian leadership and intelligentsia to find work and become absorbed within Arab countries. But for the sake of the political goal they were callous to the suffering of their people and exerted pressure upon them not to become absorbed but to remain in their camps. This duplicity was not hidden from the refugees, who accordingly regarded the Palestinian leadership with a great deal of reservation. It is difficult to place trust in a leadership which establishes itself in convenient positions and leads a normal way of life while at the same time demanding of its flock to live wretchedly. This may have been one of the reasons why the tendency among the refugees to organize themselves was late in coming.

It is understandable that among the Palestinians especially, along with their attachment to Palestine, pan-Arab sentiments would be more prevalent than among other Arab groups. Through their dispersion and wanderings many of the Palestinians became acquainted with Arab countries and sometimes even attached to them, whereas Egyptian, Syrian and Lebanese Arabs tend to know one country, and patriotism toward their homeland predominates over pan-Arab sentiments.[3] In this they can draw an analogy with Jews. Just as the Jews, owing to their dispersion, tended toward cosmopolitanism, so the Palestinians tended toward pan-Arabism. It is not accidental that the Qawmiyyūn al-'Arab movement, which so emphasized the idea of Arab unity, emerged from amid the Palestinians.

Acquaintance with the Arab states did not always endear these states to the Palestinians, for they indeed had their fill of bitters with them. Their loyalty to ideas of pan-Arabism may indeed have arisen among them partly in compensation for the grievances they had against the individual Arab countries. The Palestinians had complaints against the Arab countries for several reasons: they did not fulfill their obligations to the Palestinians, imposed discriminatory restrictions upon them, and manipulated the Palestinian problem for the purposes of their own rivalries. The Palestinians were a fermenting factor in the Arab countries. Several of the Arab states were apprehensive about their influence and consequently clipped their wings. The Palestinians have also had many grievances on the social level, for many Arabs were indifferent to their suffering and did not treat them as brethren in distress.

The Palestinians gave vent to their grievances in their literature (Ghassan Kanafani's novels for example). But it would be simplistic to conclude from these literary accounts that, because of their resentment of Arab countries, they will be amenable to agreement with Israel. The heart of man is sufficiently wide to encompass hostility toward more than one enemy, and the enemy of his enemy does not automatically become his friend. Along with grievances toward the Arab countries the Palestinians also have feelings of gratitude, for they did derive benefits from these countries. Even if they experienced difficulties of absorption, they could find work and send their children to study in their colleges. The recognition that in the confrontation against Israel they ultimately depend on the support of the Arab countries, especially in the military struggle, is another factor which inhibits the development of enmity toward them. The result, therefore, is not dissociation from the Arab countries but a complex attitude that contains elements of ambivalence: friendship and distrust at the same time.

Arabic belles-lettres are certainly a more faithful mirror of what is happening in the public than the political literature written according to the dictate of rulers. There is more spontaneity in its expressiveness than there is in the writings of political publicists. However, in evaluating political positions one should distinguish well between the position on the popular level and that on the governmental level.

For example, in the literary depiction of English life in the year 1938–39 enmity toward the Germans was not at all conspicuous, but an inference from this to England's position as a state would be misleading. From literary descriptions of the life of the Japanese farmer it was probably impossible to infer that there existed a conflict between Japan and the United States critical enough to produce an explosion as great as the attack on Pearl Harbor. In general, the individual is not preoccupied in his private life with a national conflict. He worries about his personal problems, first and foremost his daily bread, especially in countries where poverty prevails.

For this reason, it would also be an error to derive lessons concerning the political position of the Palestinians or the Egyptians from literary descriptions of the life of the Palestinian or Egyptian individual. If the conflict preoccupies the Egyptian as an individual slightly, this by no means implies that it is marginal to Egypt as a state. If the average Egyptian is not filled with enmity toward Jews and Israel, this may not be reflected in the political position. Egypt as a state may be still bitterly hostile toward Israel. Political leadership determines political objectives, and it is not necessarily influenced daily by popular conceptions. The direction of influence is generally the opposite, for recognized and accepted leaders influence their people more than their people influence them. Political opinions and views among the public are not formed spontaneously as much as they are the effect of influence by that circle called "the molders of public opinion": local leaders, journalists, authors and, at their head, the political leadership. Popular emotions do not necessarily create an international conflict. For the most part, people do not make war because they hate; they hate because they make war. It is political conflict that incites hatred. Notions that are current among the people may have significance insofar as they bear upon their

support of the government. But again, this requires qualification, especially as regards Arab countries. Regimes did
not necessarily come to power in Arab countries because
they had popular support, but having achieved power they
could create it. The regimes in Arab countries can be unpopular, or become unpopular, and nevertheless retain their
position for a long time.

A question that is being argued with great fervor is
whether the Palestinians are a people or nation. But there is
no accepted criterion or definition by which to decide what
constitutes a people or nation. It cannot be determined, for
example, what necessary components form a nation. Neither
territory nor language are a necessary criterion. The Jews,
for example, had no territory, and there are nations which
have no language of their own, or which speak a number of
languages. It was not without reason that Ernest Renan
defined the nation subjectively as "a daily plebiscite." That
is, the human group determines according to its feelings and
mutual attachment whether it is a nation or not. The argument that the Palestinians are not a nation because such a
nation has not existed in the past is not persuasive. No
nation existed primordially; all were the product of an
historical process, generally by interaction with a governmental center. The distinction between people and nation on
the one hand, and non-people and non-nation on the other,
is not dichotomous. It seems better to view nationhood as
a continuum, at the one end of which there is a group of
people among whom there is no cohesion, and at the other
end of which there is a group whose cohesion has been
realized. This continuum implies that the existence of the
nation is relative. For example, the Swedes, so to speak,
are "more a nation" than the Pakistanis, the Pakistanis
more a nation than the Tanzanians, and so on. The Palestinians are found somewhere on this continuum, and their
national status will be determined by what happens to them.

If at some point a Palestinian state is created, this status will reach maturity and be reflected also in subjective feelings.

Until 1948 the conflict was basically between Israel and the Palestinians. The intervention of the Arab states caused the role of the Palestinians to diminish. After May 1948 their position in the conflict became marginal. The pendulum swings back in the first half of the 1960's, when the Palestinians again win prominence. It should be noted that this emergence parallels a process of *radicalization* in the concept of the form of warfare against Israel. Ideas appear to the effect that the conflict involves "a war of national liberation," in which the Palestinians will be the vanguard, and the war, at least in its early stages, will take on the form of guerrilla warfare. It should be remembered that, in the meantime, changes of the guard had begun in the Palestinian leadership, and a younger generation emerged, of a predominantly Leftist state of mind, which advocated activism in the struggle with Israel and disparaged the "passivity" (*salbiyya*) of the previous generation. This state of mind of the younger generation was first given a literary expression. The younger generation expressed ideas in periodicals and books concerning the most efficient form of combating Israel. Only afterwards were these ideas given organizational form in the shape of the fedayeen groups, the chief of them being Fatah.

A great change took place in the status of the Palestinians as a result of the Six-Day War. Their stature, which was bowed by their defeat in 1948 and their exile, was raised, for after the downfall of the Arab armies fedayeen actions gained renown for them in Arab countries and outside, and the Palestinians were transformed from an inferior factor into standard-bearers of Arab nationalism and a source of pride. Again, this is not always translated into the concrete, practical attitude of the population in Arab countries toward them. Their support remains on a national and political level and is not always expressed in real action to mitigate the suffering of the Palestinian refugees.

In the past the conflict was presented as though it had two levels: the first, the national-geopolitical antagonism between Israel and Arab nationalism; and the second, the problem of the Palestinians. Arab ideologues emphasized that the antagonism on the international level was the principal one, and that even if the issue of the Palestinians were solved and the refugees settled, the principal antagonism between Israel and Arabdom would still remain.

As a result of the war the situation has been reversed and, according to current fashion, the collision with the Palestinians is presented as the essence of the conflict, for this is allegedly a struggle for "national liberation." Arabs explain, especially to foreigners, that the antagonism is not that of the large Arab states versus a small state like Israel but of an oppressed people against a strong, colonialist, oppressive state. David has become Goliath. It is maintained that the antagonism of the rest of the Arab states is a by-product of the Palestinian cause. Thus, the geopolitical issue is demoted, if only temporarily and for purposes of presentation. The focus of the conflict is shifted. It is not between states but between a government and a people struggling for its liberation, which by definition is a just war that deserves support. The "liberation" of the Palestinians (in this version) is not the elimination of their subjugation but the establishment of their sovereignty over Palestine.

The paradox in this switch is that when the conflict was marginal for public opinion in Arab countries it was represented as a conflict between the Arab states and Israel, while precisely when the importance and saliency of the conflict increased in the national life of neighboring states it is not represented as a conflict between them and Israel but between the Palestinians and Israel.

Since the importance of the Palestinians in the conflict

has grown, the question arises: can a settlement be reached
with them?

Palestinians of the West Bank and Gaza

The Palestinians are divided into two main groups. The
first consists of those who live in the West Bank (Judea and
Samaria) and the Gaza Strip. Many in this group are
apprehensive about a renewal of the war, for they may
assume by extrapolation that in the contest between Israel
and the Arabs they are liable to be the principal victims.
For this reason, it is no wonder that these people would
want a settlement which might prevent a renewed eruption
of the war. They could also explain to the Arab countries
that such a settlement with Israel will benefit the Arabs,
for it would bring about withdrawal of the Israeli military
presence from the territories that are occupied. This settlement, they could contend, is not the final word, and would
not be a barrier when the Arab states regain their strength
and are able to reopen the war. In fact, the idea of a Palestinian state arose in Arab countries. It was raised by the
Egyptian journalist, Ahmad Baha' ad-Din (in his book,
*The Proposal for a State of Palestine and the Controversy
Surrounding It*). However, he did not intend a state that
would make peace with Israel but "a confrontation state"
that would include Jordan. This state would make a military
pact with the other Arab states and serve as the base for the
onslaught against Israel. It should be noted that the concept
is not new: it is merely the metamorphosis of an idea that
arose previously concerning the establishment of "The
Republic of Palestine." The issue was brought up by General
Qassem in 1959 and emerged again during the first stages of
the establishment of the Palestine Liberation Organization at
the beginning of 1964, and then afterwards when relations

between the organization and the Jordanian rulers became strained.

The leaders of the Arab states, including the leaders of the Palestinian organizations, took a strong, unequivocal stand against a Palestinian state in any agreement with Israel. Most of those who debated the proposal of Baha' ad-Din, whose articles he includes in his book, rejected it. They pointed out that the present time is not appropriate for this proposal because the establishment of a Palestinian state would arouse opposition among circles close to the government of Jordan and thus produce an internal rift, weakening the front against Israel.

An agreement by the Palestinians of the West Bank to a settlement with Israel in face of opposition by the Arab rulers would brand them as traitors. One must not underestimate the deterrent force of this stigma for them. Even more serious from their point of view is the fear that a settlement with Israel would cut them off from the places of dispersion where their families are—from sons, daughters and relatives in Arab countries. This is how the Arab countries might penalize them. The Palestinians on the West Bank cannot, therefore, allow themselves a settlement because of human and family reasons. It is no surprise that so few expressed support for the idea of a Palestinian state.

The Palestinians of the West Bank want two things; the flaw is that they are incompatible. It is possible that many of them want a settlement with Israel, but on condition that the Arab League and the Arab states endorse it. They face a dilemma: on the one hand, fear of war and the desire for a settlement that would prevent it; and on the other, apprehension of separation from their families and national ostracism within the Arab world. It is no wonder that, when they are forced to choose between leaving the situation as is with all its dangers and a settlement in defiance of the Arab countries, they tend to elect the first alternative.

A strong stand against the idea of a Palestinian state on the West Bank was taken by the Palestinian National Council in its Fourth Congress, which took place in Cairo beginning on July 10, 1968. (The Palestinian National Council is the highest institution of the Palestine Liberation Organization, which now embraces virtually all the Palestinian organizations.) Among its political resolutions, under the heading, "The Dubious Calls for Creation of a Fraudulent Palestinian Entity," it is stated:

The Zionist movement, imperialism and Israel, the tool of both, are making efforts to reinforce the Zionist aggression against Palestine and to strengthen the Israeli military victory of 1948 and of 1967 by establishing a Palestinian entity in the territory conquered after the agression of June 5th, an entity which will bestow legality and permanence on the State of Israel. This is an act which utterly contradicts the right of the Palestinian Arab people to the whole of its homeland of Palestine. This fraudulent entity is actually an Israeli colony which will finally liquidate to Israel's advantage the Palestinian problem. At the same time, it will be a temporary stage which will enable Zionism to evacuate the Arab inhabitants from the Palestinian territories which were conquered after the aggression of June 5th. Moreover, there will be the possibility of setting up a vassal (*'amīl*) Palestinian Arab administration, upon which Israel will depend in its contest with the Palestinian revolution. There also enter into this framework the imperialist and Zionist programs to place the Palestinian territories conquered after June 5th under international administration and protection.[4] Whence the National Council declares its absolute denunciation of the idea of the fraudulent Palestinian entity in the territories of Palestine conquered after June 5th and, together with this, denunciation of every form of international protection. Likewise, it declares that every Arab individual or group, Palestinian or non-Palestinian, calling for the vassal entity and international protection, or supporting it, is the enemy of the Palestinian Arab people and the Arab nation. (The official report of the Congress, pp. 39–40.)

The declaration concerning "the enemy of the people" is, in in effect, a threat against the life of any Arab who may take a less extremist position.

Presenting the problem as though what is required for a settlement with the Palestinians is Israel's recognition of them is a distortion. This indictment by Israelis only supports the slander against Israel, that Israel is the principal barrier to peace. If in some circles in the world Israel's image has become cloudy, not only the extremist Israelis, but also many of those Israelis who claim to be men of peace, are responsible. Israel, in fact, has already recognized a Palestinian entity, as implied in its very acceptance of the Partition Resolution in 1947, which stipulated the establishment of a Palestinian Arab state alongside the Jewish state. The problem was, and remains, quite the opposite: not recognition on Israel's part of the Palestinian's right to a section of country but the non-recognition on the part of the Palestinians and the Arabs of Israel's national right to a separate national existence of its own. In the Palestinian position there was a consistent totalistic demand for exclusive possession. This appeared in the form of opposition to the Partition Plan, and appears today in the demand for "entire liberation" and sovereignty over the whole territory of Palestine. (The reader will find documentation of this in the Palestinian National Covenant.) For Israel to proclaim day and night that it recognizes the Palestinians is irrelevant to the possibility of establishing a Palestinian state by agreement even within the Armistice demarcation lines.

Palestinians in the Arab States

The second Palestinian group consists of those found outside the present boundaries of Israel. They have nothing to lose from the continuation of the conflict, as have the Arabs of the West Bank. Their leaders have capitalized on the conflict and thrive on it. Men like Yassir Arafat and George Habash acquired a high status only owing to the conflict. In their case there is rabid opposition to a compromise solution. They vehemently oppose any political settlement, regardless of boundaries or conditions, because their opposition is to the principle of a Jewish state in any size or shape. They formulated this opposition to a political settlement in their National Covenant, in its new version adopted by their Congress in Cairo in July 1968 and reinforced it with explicit resolutions. The National Covenant is the Palestinians' basic political document and it was approved by all the terrorist organizations. Concurrence with it is a condition for joining the "Command of Armed Struggle," which now makes joint announcements for most of the terrorist organizations. What is said in it has more weight than the declaration of any Palestinian spokesman. For an understanding of the Arab position, especially that of the Palestinians, there is no more important document. Article 21 of this charter asserts: "The Arab Palestinian people, expressing themselves by the armed Palestinian revolution, reject all solutions which are substitutes for the total liberation of Palestine. . . ." The right of self-determination becomes the right of "restoring" the whole territory of Palestine. The Jews now living in the country have no right of national self-determination. Many Palestinian leaders outside the country affirm that they do not fear another war, nor even another defeat of the Arab states. On the contrary, it appears that they are interested in embroiling the Arab states in the conflict as much as possible. The position of these Palestinians toward Israel has become polarized. Their hostility toward Israel is much more central in their worldview than was the hostility of the Nazis to Jews. However, they now choose to hide their aim of destroying Israel in euphemisms, such as, "the dezionization of Israel," or "the restoration of the rights of the Arabs in Palestine," which does not alter the basic meaning, namely, the annihilation of Israel.

Even though the Arab's confidence in their ability to achieve their aim was shaken by the Six-Day War, the radicalism of the Palestinian leadership outside the country increased as a result of the war. This can be deduced from comparison of the Covenant in its first version of May 1964, from the time of Shukeiry, with the version adopted under the influence of Yahya Hamuda and Yasser Arafat concerning the fate of the Jews in the free Palestinian Arab state after it is "liberated" and Israel annihilated. The former version can be interpreted to the effect that the Jews who lived in Palestine in 1947 would be recognized as Palestinians, that is, would be able to remain; whereas in the new text, as revised in the fourth session of the National Council (July 1968), it is explicitly stated that only Jews who lived permanently in Palestine before 1917 would be recognized as Palestinians. This implies that the rest are aliens and must leave. It is indeed difficult to agree with the claim of some people, that the Arabs have become more realistic and their position more moderate, if a hallowed and authoritative document like the National Covenant specifies the aim of banishing almost two and a half million Jews.

What can be a more flagrant contradiction of the slogan they brandish today concerning a "pluralistic society"? It should be mentioned that the representatives of all the Palestinian organizations participated in the National Council, including the principal fedayeen groups. The Popular Front for the Liberation of Palestine, which is critical of the Palestine Liberation Organization, did not criticize this article. The importance of such articles in the Covenant is not in their practical value but in the state of mind reflected in them. Shukeiry did speak of throwing the Jews into the sea and used many vilifying expressions, but his position was in principle less radical. In view of the extremism of the official Palestinian and Arab position, what value is there to the words of an Arab student outside the country who tries to lend moderation to his stand, out of false piety or an effort to conform to the general atmosphere and find favor in foreigners' eyes, while in closed gatherings of Arab students he holds the official position, and upon returning to his country shows the same tendency to conform to the radical atmosphere of the Arab countries? Even if we assume that he was sincere in his remarks, their value is nil against the collective position. Moreover, there is no sign of any dissociation from this formulation of the Covenant by any Arab group, including Arab student organizations abroad. In no Arab newspaper or other publication was there even the slightest afterthought about the wisdom of this formulation. In the meantime, three more congresses were held and the Covenant was not amended. It seems that there is no more decisive evidence regarding the essence of the Palestinian Arab position.

One may ponder what induced the Palestinian Congress which assembled in Cairo on July 10, 1968 to introduce this change regarding the Jews "who would be permitted" to remain in a Palestinian state. We shall probably have to wait for solid information until clarifications are published by the participants in the Congress, or until its minutes or those of the Covenant Committee appointed to formulate it become known. In the meantime, it is possible to guess what factors prompted this. It may be that the very emphasis by Palestinian spokesmen that the state will be "democratic" necessitates the reduction of the number of Jews to a small minority. It is also possible that the radicalization of their position as a result of Fatah's gaining control of the Palestine Liberation Organization produces greater doctrinal consistency: since Zionism is despicable, their argument would run, it is necessary to purge the country of all the Jews who came after the first political recognition that was granted to Zionism in the Balfour Declaration. Fatah defines the purpose of the war thus: "The action of liberation is not only the liquidation of an imperialistic base but the obliteration of a society" (Fatah pamphlet, *Taḥrir al-Aqṭār al-Muḥtalla wa-Uslūb al-Kifāḥ ḍidd al-Istiʿmār al-Mubāshir* ("The Liberation of the Occupied Territories and the Means of Combating Direct Colonialism"), new edition, September 1967, p.16; Fatah Yearbook, 1968, p. 39). It may also be that the qualitative superiority of the Israeli and Israeli society, which was conspicuous in the Six-Day War, in contrast to Arab weakness, engenders apprehensions about living together with a significant Jewish minority; hence the need that it be small. Reduction of the number of Jews in Palestine is inherent in the Arab position. If to the outside world they now prudently avoid specifying that it will be done by violent means, as a compensation, the dimensions of the designed reduction have increased.

The Palestinian Arab position, as expressed in pronouncements of Palestinian spokesmen, is not only a demand to return to Palestine as its sovereigns but that Palestine should return to the Arabs as Arab, that is, after its foreign population is purged from it. It is not accidental that in their descriptions of its "liberation" they frequently use the verb "purify." Professor Fayez Sayegh, who was a member of the Executive Committee of the Palestine Liberation Organization and the founder of the Palestine Research Center, formulates the position in the following words: "Peace in the land of Palestine and its neighbors is our fondest desire. The primary condition for this is the liberation of Palestine, that is, the condition is our return to an Arab Palestine and the restoration of Palestine to us *as Arab*" ([emphasis added], *Ḥafna min Ḍabāb* ("A Handful of Mist"), PLO Research Center, Beirut, July 1966, p. 19). Shafiq al-Hut, the head of the Beirut branch of the Palestine Liberation Organization, writes in the same spirit: "Disregarding the Palestinian entity is only a part of the Zionist imperialist plot, the aim of which is the liquidation of the people of Palestine and prevention of its attaining its right in the struggle for liberation of its usurped country, restoration of it as free and Arab, and returning its people to it as free and sovereign, abounding with honor and glory" (*Ḥaqā'iq 'alā Ṭarīq at-Taḥrīr* ("Truths on the Way of Liberation"), PLO Research Center, Beirut, November 1966, p. 6).

Among the Arabs the Palestinians outside the country are the most radical and uncompromising group. Their leaders and intellectuals acquired positions and influence in Arab public life, and they are most vehement in incitement against Israel. These Palestinians are not hostile to Israel on account of the hostility of the Arab states. The converse is rather more accurate: the hostility of the Arab states is caused to a great degree by the hostility of the Palestinians. Nasser reiterated the statement, "We shall not concede the rights of the Palestinians," that is, he presented himself as fighting their war. Nasser repeatedly defined the Palestinian problem as one of "a people" and its "fatherland," that is, the people must become sovereign over its fatherland. Nasser indicated that he would agree to a peace settlement after a just solution from the point of view of the Palestinians was found. He could agree to the Security Council Resolution of November 22, 1967 because this condition was included in it, according to Arab interpretation. The problem is that according to this interpretation justice means the eventual sovereignty of the Palestinians over their homeland. The injustice inflicted on the Palestinians is not only in their loss of property but is implicit in the circumstance that their homeland and sovereignty were taken from them. Less than restoration of sovereignty is not "just," and a partial justice is a self-contradiction because it permits the injustice to remain. Thus, the use of the language current among the Arabs, "a just solution of the problem of the Palestinians," is actually a euphemism for the destruction of Israel. The existence of Israel and a just solution of the problem of the Palestinians, as the Palestinians and Arabs define it, are thus incompatible.

A complication is created which is the essence of the Arab-Israeli conflict at the present stage. The Palestinians on the West Bank can hardly allow themselves to reach a settlement with Israel at the expense of the Arab states. The Arab states are bound to a degree that should not be under-rated by their commitment to the Palestinians, especially those outside Israel's borders. In this triangle, therefore, the Palestinian leadership outside Israel's borders is the principal barrier to a settlement.

At the present stage the Palestinians outside the country are more influential than those of the West Bank. The relationship is asymmetrical. The Palestinian leaders outside the country have influence over the Palestinians of the West Bank, but it is doubtful whether the leaders of the West Bank could influence the Palestinians outside to change their position. This change is possible only by means of the suppression of their organizations by the Arab states. Indeed, between them and the Arab states there are seeds of antagonisms which may develop into a confrontation.

One should not overlook the status and influence this Palestinian leadership outside the country has. However, when it becomes clear to what extent it has failed, especially in relying on fedayeenism, when this does not produce the anticipated results, its status is bound to be undermined. When the Arab states discover to what extent continuation of the conflict is destructive from their point of view, draws them into political disintegration, and denies them the possibility of national progress and recovery, they may take action against the Palestinian organizations outside the country. Then there will be an opening for negotiation and a settlement between Israel and the Palestinians nearby, and between Israel and the Arab countries.

Notes

1 A. L. Tibawi, "Visions of the Return: The Palestine Refugees in Arabic Poetry and Art," *The Middle East Journal*, 17 (1963), pp. 507–526.
2 A village east of Tiberias which is frequently mentioned in Arabic literature as an example of Jewish terrorism. 'Arif al-'Arif relates that ten Arabs were killed there (*an-Nakba*, Vol. I, p. 205).
3 Arab ideologues tend now to distinguish between the one Arab "nation" and the many Arab "peoples," such as the Egyptians, Iraqis and so on. They call attachment to the nation *qawmiyya*, "nationalism," whereas attachment to the people, and especially its land, they call *waṭaniyya*, which recently took on the sense of "patriotism." Correspondingly, there are also those who distinguish between the general homeland of all the Arabs, *al-waṭan al-'āmm*, and the homeland of a specific people, which is called *al-waṭan al-khāss*.
4 This has to do with the idea of demilitarizing the West Bank for a number of years under UN protection. It was suggested by foreign consuls in conversations with men of the West Bank and was considered by its leaders.

Works Cited

al-'Arif, 'Arif. *an-Nakba: Nakbat Bayt al-Maqdis wal-Firdaws al-Mafqūd* ("The Disaster: The Disaster of Palestine and the Paradise Lost"), Five vols. Sidon-Beirut: al-Maktaba al-'Asriyya, 1947–1955.

Baha' ad-Din, Ahmad. *Iqtirāh Dawlat Filastīn wa-mā Dāra thawlahā min Munāqashāt* ("The Proposal for a State of Palestine and the Controversy Surrounding It"). Beirut: Dar al-Adab, 1968.

Galtung, I. and J. *A Pilot Project from Gaza.* Peace Research Institute, Oslo, February 1964.

al-Hut, Shafiq. *Haqā'iq 'alā Tarīq at-Tahrīr* ("Truths on the Way to Liberation"). PLO Research Center. Beirut, November 1966.

Munazzamat at-Tahrīr al-Filastīniyya (PLO). *al-Majlis al-Watani al-Filastini al-Mun'aqad fi al-Qāhira fi 10–17 Tammūz (Yūliyō), 1968* ("The Palestinian National Council, which Convened in Cairo July 10–17, 1968"). Official Report.

an-Nashashibi, Nasir ad-Din. *Tadhkirat 'Awda* ("Return Ticket"). Beirut: al-Maktab at-Tijari, 1962.

Sayegh, Fayez. *Hafna min Dabāb* ("A Handful of Mist"). PLO Research Cênter. Beirût, July 1966.

Tibawi, A. L. "Visions of the Return: The Palestine Refugees in Arabic Poetry and Art," *The Middle East Journal,* 17 (1963), pp. 507–526.

3

The Palestinian National Covenant

The Palestinian National Covenant is perhaps the most important document at this stage of the Arab-Israel conflict, especially with regard to the Palestinian side. It represents a summation of the official position of the Palestinian organizations in the conflict.[1]

The previous version of the Covenant was adopted by the First Palestinian Congress, which convened in Jerusalem in May 1964 at the time of the establishment of the Palestine Liberation Organization. In the official English translation of the previous version it was called "Covenant" and not "Charter," in order to emphasize its national sanctity, and the introductory words to the Covenant conclude with an oath to implement it. The Congress stipulated that a Palestinian National Council, the highest institution of the Palestinian organizations, would meet periodically, and that a two-thirds majority of the Council members would be required to amend the Covenant. As a result of the changes which came about in the Palestine Liberation Organization after the Six-Day War, the Palestinian National Council convened in Cairo for its fourth session on July 10–17, 1968 and amended the Covenant. The membership of the Council had undergone a radical change. The number of delegates was reduced from some 400 (present at previous Congresses) to 100. The traditional dignitaries of the Shukeiry period completely disappeared. It should be noted that representatives of almost all the Palestinian organizations existing in

Arab countries participated in this session, including all the fedayeen organizations. Fatah and the fedayeen organizations affiliated to it had 37 representatives in the National Council of 100 members and the Popular Front had ten. Fatah's style is recognizable in the new Covenant. This amended version was certainly not formulated casually; it represents a position that was seriously considered and weighed. The amended version is here presented. In order to highlight the changes we shall compare this version with its predecessor.

The main principles which were set down in the Covenant are:

In the Palestinian state only Jews who lived in Palestine before 1917 will be recognized as citizens (Article 6).

Only the Palestinian Arabs possess the right of self-determination, and the entire country belongs to them (Articles 3 and 21).

Any solution that does not involve total liberation of the country is rejected. This aim cannot be achieved politically; it can only be accomplished militarily (Articles 9 and 21).

Warfare against Israel is legal, whereas Israel's self-defense is illegal (Article 18).

The Covenant is presented here in its entirety. This version is still in force and has not been amended by subsequent Palestinian National Councils, including the last one (the twelfth) which convened in June 1974. The final communiqué of the Palestinian Popular Congress on April 10, 1972 proclaimed: "The Palestine Popular Congress reaffirms its belief in, and adherence to, the Palestine National Charter" (*Journal of Palestine Studies*, Vol. 1, No. 4, Summer 1972, p. 177; Arabic original in the Official Report of the Congress, p. 142).

The full text of the Covenant is given below in italics, each article being followed by commentary by Y. Harkabi. The English rendition is taken from Leila S. Kadi (ed.), *Basic*

Political Documents of the Armed Palestinian Resistance Movement, PLO Organization Research Center, Beirut, December 1969, pp. 137–141.

The Palestinian National Covenant

This Covenant will be called "The Palestinian National Covenant" (al-Mīthāq al-waṭanī al-filasṭīnī).

In the previous version of the Covenant of May 1964 the adjective "national" was rendered by *qawmī*, the usual meaning of which in modern Arabic is pan-Arab and ethnic nationalism, whereas here the adjective *waṭanī* is used, which signifies nationalism in its narrow, territorialistic sense as patriotism toward a specific country. This change is designed to stress Palestinian patriotism.

Articles of the Covenant

Article 1: Palestine is the homeland of the Arab Palestinian people; it is an indivisible part of the Arab homeland, and the Palestinian people are an integral part of the Arab nation.

In most Arab constitutions it is simply stipulated that the people of the particular country constitutes an integral part of the Arab nation. Here, because of the special problem of territory, it is also stressed that the land is an integral part of the general Arab homeland. The previous version in the Covenant of 1964 was more vague: "Palestine is an Arab homeland bound by strong Arab national ties to the rest of the Arab countries which together form the Great Arab Homeland." The combination "the Palestinian Arab people" recurs often in the Covenant and is also intended to stress the special status of the Palestinians, though as Arabs.

Article 2: Palestine, with the boundaries it had during the British mandate, is an indivisible territorial unit.

The same formulation as in the previous version. It is implied that Palestine should not be divided into a Jewish and an Arab state. Although it is an accepted tenet of Arab nationalism that existing boundaries should one day be abolished, since they were artificially delineated by the imperialist powers, here they are sanctified. The expression "that existed at the time of the British Mandate" is vague. The article is subject to two interpretations: 1) The Palestinian State includes also Jordan; 2) The whole area west of the Jordan.

Article 3: The Palestinian Arab people possess the legal right to their homeland and have the right to determine their destiny after achieving the liberation of their country in accordance with their wishes and entirely of their own accord and will.

The decision concerning the problem of the internal regime is deferred until after the liberation. The crux of this article is to postpone the decision concerning the relation to the Kingdom of Jordan and Hashemite rule. There is also the emphasis here that only the Palestinian Arabs possess a national legal right, excluding of course the Jews, to whom a special article is devoted below.

Article 4: The Palestinian identity is a genuine, essential and inherent characteristic, it is transmitted from parents to children. The Zionist occupation and the dispersal of the Palestinian Arab people, through the disasters which befell them, do not make them lose their Palestinian identity and their membership of the Palestinian community, nor do they negate them.

The Palestinian, therefore, cannot cease being a Palestinian. Palestinianism is not citizenship but an eternal characteristic that comes from birth. The Jew is a Jew through the maternal line, and the Palestinian a Palestinian through the paternal line. The Palestinians, consequently, cannot be assimilated. This article implies that Palestinian citizenship follows from the Palestinian characteristic. This is the Palestinian counterpart to the Israeli Law of Return.

Article 5: The Palestinians are those Arab nationals who, until 1947, normally resided in Palestine regardless of whether they were evicted from it or have stayed there. Anyone born, after that date, of a Palestinian father—whether inside Palestine or outside it—is also a Palestinian.

A reinforcement of the previous article. This definition refers solely to the Arabs. With reference to the Jews the matter is different. This is because being Palestinian assumes being Arab.

Article 6: The Jews who had normally resided in Palestine until the beginning of the Zionist invasion will be considered Palestinians.

In the section on resolutions of the Congress, in the chapter entitled "The International Palestinian Struggle" (p. 51), it is stated: "Likewise, the National Council affirms that the aggression against the Arab nation and its land began with the Zionist invasion of Palestine in 1917.[2] Therefore, the meaning of 'removal of the traces of the aggression' must be removal of the traces of the aggression which came into effect from the beginning of the Zionist invasion and not from the war of June 1967. . . ."

"The beginning of the Zionist invasion" is therefore at the time of the Balfour Declaration. This conception is current in Arab political literature. In the 1964 version the corresponding article was: "Jews of Palestinian origin will be considered Palestinians if they are willing to endeavor to live in loyalty and peace in Palestine." The expression "of Palestinian origin" is vague, for the article does not specify which Jews are to be considered of Palestinian origin. Since in the previous article (5 in the new version, 6 in the old) the date which determines being Palestinian is set at 1947, the implication could be that this applies also to the Jews, i.e., the Jews who could have become naturalized in Mandatory Palestine and presumably their offspring. Since the aim is the return of the Arab Palestinians, it is necessary to make room for them. However, in the meantime, Jews have taken up residence in Arab dwellings, especially those Jews who immigrated after 1947; hence also from a practical aspect it is necessary to remove these Jews in particular.

The Jews who will not be recognized as Palestinians are therefore aliens who have no right of residence and must leave.

The National Covenant is a public document intended for general distribution. The Executive Committee of the Palestine Liberation Organization specified in its introduction to the official report of the proceedings of the Congress as follows: "In view of the importance of the resolutions of the Palestinian National Council in its session convened in Cairo from July 10 to 17, 1968, we published them in this booklet so that the Palestinians in every place may read them and find in them a policy and a program. . . ." (pp. 17–18).

One might expect that those hundred members of the National Council would have recoiled from adopting such an extreme position which could serve as a weapon against the Palestinians. The fact that they did not is itself of great significance and testifies to the vehemence of the Palestinian Arab position.

The amended version of this article points to a radicalization of the Palestinian Arab position. It contains decisive evidence as to the nature of the slogan which Arab leaders brandish concerning a "pluralistic, democratic state." Pluralism that is expressed in expelling 2,400,000 Israeli Jews is nothing but throwing dust in the eyes.

The existence of Article 6 was an inconvenience to Arab spokesmen. It is no wonder that they tried to explain it away. This article has been misrepresented by Hishām Sharābi, professor of history at Georgetown University, Washington D.C. His version is:

Jews living in Palestine until the time of the Zionist occupation (1948) are also Palestinians (*Palestine and Israel: The Lethal Dilemma*, Pegasus, New York 1969, p. 201).

The original document reads in arabic:

Al-Yahud alladh'īna kānū yuqimūna iqāmatan 'ādīyatan fi Filastīn hatta bad'i alghazui alzahiuni laha yu'tabrana filastiniyyin.

Professor Sharabi replaces the term "invasion" by "occupation," adding "(1948)." This was not done inadvertently. It is disconcerting to note how a renowned scholar resorts to such distortions.

In contrast, *The Yearbook of the Palestinian Problem for the Year 1968* (Arabic, Beirut 1971, p. 71) faithfully described the amended article: "One of the important amendments of the National Palestinian Covenant is of Article 6, which . . . means that the National Covenant considers only those Jews living in Palestine before 1917 as Palestinians."

Article 7: That there is a Palestinian community and that it has material, spiritual and historical connections with Palestine are indisputable facts. It is a national duty to bring up individual Palestinians in an Arab revolutionary manner. All means of information and education must be adopted in order to acquaint the Palestinian with his country in the most profound manner, both spiritual and material, that is possible. He must be prepared for the armed struggle and ready to sacrifice his wealth and his life in order to win back his homeland and bring about its liberation.

The second part, the preparation for the struggle, is new

and was formulated under the influence of the special place that is now given to fedayeenism.

*Article 8: The phase in their history, through which the Palestinian people are now living, is that of national (*waṭanī*) struggle for the liberation of Palestine. Thus the conflicts among the Palestinian national forces are secondary, and should be ended for the sake of the basic conflict that exists between the forces of Zionism and of imperialism on the one hand, and the Palestinian Arab people on the other. On this basis the Palestinian masses, regardless of whether they are residing in the national homeland or in diaspora (*mahajir*) constitute—both their organizations and the individuals—one national front working for the retrieval of Palestine and its liberation through armed struggle.*

It is necessary to postpone internal disputes and concentrate on warfare against Israel. The style of "secondary contradictions" and "fundamental contradictions" is influenced by the language of Fatah and the younger circles. In the previous corresponding article it is stated: "Doctrines, whether political, social or economic, shall not divert the people of Palestine from their primary duty of liberating their homeland. . . ."

Article 9: Armed struggle is the only way to liberate Palestine. Thus it is the overall strategy, not merely a tactical phase. The Palestinian Arab people assert their absolute determination and firm resolution to continue their armed struggle and to work for an armed popular revolution for the liberation of their country and their return to it. They also assert their right to normal life in Palestine and to exercise their right to self-determination and sovereignty over it.

The expression "a strategy and not tactics" is from the lexicon of Fatah expressions (see Y. Harkabi, *Fedayeen Action and Arab Strategy* (Adelphi Papers, No. 53, The

Institute for Strategic Studies, London, 1968), p. 8). They use it with reference to fedayeen activities: they are not a support weapon but the essence of the war. "The armed struggle" is a broader concept, but here too stress is placed on action of the fedayeen variety. "The armed popular revolution" signifies the participation of the entire people in the war against Israel. It is depicted as a stage that will be reached by means of broadening the activity of the fedayeen. They are merely the vanguard whose role is to produce a "detonation" of the revolution until it embraces all levels of the people.

The radicalism in the aim of annihilation of the State of Israel and the "liberation" of all its territory eliminates the possibility of a political solution, which is by nature a compromise settlement. Such is the reasoning in this article and in Article 21. There remains only the way of violence.

*Article 10: Commando action constitutes the nucleus of the Palestinian popular liberation war. This requires its escalation, comprehensiveness and the mobilization of all the Palestinian popular and educational efforts and their organization and involvement in the armed Palestinian revolution. It also requires the achieving of unity for the national (*waṭanī*) struggle among the different groupings of the Palestinian people, and between the Palestinian people and the Arab masses so as to secure the continuation of the revolution, its escalation and victory.*

This article is new. It describes the "alchemy" of fedayeenism, how its activity broadens and eventually sweeps the entire people. The masses in Arab countries are described in the language of Fatah as constituting "the supportive Arab front," the role of which is not only to offer aid but to assure that the Arab states will not deviate, on account of local interests and pressures, from their obligation to support the Palestinian revolution.

As fedayeenism ebbed the Arab groups supporting the PLO were promoted at the Tenth National Council (April 1972) by being named the "Participating Front."

*Article 11: The Palestinians will have three mottoes: national (*waṭanīyya*) unity, national (*qawmiyya*) mobilization and liberation.*

Here there is no change. These mottoes are inscribed above the publications of the Palestine Liberation Organization.

Article 12: The Palestinian people believe in Arab unity. In order to contribute their share towards the attainment of that objective, however, they must, at the present stage of their struggle, safeguard their Palestinian identity and develop their consciousness of that identity, and oppose any plan that may dissolve or impair it.

The idea of Arab unity requires the giving of priority to the pan-Arab character over the local character. From the aspect of a consistent doctrine of unity, the stressing of a local character or distinctiveness is divisive because it strengthens difference, whereas unity rests on what is common and uniform. The issue of the relation between local distinctiveness and pan-Arab unity has much preoccupied the ideologues of Arab nationalism. The conservative circles tend to stress the need for preserving local character even after unity has been achieved. By this means Arab unity will be enriched through variegation. The revolutionary circles, on the other hand, stress unity and homogeneity. This is based either on a practical consideration, that internal consolidation will be reinforced in proportion to the reduction of distinctive factors, or on the view that the local character is part of the heritage they desire to change. The controversy between distinctiveness and unity is also reflected in the conception of the structure for unity. Those who seek to preserve distinctiveness deem it necessary to conserve the existing political frameworks in a loosely confederated unified structure. Those who stress unity call for the obliteration of the existing political frameworks, along with their boundaries, which were merely the adjunct of a colonial system, with the object of achieving a more consolidated political structure. This controversy may be represented as an antinomy in which Arab nationalism is caught: unity which tries to suppress the distinctive character of its parts will arouse local opposition; unity which conserves the local distinctive character may strengthen divisive tendencies.

This article seems designed to answer the charge that stressing Palestinian distinctiveness is an objective that conflicts with Arab unity (in the language of Arab nationalism, the sin of *Shu'ūbiyya* or *Iqlīmīyya*). This charge was heard, for example, from within circles of the Qawmiyyūn al-'Arab movement, who were dedicated to the idea of Arab unity. Prior to the Six-Day War this charge also had a practical aspect, namely, the assessment that excessive stress on the Palestinianism of the struggle against Israel diminished the role of the Arab states as direct participants in this confrontation. The response to this charge is, therefore, that preservation of Palestinian distinctiveness is merely a temporary necessity, to be transcended in favor of Arab unity. However, there is an obvious contradiction between this contention and the previous assertion of the eternity of the Palestinian personality.

Article 13: Arab unity and the liberation of Palestine are two complementary objectives, the attainment of either of which facilitates the attainment of the other. Thus, Arab unity leads to the liberation of Palestine; the liberation of Palestine leads to Arab unity; and work towards the realization of one objective proceeds side by side with work towards the realization of the other.

This again is an antinomy. Victory over Israel requires

concentration of all Arab forces upon the struggle, a concentration made possible only by the establishment of a supra-state authority to control all these forces, that is, a common government. Nasser repeatedly warned that unity is a precondition for initiating war against Israel. But attaining unity is a long-range affair. Consequently, war against Israel was deferred until a remote time, because undertaking a war without unity would only lead to defeat. On the other hand, unity can be attained only by the "detonation" of a spectacular event, like victory over Israel. The ideologues of Fatah were much preoccupied with this issue (see *Fedayeen Action and Arab Strategy*, p. 9). Their response is contained in their slogan: "The liberation of Palestine is the road to unity, and this is the right substitute for the slogan, 'unity is the road to the liberation of Palestine.'" Actually, this article offers a verbal solution, circumventing the problem of priority by characterizing both events as simultaneous, just as in the previous version of the Covenant.

*Article 14: The destiny of the Arab nation, and indeed Arab existence itself, depends upon the destiny of the Palestine cause. From this interdependence springs the Arab nation's pursuit of, and striving for, the liberation of Palestine. The people of Palestine play the role of the vanguard in the realization of this sacred national (*qawmī*) goal.*

This is a common notion in the Arab position. It is often stated in Arab political literature that the Palestine issue is *fateful* for the very Arab existence. It is maintained that the existence of Israel prevents the Arabs from achieving their national goal. Furthermore, the existence of Israel necessarily leads to its expansion and the liquidation of the Arabness of additional Arab lands. The Palestinians have an interest in stressing the fatefulness of the struggle against Israel and its centrality for the whole Arab world. They thus spur on the others to take an active role in the struggle against Israel. It may be that there is also implicit here the intention to lend symmetry to the conflict. Thus, both sides threaten each other with extinction, and the Arabs are not alone in this. A formula for division of labor is also presented here. The Palestinians will be the vanguard marching before the Arab camp.

Article 15: The liberation of Palestine, from an Arab viewpoint, is a national (qawmī) duty and it attempts to repel the Zionist and imperialist aggression against the Arab homeland, and aims at the elimination of Zionism in Palestine. Absolute responsibility for this falls upon the Arab nation—peoples and governments—with the Arab people of Palestine in the vanguard.

The goal is, therefore, twofold: defense of the rest of the Arab countries and removal of Zionism from Palestine.

Accordingly the Arab nation must mobilize all its military, human, and moral and spiritual capabilities to participate actively with the Palestinian people in the liberation of Palestine. It must, particularly in the phase of the armed Palestinian revolution, offer and furnish the Palestinian people with all possible help, and material and human support, and make available to them the means and opportunities that will enable them to continue to carry out their leading role in the armed revolution, until they liberate their homeland.

There is the implied concern that without the support of the Arab states, the drive of "the Palestinian revolution" will dissipate. The distinction of this version as compared with its predecessor is mainly in the accentuation of "the active participation" of the Arab states and the issue of "the armed Palestinian revolution," which is certainly to be attributed to Fatah's ideological influence upon the Palestine Liberation Organization.

Article 16: The liberation of Palestine, from a spiritual point of view, will provide the Holy Land with an atmosphere of safety and tranquility, which in turn will safeguard the country's religious sanctuaries and guarantee freedom of worship and of visit to all, without discrimination of race, color, language, or religion. Accordingly, the people of Palestine look to all spiritual forces in the world for support.

Article 17: The liberation of Palestine, from a human point of view, will restore to the Palestinian individual his dignity, pride and freedom. Accordingly the Palestinian Arab people look forward to the support of all those who believe in the dignity of man and his freedom in the world.

The very existence of Israel and the lack of a Palestinian homeland create alienation in the Palestinian, for these deprive him of his dignity and bring him to a state of subservience. As long as Israel exists the Palestinian's personality is flawed. This is an addition in the spirit of Fatah which was not in the previous version, and it is probably influenced by recent revolutionary literature, such as the teaching of Franz Fanon.

Article 18: The liberation of Palestine, from an international point of view, is a defensive action necessitated by the demands of self-defence. Accordingly, the Palestinian people, desirous as they are of the friendship of all people, look to freedom-loving, justice-loving and peace-loving states for support in order to restore their legitimate rights in Palestine, to re-establish peace and security in the country, and to enable its people to exercise national sovereignty and freedom.

As in the previous version, the existence of Israel is "illegal"; therefore war against it is "legal". In Palestinian literature there is a frequent claim that the fedayeen assaults against Israel are legal, while the self-defense and reactions of Israel are illegal, for their aim is to perpetuate the state which embodies aggression in its very establishment and existence. To the foreign observer this distinction between the legality of attacking Israel and the illegality of the response thereto may appear as sham innocence that is indeed even ludicrous. Nevertheless, it may be assumed that there are Arabs for whom this is not only a matter of formal argument but a belief.

Ibrahim al-'Abid, in an article entitled "The Reasons for the Latest Israeli Aggression" (the Six-Day War), writes: "Fedayeen action is a right of the people of Palestine because the right of national liberation is an extension of the right of peoples to self-defense, and it is the right which the United Nations Charter affirmed as an original natural right" (Anis Sayegh, ed., *Filastiniyyāt,* PLO Center for Research, Beirut 1968, p. 107).

Article 19: The partition of Palestine in 1947 and the establishment of the state of Israel are entirely illegal, regardless of the passage of time, because they were contrary to the will of the Palestinian people and to their natural right in their homeland, and inconsistent with the principles embodied in the Charter of the United Nations, particularly the right to self-determination.

It is often found in Arab literature that the Mandate and the Partition Resolution, though accepted by the League of Nations and the United Nations Organization, are simply denied all legal force. They represent (as it were) an aberration and not a norm of international law. The "reason" for this is that they contradicted the fundamental principle of the right of self-determination. This article is copied from the previous version.

Article 20: The Balfour Declaration, the mandate for Palestine and everything that has been based upon them, are deemed null and void. Claims of historical or religious ties of Jews with Palestine are incompatible with the facts of history and the true conception of what constitutes statehood. Judaism, being a religion, is not an independent nationality. Nor do Jews constitute a single nation with an identity of its own; they are citizens of the states to which they belong.

Again an identical formulation. This article incorporates the principal claims concerning historical right: The Jews lived in Palestine for only a brief time; their sovereignty over it was not exclusive; the Arabs did not conquer it from them and need not restore it to them; and the Arabs remained in the country longer than the Jews. Moreover, a state embodies a national, not a religious, principle. The Jews, having merely religious distinctiveness, do not need a state at all, and a Jewish state that makes of Judaism a nationalism is a historical and political aberration. Therefore, Zionism, as a manifestation of Jewish nationalism, distorts Judaism.

On the alleged ground that the State of Israel is not based on a true nationalism, it is very often described in Arabic as "an artificial entity." This is also brought as proof that Israel can be destroyed. This conception is also at the basis of fedayeen theory: since the Jews have no real nationalism, terror will cause their disintegration to the point that they will consent to relinquish Jewish statehood.

The conception that the Jews do not constitute a national entity is a vital principle for the Arab position. For if the Israelis do constitute a nation, then they have the right of self-determination, and the claim that only the Palestinian Arabs have the right of self-determination, and that only they must decide the national character of the country, is invalid. Moreover, the Arab claim for exclusive national self-determination appears in all its starkness as chauvinism that demands rights for itself which are denied to the other.

Article 21: The Arab Palestinian people, expressing themselves by the armed Palestinian revolution, reject all solutions which are substitutes for the total liberation of Palestine and reject all proposals aiming at the liquidation of the Palestinian problem, or its internationalization.

This rejection of any compromise settlement is an addition to the previous version. In the resolutions of the fourth session of the Palestinian National Council a long and detailed section is devoted to the rejection of the Security Council Resolution of November 22, 1967 and any peaceful solution, with insistence upon the intention to undermine any attempt in this direction.[3]

Article 22: Zionism is a political movement organically associated with international imperialism and antagonistic to all action for liberation and to progressive movements in the world. It is racist and fanatic in its nature, aggressive, expansionist and colonial in its aims, and fascist in its methods. Israel is the instrument of the Zionist movement, and a geographical base for world imperialism placed strategically in the midst of the Arab homeland to combat the hopes of the Arab nation for liberation, unity and progress.

In this new version there is an accentuation of Israel's alleged relation to world imperialism and intensification of its denunciation. This is in the spirit of the Leftist sentiments that prevail among the up-and-coming Arab generation. The claim that the hostility of Zionism is directed not only against the Arabs but against all that is good in the world, is also an addition. Thus, warfare against Israel is elevated from an Arab interest to a universal humanistic mission.

Israel is a constant source of threat vis-à-vis *peace in the Middle East and the whole world. Since the liberation of Palestine will destroy the Zionist and imperialist presence and will contribute to the establishment of peace in the Middle East, the Palestinian people look for the support of all the progressive and peaceful forces and urge them all, irrespective of their affiliations and beliefs, to offer the Palestinian people all aid and support in their just struggle for the liberation of their homeland.*

Article 23: The demands of security and peace, as well as the demands of right and justice, require all states to consider Zionism an illegitimate movement, to outlaw its existence, and to ban its operations, in order that friendly relations among peoples may be preserved, and the loyalty of citizens to their respective homelands safeguarded.

The attachment of Jews to Israel expressed in Zionism creates dual-nationality and political chaos. Arabs apparently do not sense the contradiction in this claim. Despite the prevalence of supra-national tendencies among circles in the progressive world, with which the Palestinians claim to have an affinity, a narrow, formal nationalistic approach is stressed here, which maintains that a man cannot cherish a loyal attachment to any factor apart from his own state.

Article 24: The Palestinian people believe in the principles of justice, freedom, sovereignty, self-determination, human dignity, and in the right of all peoples to exercise them.

Article 25: For the realization of the goals of this Charter and its principles, the Palestine Liberation Organization will perform its role in the liberation of Palestine in accordance with the Constitution of this Organization.

This article (with the omission of the conclusion, "in accordance with the Constitution of this Organization") is identical to the previous version. In this and the next article the Palestine Liberation Organization is presented as the umbrella organization bearing the overall responsibility for the struggle of all the Palestinians against Israel.

Article 26: The Palestine Liberation Organization, representative of the Palestinian revolutionary forces, is responsible for the Palestinian Arab people's movement in its struggle—to retrieve its homeland, liberate and return to it and exercise the right to self-determination in it—in all military, political and financial fields and also for whatever may be required by the Palestine case on the inter-Arab and international levels.

The addition here, as compared with the previous version, is that the organization also assumes the role of bringing into effect the regime it prefers after the victory.

Article 27: The Palestine Liberation Organization shall cooperate with all Arab states, each according to its potentialities; and will adopt a neutral policy among them in the light of the requirements of the war of liberation; and on this basis it shall not interfere in the internal affairs of any Arab state.

The obligation of neutrality, therefore, is not absolute but is qualified by the requirements of the struggle for liberation.

*Article 28: The Palestinian Arab people assert the genuineness and independence of their national (*waṭaniyya*) revolution and reject all forms of intervention, trusteeship and subordination.*

The Palestinian movement is not the tool of any Arab state and does not accept orders from any outside authority.

Article 29: The Palestinian people possess the fundamental and genuine legal right to liberate and retrieve their homeland. The Palestinian people determine their attitude towards all states and forces on the basis of the stands they adopt vis-à-vis the Palestinian case and the extent of the support they offer to the Palestinian revolution to fulfill the aims of the Palestinian people.

This is a new article, which includes a threat that the friendship of any state toward Israel will entail the enmity of the organization. A similar principle was established in the First Arab Summit Conference.

Article 30: Fighters and carriers of arms in the war of liberation are the nucleus of the popular army which will be the protective force for the gains of the Palestinian Arab people.

In other words, there is a future military career in joining the fedayeen.

Article 31: The Organization shall have a flag, an oath of allegiance and an anthem. All this shall be decided upon in accordance with a special regulation.

Article 32: Regulations, which shall be known as the Constitution of the Palestine Liberation Organization, shall be annexed to this Charter. It shall lay down the manner in which the Organization, and its organs and institutions, shall be constituted; the respective competence of each; and the requirements of its obligations under the Charter.

Article 33: This Charter shall not be amended save by (vote of) a majority of two-thirds of the total membership of the National Congress of the Palestine Liberation Organization (taken) at a special session convened for that purpose.

Notes

1 Acceptance of the Covenant is a formal requirement of all members of the PLO. The Regulations of Popular Organization (*at-Tanzīm ash- Sha'bī*) stipulates in Article 5: "Active membership in the Palestine Liberation Organization is open to every Palestinian Arab, male or female, on condition that he register his name with the Organization and adhere to its Covenant (*yaltazim mīthāqahā*)." The same requirement is repeated in Article 9 (The Institute for Palestine Studies, *Documents on Palestine*, 1965 (Beirut 1967), pp. 297–98).

2 Yahya Hamuda, Shukeiry's successor as head of the PLO, declared: "L'agression sur notre sol a commencé en 1917 avec

la declaration Balfour" (Vick Vance and Pierre Lauer, *Hussein de Jordanie: ma guerre avec Israël*, Paris: Albin Michel, 1968, p. 166). Naji 'Alush stated that the Palestinian Organization should "declare by every means at its disposal its absolute rejection in the name of the Palestinian people of all that has been accomplished after 1917" (*al-Masira ilā Filasṭin* ("The Way to Palestine"), Beirut: Dar at-Tali'a, 1964), p. 50).

3 Rejection of the Security Council Resolution of November 22 (Resolution 242) as a political means of ending the conflict is a common feature in all subsequent Council resolutions until the eleventh (which convened in January 1973).

4
The Meaning of "A Democratic Palestinian State"

1. The Internal Debate

The crux of the Arab conflict with Israel has been the problem of safeguarding the country's Arab character. Arab demands during the Mandate for the prohibition of the sale of land to Jews and curtailment of Jewish immigration served the same purpose: that of keeping the ownership of land and Palestine's ethnic character inviolate. The difficulties confronting the Arabs in their attempt to halt Judaization were aggravated with the end of the Mandate and the foundation of the State of Israel; from then on it was a question of turning back the wheel of history and erasing the Jewish state.

The problem of eliminating the Jewish state is heightened by the presence of a considerable Jewish population. For a Jewish state depends upon the existence of Jewish citizens, and therefore elimination of the state requires in principle a "reduction" in their number. Hence the frequency and dominance of the motif of killing the Jews and throwing them into the sea in Arab pronouncements. Their position, insofar as it was *politicidal* (i.e., calling for annihilation of a state), was bound to have *genocidal* implications, even had the Arabs not been bent upon revenge.

When, after the Six-Day War, the Arabs realized that their wild statements had harmed their international reputation, they moderated their shrill demands for the annihilation of Israel. Arab propagandists denied that they had ever advocated the slaughter of the Jewish population, asserting that, at most, "Jewish provocations" had aroused their anger and wild statements which, they alleged, were not meant to be taken literally. Ahmed Shukeiry insisted that he never advocated throwing the Jews into the sea, that the whole thing was merely a Zionist libel. What he meant, he explained, was that the Jews would return to their countries of origin by way of the sea: "They came by the sea and will return by the sea" (*Palestine Documents for 1967*, p. 1084).

After the Six-Day War, Arab spokesmen put forward the concept of "a Democratic Palestinian State in which Arabs and Jews will live in peace." This slogan was well recieved and regarded by the world at large as evidence of a new Arab moderation. Many people overlooked the ambiguity of the pronouncement and disregarded the fact that it did not contradict basic Arab contentions: for the wording might well imply the reduction of Jews to an insignificant minority, which would then be permitted to live in peace. Once this line was adopted, its meaning was keenly debated among the Palestinian Arabs.

An indication of the slogan's true significance, as understood by the Palestinian organizations, is found in a circular to its members sent by the Popular Democratic Front for the Liberation of Palestine, reporting on the deliberations of the sixth session of the Palestinian National Assembly. This fedayeen organization, headed by Na'if Hawatmeh, broke away from George Habash's Popular Front for the Liberation of Palestine in February 1969. A delegation of the Popular Democratic Front proposed to the Assembly that the slogan "Democratic State" should be given "a progressive content." The Assembly rejected their proposal suggesting that the main purpose of the "Democratic State" concept was to improve the Arab image. Moreover, the inclusion of this slogan in the national program would, it was stressed, impair the Arab character of Palestine. Nevertheless, since it had been well received abroad, the Assembly considered it worth retaining.

The relevant passage in the Popular Democratic Front's report entitled "Internal Circular concerning Debates and Results of the Sixth National Assembly" reads:

The slogan "The Democratic Palestinian State" has been raised for some time within the Palestinian context. Fatah was the first to adopt it. Since it was raised, this slogan has met with remarkable world response. Our delegation presented the Congress [i.e., the Assembly] with a resolution designed to elucidate its meaning from a progressive aspect, opposing in principle the slogan of throwing the Jews into the sea, which has in the past seriously harmed the Arab position.

When the subject was first debated, it was thought that there was general agreement on it. But as the debate developed, considerable opposition showed itself. In the course of the discussion the following views came to light:

1. One which maintains that the slogan of "The Democratic Palestinian State" is a tactical one which we propagate because it has been well received internationally.

2. Another suggests that we consider this slogan to be strategic rather than tactical, but that it should be retained even though it is not a basic principle. This position, but for a mere play of words, corresponds to the previous one.

3. The third view was more straightforward in rejecting the slogan and its progressive content as proposed by our delegation. The position of this faction was based on the assertion that the slogan contradicts the Arab character of Palestine and the principle of self-determination enshrined in the National Covenant of the [Palestine] Liberation

Organization, and that it also advocates a peaceful settlement with the Jews of Palestine.

This means that the Arab character which the country is to have after its "liberation" would be undermined, if, taking the concept literally, a large group of Jews were permitted to remain. The Palestinian National Covenant stipulated that only the Palestinian Arabs had the right to self-determination, whereas the slogan of a "Democratic State" makes the Jews partners.

These were the contending views concerning the slogan of "The Democratic Palestinian State." We were able to arrive at a recommendation to continue in the adoption of the slogan and its brandishment and that the Executive Committee of the [Palestine] Liberation Organization will undertake to study its meaning and present the results of its investigation to the National Assembly at its next session for discussion.

Echoes of the debate in the Arab press also reveal something of the mood of the Congress. *Al-Hurriyya* (29.9.69), the Popular Democratic Front weekly, stated:

Even general slogans like "Democratic State," which had won support from the Palestinian Right, were rejected by the Sixth National Assembly. There appeared among the rightist ranks in the Assembly manifest racist tendencies in the solutions they proposed which were reminiscent of the well known Shukeirian ones.

(The Popular Democratic Front calls itself "The Left," and most other groups, especially Fatah, "The Right.") *Al-Muharrir* (9.9.69) reports:

After a long debate on this point ["Democratic State"] the need was expressed to reconcile the propaganda aspects of the issue with the necessary strategic aims. It was agreed that statements concerning the "Democratic State" should be made only in the context of the entire liberation of Palestine and annihilation of the Israeli entity, so that there can be no misunderstanding or comparisons between the waves of European Jewish immigrants into Palestine and the original sons of the country.

The Popular Democratic Front, on its own testimony, prepared more conscientiously than the other participants for the Sixth Congress of the Palestinian National Assembly, the first at which it was represented. It formulated memoranda and draft resolutions. This material was collected in a book of 167 pages entitled *The Present Situation of the Palestinian Resistance Movement: A Critical Study* (Beirut 1969), for which Na'if Ḥawatmeh wrote an Introduction. The proposed resolution concerning the Democratic State reads (p. 165):

The Palestinian National Assembly, in accordance with the Palestinian people's belief in democratic solutions for the Palestine question, resolves as follows:
1. To reject the chauvinist and reactionary Zionist-colonialist solutions advocating recognition of the State of Israel as one of the facts of the Middle East region, for these solutions contradict the right of the Palestinian people to self-determination in its country, and sanction the expansionist Zionist entity which is linked to colonialism, and hostile to the Palestinian and Arab national liberation movement and to all forces of liberation and socialism in the world.
2. To reject the Palestinian and Arab chauvinistic solutions advanced before and after June 1967, which advocate the slaughter of the Jews and throwing them into the sea, and also to reject reactionary solutions which support the consolidation of the State of Israel within secure and recognized boundaries as expressed in the ill-begotten

resolution of the Security Council. These solutions are at the expense of the right of the Palestinian people to self-determination in their country, and introduce into the Middle East a racist-capitalist-expansionist state linked dialectically to international capitalism, which is hostile to the Palestinian-Arab and to world liberation movements as well as to all forces of socialism and progress in the world.

3. The struggle for a democratic popular solution to the Palestine and Israel question is based on the elimination of the Zionist entity in all institutions of the state (army, administration and police) and all chauvinist and Zionist political and cooperative bodies. It is based on the establishment of a Democratic Popular Palestinian State in which Arabs and Jews will live without discrimination, a state opposed to all forms of class and national suppression, conferring the right to both Arabs and Jews to develop their own national *(wataniyya)* culture.

4. By virtue of links which history and destiny have forged between Palestine and the Arab nation, the Democratic Popular State of Palestine will be an organic part of an Arab federal state of democratic content, hostile to colonialism, imperialism, Zionism and to Arab and Palestinian reaction.

In this way the "democratic solution" is presented as a compromise between two chauvinistic alternatives—a Jewish state, and driving the Jews into the sea—as if these were comparable propositions. By this supposedly fair solution, the Arabs renounce the extermination of Jews, and the Jews renounce their state. Although the Palestinian state will become a popular democracy, its Arab character will be preserved by being part of a larger "democratic" Arab federation. The final paragraph is meant to repudiate objections that a democratic Palestine would remain, owing to its mixed population, an anomaly among the Arab states and difficult to digest within the framework of Arab unity.

The Democratic Front's pronouncement may be mistakenly interpreted as favoring a binational state: "The Palestinian state will eliminate racial discrimination and national persecution and will be based on a democratic solution to the conflict brought about by the coexistence *(ta'āyush)* of the two peoples, Arabs and Jews" (*The Present Situation* . . ., p. 136). The recognition of "a Jewish people" is a significant innovation. Hitherto Arabs have mostly held that Jews constitute only a religion and do not therefore deserve a national state. However, this admission of a Jewish nationhood is qualified, for Jews as a people are not entitled to a state of their own but must settle for incorporation in a state of Palestinian nationality. Their nationhood, therefore, has only cultural and not national-political dimensions. Thus, Ḥawatmeh tells Lutfi al-Khuli, editor of *at-Tali'a:*

> We urged initiation of a dialogue with the Israeli socialist organization Matzpen, which advocates an Arab-Jewish binational state. But we have not been able to convince Matzpen to adopt a thoroughly progressive, democratic position on the Palestine question which would mean liquidation *(tasfiaya)* of the Zionist entity and establishment of a democratic Palestinian state opposed to all kinds of class and national suppression (*at-Tali'a,* November, 1969, p. 106).

The proposal for a binational state, as advocated by Matzpen, is not sufficiently progressive for Ḥawatmeh. In his view, Jewish nationhood implies only cultural autonomy for a religious community. But this is no innovation; Mr. Shukeiry was prepared to grant the same.

To be accepted in the Command of Armed Struggle, an arm of the Palestine Liberation Organization, the

Democratic Front was required to declare itself "loyal to everything written in the National Covenant as the minimal program for the relations in the Command of Armed Struggle" (Abu Iyad in a conversation with al-Khuli, *at-Tali'a,* June 1969). It is astonishing that the Front's "democratic" proposals can be reconciled with the Palestine National Covenant (1968) and particularly with the status of Jews allowed to remain in the liberated state (Article 6).

Thus, despite all pretensions, the difference between the Popular Democratic Front and the other Palestinian organizations may relate mostly to the size of the tolerated Jewish minority. A current notion among many Arab spokesmen suggests that a considerable number of Israelis are in Israel against their will and would leave if Zionism and the "national coercion" it imposes were abolished. European Jews would not wish to live in a Palestinian Arab state, preferring to emigrate, while Jews from Eastern countries would "rejoice" at the opportunity afforded them to return to their countries of origin. These are themes harped on by the Arab mass media. Contact with the Jewish community in Israel across the open bridges has not yet shaken these ideas. It seems that they play so vital a role in Arab thinking that it is difficult to change them. If a voluntary Jewish exodus after victory is a foregone conclusion, why spell out solutions involving violence? What do the Arabs lose if they declare that Palestinian citizenship will be given to all Israelis?

The Popular Democratic Front, by dissociating the annihilation of the State of Israel from the necessity of having "to reduce" the number of her Jewish inhabitants, tries to humanize the Arab position. It should be noted, however, that its approach is basically neither moderate nor conciliatory. In the Arab-Israel conflict, the relevant political question is that of the attitude to Israel as a state and to its sovereignty. The Popular Democratic Front has unequivocally rejected Israel's right to statehood, as if it had to atone for its "softness" toward individual Jews by a corresponding harshness against their state. In its view, Israel is not an independent country with individual, though odious, characteristics; it is rather part of everything sinister and inhuman in international life—imperialism, colonialism and capitalism—phenomena which must be fought to the bitter end. From World War I onwards, Arabs insisted that Israel was set up and aided by colonialist powers and that only American imperialism assured its continuing survival. But leftists now regard the link between Israel and colonialism or imperialism as organic, and their opposition to its existence is thus intensified.

The Popular Democratic Front utterly rejects the Security Council Resolution and indeed any possibility of a peaceful solution. Its stand on this issue is far more radical than that of most Arab states. Even the Khartoum Summit Conference resolutions are treason in its eyes:

> This conference offered the Arab peoples hollow promises, "no peace, no recognition, no negotiation with Israel," as though the question on the agenda were that of negotiation and peace and not of overcoming the aggression and annihilating its bases (*The Present Situation . . .,* p. 85).

Acceptance of the Security Council Resolution is treason even more infamous; for it implies recognition of Israel, even though Arab states excuse it as a tactical maneuver:

> The contention that acceptance of the Security Council Resolution is a tactical maneuver aiming at the "elimination of the traces of aggression," in order to continue action for the liberation of Palestine, is a misleading, demagogic and fraudulent claim which arouses only loathing and nausea in the souls of Arab revolutionaries (*ibid.,* p. 88).

Another paragraph of the draft resolution sponsored by the Democratic Front to the Sixth National Assembly emphasizes:

> The national liberation movement will achieve a Democratic Popular Palestinian State only by armed struggle and a people's war of liberation against Zionism, imperialism and reaction, by the destruction of the Israeli State and liberation of the Jews from the Zionist movement (*ibid.,* p. 167).

The pronouncements of Fatah itself used to contain, though not always explicitly, hints of genocide. For instance, Fatah's monthly, *The Palestinian Revolution* (June 1968, p. 38), explains why a conventional war does not suit the Palestinian goal:

> For the aim of this war is not to impose our will on the enemy but to destroy him in order to take his place *(ifnā'uhu lil-hulūli mahallahi)* . . . . In a conventional war there is no need to continue the war if the enemy submits to our will . . . while in a *people's war* there is no deterrent inhibition, for its aim is not to defeat the enemy but to extirpate *(ifnā')* him. A conventional war has limited aims which have to be observed, for the enemy must be allowed to exist so that we can impose our will on him, while in a *people's war* destruction *(ifnā')* of the enemy is the first and last duty.

The expression *ifnā'* used here is extreme, its literal meaning being "reduction to absolute nothingness." This does not mean the simple destruction of army units but the total annihilation of the enemy as a whole.

The Palestinian National Covenant's extreme line, restricting Jews to five percent of the population (those who came before 1917 and their offspring), has become common knowledge and it is not unlikely that some Palestinians will now press for a change in the Covenant in order to give it a more moderate appearance.

The position combining annihilation of the state and the murder of its inhabitants (politicide and genocide) was in itself consistent. It provided a basis for the subsequent establishment of an Arab state. But the proposition advocating destruction of the Jewish state and turning it into an Arab one without doing away with its Jewish inhabitants is self-contradictory. The Arabs avoid this contradiction by clinging to the illusion that the Jews, anxious to emigrate, will reduce their own numbers. They also exaggerate the number of Palestinians. Even so, one wonders how they are to return to their former dwellings unless the Jews are evicted and removed.

The declaratory recognition of partial rights for Israelis, expressed in the slogan of a "Democratic State," although adding to the persuasiveness of propaganda and diplomacy, nevertheless represents a *retreat* from previous Arab positions. The contradictions inherent in the concept will, no doubt, provoke further seminars, heartsearchings, debates and inner struggles, and will provide another issue on which Arabs will divide. The Jewish community will continue to grow and hopes of absorbing it as a minority will become correspondingly more remote. Since the internal contradictions of their politicidal position will become increasingly obvious, it would appear that from an Arab point of view the whole "Democratic State" concept tends to create more problems than it solves.

2. Bafflements and Contradictions

In Arab journalism, particularly in periodicals, interesting articles and symposia are often published concerning social problems, self-criticism and the Arab-Israel conflict. Israeli newspaper reporting usually skips over these articles because it is by its nature more concerned with political events, more with Arabs' actions and less with their ideas. Such journalistic portrayal of the Arab world becomes pallid because of the absence of the human-ideological dimension of events. Human beings not only operate, they also think about their actions. Furthermore, our concern for the opponent's reflections tends to humanize him by viewing him along with all his human problems. The Six-Day War and its aftermath raised questions for the Arabs and stimulated them to reassess their procedure in the conflict. They began to grapple with the question of their *objective* in the conflict. This wrestling is primarily concerned now with the slogan "Democratic Palestinian State."

Studying their deliberations over this question is important for we Israelis for three reasons:

1. It contributes to our understanding of the opponent's intention, however disconcerting this may be. The tension of involvement in the conflict has often engendered among Israelis a tendency toward self-deception and a desire to play down the severity of the Arab position. Arabs brandish the slogan of a "Democratic State" as a means of psychological warfare against us, in order to weaken our determination, and we should be aware of this.

2. This issue provides an aperture through which we may witness the difficulties the Arabs confront because of their genocidal position toward Israel, and it shows why the ideological structure of the Arab position will compel them to retreat from it. This may also herald a change in their position toward us.

3. The Arabs use the slogan of a "Democratic State" as a propaganda means in foreign countries. In order to discredit it, there is nothing better than to rely upon their own words, which disclose its underlying significance.

In the weekly supplement of the Beirut newspaper *al-*

Anwar (March 8, 1970), a long symposium was published concerning the meaning of the slogan "The Democratic State," in which the views of most of the prominent fedayeen organizations were represented. A translation of extracts (italicized text) from this symposium is here presented, along with comments by the author and a summary concerning its significance.

* * *

Moderator: *The main objective of the symposium is to discuss all the solutions proposed by the various groups of the resistance movement under the slogan "The Democratic Palestinian State," particularly the proposals of Fatah and the Popular Democratic Front. I omit from the discussion those solutions which were hatched apart from the groups of the resistance movement, whether openly or secretly. . . . I refer particularly to the solution adopted by the United States to establish a Palestinian State in the West Bank and the Gaza Strip, and France's proposals concerning the establishment of a Palestinian State to be connected with some Arab countries.*

At the beginning of the symposium, I thus turn to the representative of the (Popular) Democratic Front for the Liberation of Palestine: I would like you to explain to us the Front's viewpoint concerning the Democratic Palestinian State on the basis of the resolution presented to the Sixth Congress of the Palestinian National Assembly which was convened last September.

Representative of the Democratic Front: *. . . The adoption of a particular slogan, in our estimation, does not stem from a subjective position or a subjective desire but from a study and analysis of the evolution of the objective situation, the objective possibilities present in society and within history— moving forces, as well as the nature of the potential evolution of these forces in the future. . . .*

Coexistence (taʿāyush) *with this entity (Israel) is im-*

possible, not because of a national aim or national aspiration of the Arabs, but because the presence of this entity will determine this region's development in connection with world imperialism, which follows from the objective link between it and Zionism. Thus, eradicating imperialist influence in the Middle East means eradicating the Israeli entity. This is something indispensable, not only from the aspect of the Palestinian people's right of self-determination, and in its homeland, but aslo from the aspect of protecting the Arab national liberation movement, and this objective also can only be achieved by means of armed struggle. . . .

We believe that hypothetical questions, such as what will happen if the working class or the Communist Party takes over the government in Israel, are irrelevant. For there are no signs indicating that the working class will be capable of taking over the government in the near or distant future without armed struggle under the leadership of the Palestinian national liberation movement. Moreover, the status of the Israeli entity as a foreign colony implanted in the region impels the majority of the workers in the Zionist State to consolidate themselves around the ruling class, consequently obstructing the development of class war within Israel. This phenomenon is observable in the case of many colonialist settlements. This is observable in Algeria, where most of the sectors of the French colony that were Fascist and radically opposed to the Algerian revolution were from the petty bourgeoisie and the workers. Therefore, the liberation of Palestine is indissolubly linked with the victory of the Palestinian national liberation movement.

The problem is: Israel as "reactionary" deserves to be attacked; but what will happen if Israel becomes Socialist and progressive? This possibility according to the stand common in Arab radical publications, is summarily dismissed as out of the question. Israel is congenitally aggressive and inherently reactionary and cannot become Socialist. Socialist movements in Israel are only a sham.

Farīd al-Khatīb: *I don't consider my view to be identical with that of Fatah. I am a friend of Fatah, and my view is very close to its view. . . . The idea of coexistence in a Palestinian State is not new. This idea was first brought up officially by Yaḥya Ḥamuda (chairman of the Palestinian National Assembly) . . . Then in October 1967, I believe, Abu Iyad (a Fatah leader—Salāḥ Khalaf) announced, at a press conference held by the Beirut newspaper* al-Yawm, *the adoption by Fatah of the idea of the Democratic Palestinian State as a solution for the Zionist contradiction presently found on Arab soil. . . .*

The Democratic Palestinian State, as conceived by Fatah, I believe is as follows. There is a basic condition for establishing the Democratic Palestinian State: the winning of victory. Otherwise it cannot be brought into effect. The slogan of the (Palestinian Democratic) State is one of struggle; it can in no way be isolated from the Palestinian national liberation movement. . . .

In short, the Democratic State is linked to the Palestinian national liberation movement. I believe it is necessary to present the details of the Palestinian State gradually, for in presenting the idea Fatah wished to say to the world that the objective of the Palestinians and the Arabs is not to throw the Jews into the sea but to disband the Zionist State and establish a new one. What is sought is not the development of Israel into a form acceptable to the Arabs, as Member of Knesset Uri Avneri advocates; the objective is to disband the Zionist State and establish a new one, according to the will of the Palestinian national liberation movement and the will of the Jews who lived in Palestine originally, that is, before 1948, and those who came later. . . .

The common Arab position rejected in principle the very

existence of Israel; it was not critical of a certain kind of Israel, as some people tended to think. It is true that Arabs used to express their fundamental opposition to the existence of Israel first, and then go on to enumerate its sins: expansionism, aggression, and so on. This enumeration is intended to reinforce the basic denial of Israel's existence; it does not mean, as some may mistakenly suppose, that if Israel were without sin, Arabs would be reconciled to its existence. In this manner, the sins they ascribe to Israel are irrelevant to the judgment they have passed upon it.

There is no benefit in discussing details of the Democratic State at present, for the objective in presenting this slogan at the present stage is to leave a narrow opening for the Israeli enemy, while the resistance groups strike relentless blows at the enemy within Palestine, to the point that his military, economic and political forces are exhausted and he is sore pressed. Then the enemy will have no possibility but to look toward that narrow aperture, attempting to find an outlet. Then the Palestinian revolution can remove the veil, so that the Israeli enemy may find deliverance. Thus, it is not beneficial to remove the veil now. . . .

The reluctance to specify in detail how this state would be established probably stems from the wish to evade this issue. Many Israelis would be forced to evacuate their present dwellings to make room for the Palestinians flocking to the country and demanding their former lands. Thus the erection of a Democratic Palestinian State presupposes large displacement of the Jewish population and havoc in the country. This havoc lies beneath the "veil" which al-Khatib refuses to lift.

The representative of the Arab Liberation Front *(a fedayeen organization under Iraqi influence): There is no special [separate] solution for the Palestine issue. The solution must* *be within the framework of the Arab revolution, because the Palestine issue is not merely the pramount Arab issue but the substance and basic motivation of the Arab struggle. If the Arab nation suffers from backwardness, exploitation and disunity, these afflictions are much more severe in Palestine. That is, the Arab cause in the present historical stage is epitomized in the Palestine issue. . . .*

The liberation of Palestine will be the way for the Arabs to realize unity, not to set up regional State No. 15, which will only deepen disunity. The unified State will be the alternative to the Zionist entity, and it will be of necessity democratic, as long as we understand beforehand the dialectical connection between unity and Socialism. In the united Arab State all the minorities—denominational and others—will have equal rights . . .

The intention is not to set up a Palestinian State as an independent unit, but to incorporate it within a unified Arab State which will be democratic because it is progressive, and which will grant the Israeli Jews minority rights. Achieving Socialism and unity are interconnected, as Socialism needs a large state to withstand pressure from outside and unity cannot be achieved unless socialism wins in the Arab world.

When this slogan was put forth, it was understood that it was intended to conciliate progressive public opinion and the world leftist movement, but this cannot be accomplished with impractical slogans. The tactical nature of this slogan cannot elude public opinion . . .

The Arab Liberation Front considers the slogan of the (Democratic) Palestinian State, whether tactical or strategic, as incorrect, especially in the present situation, in which the Israeli enemy enjoys political, economic and military superiority, and any settlement is liable to consecrate this superiority of the enemy. . . .

The Liberation Front rejects this idea as a tactical step because if, let us assume, Israel agrees to it, the sponsors of the idea will have to accept it. . . .

As I have already mentioned, the slogan of the Democratic State does not presently serve Arab interests. It is identical with what some regimes have proposed, that, since Israel has not accepted the Security Council Resolution, we should accept this Resolution, which consecrates the Zionist presence on Arab land.

The Arab Liberation Front vehemently opposed the idea of a Palestinian Democratic State and even rejected the stand of the Popular Front for the Liberation of Palestine (Dr. Habash) to adopt it as a tactical propagandist device.

Shafiq al-Ḥūt *(a leader of the PLO and head of its Beirut office):* . . . *The Palestinian problem is that of a Zionist-colonialist invasion at the expense of a land and a people known for thirteen centuries as the Palestinian Arab people.* . . .

This is an example of the tendency to depict the Palestinian people as though it existed from yore. It is designed to counter the claim that Zionism did not encounter a Palestinian people, and the contention that it was colonialism that created the Palestinian people since the Mandate Powers delineated the national borders in the Middle East. Indeed, in the past, describing Palestine as an independent unity was considered betrayal of Arab nationalism, and Palestinian Arab spokesmen insisted at the beginning of the Mandatory period, though only for a short time, that they were Southern Syrian Arabs, not Palestinians.

I side with Farid al-Khatīb in holding that there is no benefit in expatiating upon the slogan "Democratic Palestinian State." I hope the fedayeen organizations will not do so, although I would encourage discussion of it by those who are not in responsible positions. Whatever discussion of it there is on the part of the fighting groups may cause a sense of helplessness, despair or weakness. . . .

As far as it concerns the human situation of the Jews, which Farīd al-Khatīb mentioned, we should expose the Zionist movement and say to the Jew: The Zionist movement which brought you to Palestine did not supply a solution to your problem as a Jew; therefore you must return whence you came to seek another way of striving for a solution for what is called "the problem of the persecuted Jew in the world." As Marx has said, he (the Jew) has no alternative but to be assimilated into his society. . . .

Even if we wished, by force of circumstances, a Democratic Palestinian State "period," this would mean its being non-Arab. Let us face matters honestly. When we speak simply of a Democratic Palestinian State, this means we discard its Arab identity. I say that on this subject we cannot negotiate, even if we possess the political power to authorize this kind of decision, because we thereby disregard an historical truth, namely, that this land and those who dwell upon it belong to a certain environment and a certain region, to which we are linked as one nation, one heritage and one hope—Unity, Freedom and Socialism. . . .

The implication that the Israeli Jews would be allowed to stay in the Democratic State raises difficulties concerning its Arab character.

If the slogan of the Democratic State was intended only to counter the claim that we wish to throw the Jews into the sea, this is indeed an apt slogan and an effective political and propaganda blow. But if we wish to regard it as the ultimate strategy of the Palestinian and Arab liberation movement, then I believe it requires a long pause for reflection, for it bears upon our history, just as our present and certainly our future.

I conclude with a warning that this may be the beginning of a long dispute resulting in a substitute for the basic objective of the Palestinian revolution, which is the liberation of the Palestinian land and individual within the national totally Arab framework to which we belong.

Representative of as-Saʻiqa *(a Syrian fedayeen organization): I agree with Shafīq al-Ḥūt that there is no group which may determine independently the meaning of this slogan, or consent to its implementation. This problem does not belong to the Palestinians alone, because the Zionist design threatens the Arab region and not only the Palestinians, and every Arab citizen has the right to express his opinion concerning presumed or proposed solutions. Neither the Palestinian alone, nor any of the resistance movements, has the right to hold an independent view concerning the destiny of Palestine regarding the procedure to be adopted after the revolution or its victory.*

It seems that this slogan has been raised prematurely, and this may be one of the principal reasons for the divergence of views concerning it. Thus, there is no consensus concerning the distinct meaning of this slogan. . . . The Jews are human beings like all others. No man can bear to live forever in tension, a state of emergency and threat. Every man seeks stability. However, the people living today in Palestine, subjected to this predicament, cannot return to the countries from which they emigrated, nor can they find an alternative to bearing arms against the Arab revolution, which continues to mean for the Jews the pulverization and ultimate liquidation of the millions living in Palestine. I think that when we propose to those Jews an alternative for their present life, for the threat of death, we can reap benefit for our cause and make great strides on the way to victory. We cannot overlook the fact that these Jews, the majority of whom were born in Palestine, know no other homeland. . . .

This is an argumentation of a pragmatic utilitarian nature.

The Israelis fight tenaciously because they have the impression that they will be in deadly danger should the Arabs win. The Arabs, therefore, have to present their objective in such a way that differentiates between their intention toward Israel as a state (its destruction), and their intentions toward its inhabitants as individuals (allow them to live).

I was among those who thought five years ago that we must slaughter the Jews. But now I cannot imagine that, if we win one night, it will be possible for us to slaughter them, or even one tenth of them. I cannot conceive of it, neither as a man, nor as an Arab.

If so, what do we wish to do with these Jews? This is a problem for which I do not claim to have a ready answer. It is a problem which every Arab and Palestinian citizen has an obligation to express his opinion about, because it is yet early for a final, ripe formulation to offer the world and those living in Palestine.

Thus, I think that among many Jews, those living in Palestine, especially the Arab Jews, there is a great desire to return to their countries of origin, since the Zionist efforts to transform them into a homogeneous, cohesive nation have failed. There is a well-known human feeling—yearning for one's homeland, one's birthplace. There are a number of known facts concerning the Jews living in Palestine today which clearly point to this feeling among them. They desire to return to their countries of origin, especially Jews from the Arab region.

It should be made clear that the Arabs initially blocked the way for Jews to return to their countries. If the Arab governments had treated these situations from the start, the problem would have "budged" by now. There are a number of known circumstances which point to this. We have made the Jews think constantly for twenty years that the sea is before them and the enemy behind, and that there was no recourse but to fight to defend their lives. . . .

For us, as the Vanguards of the Popular War of Liberation—as-Sa'iqa, the slogan is not tactical but strategic. And, as I have said, we cannot imagine how it is possible to solve the problem of these Jews without permitting them to dwell either in Palestine or in another homeland they choose. My estimation is that many of them will choose to live outside Palestine, for Palestine will not be able to absorb all the Palestinians, as well as the Jews living there. . . .

Representative of the Democratic Front: *. . . The organization mentioned above (Matzpen) advocates a Socialist Palestine, in which the Arabs and Jews will live in equality, that is, having equal rights and obligations, and that it be part of a federal union in the Middle East . . . . It is hard to say that there is responsiveness in Israel to the idea of a Democratic State. Although the idea of Matzpen is more acceptable from the Arab viewpoint, even that of Arab nationalism, Matzpen merely expresses the view of the Left; in fact, an insignificant minority of what is called the Israeli Left. Although it is a vocal and noisy organization, it represents but a minute fraction of what is called the Israeli Left . . . .*

It may be assumed that the continuing generation process, imposed upon history but actually consisting of what is called Jewish nationalism in Palestine must be terminated. This is not to be by annihilation of this human group living there, because such a solution is not only inhuman, it is also impractical. It must be terminated by the victory of the Palestinian revolution. I agree with the representative of as-Sa'iqa that the slogan of the Palestinian State is not a tactical slogan in the Machiavellian sense. We adopt this slogan not simply in order to win world public opinion, or to deceive the Jews regarding their destiny. This slogan must be presented clearly and with intellectual honesty. It should be stated that Zionism must cease to exist in Palestine, but this does not necessitate the human liquidation of the Israeli community living in Palestine. . . .

We do not adopt this slogan because we are weak, with the intention of changing it when we become strong. The matter must be explained otherwise. Our struggle must have a clear objective based on actual reality, not on our desires and wishful thinking. . . .

As for the question concerning what will happen if Israel agrees to our impractical assumptions on which we base a political position, the answer is: Israel will not agree to this slogan, and it is impossible for Israel to agree, because it means elimination of the State of Israel and all the class interests on which Israel is based. There has never been in history a class, social, or political power which has consented to its own elimination. . . .

Moderator: . . . *Can we consider the Kurdish problem and the manner of its solution as similar to the Jewish problem and its solution under the heading of the slogan of one Democratic State? . . .*

Representative of the Liberation Front: *Our view of the subject of Kurdish national rights follows from objective and historical considerations which substantially contradict the nature and objectives of the Zionist movement. The Kurds comprise a nationality having a distinct, well-known historical, geographical and human dimension. . . .*

In this connection, we must not forget the historical, religious and social ties that have bound Kurdish-Arab brotherhood for centuries. Salāḥ al-Dīn al-Ayyūbi (who was a Kurd) was the one who led the struggle against the foreign presence in the Arab region a number of centuries ago.

Farīd al-Khatīb: *I agree with the view of the representative of the Democratic Popular Front, namely, if a group of people lives together for a long time in a homeland, they become a nationality, as has happened in America. But it seems that calling the Jewish denomination a nationality is premature. . . .*

The Jews are a denomination associated with more than one people; the Arabs are a people which embraces more than one religion. . . .

As far as the Arab character of the Democratic State is concerned, the Jews in Palestine have the right to express their view concerning the Arab character of the Democratic State in a democratic manner. And although it is possible to say that the Democratic State is Arab, and to say furthermore that it is a union, it is advisable to hold back additional information until the appropriate stages in the evolution of the resistance are reached. When the Zionist movement came to Palestine, it first sought a refuge, afterward a homeland, and then a State; and now it is striving to build an empire within and outside Palestine.

Zionism also disclosed its objectives in stages.

There is nothing to be gained by summoning the Jews in the Zionist State to join the national liberation movement, as Shafiq al-Ḥūt proposed, when he advocated convening the unified State at once. This will not convince the Jews of the world and world public opinion.

As far as it concerns the number of Palestinians, all those who emigrated to Latin America in the nineteenth century, and those who live in the desert, in exile, under conquest, or in prison, all are citizens in the State. For example: the number of Bethlehemite residents living in South America exceeds the number of those Bethlehemites living in occupied Palestine, and the combined total [of all Palestinians] is not less than that of the Jews now living in the Zionist State. . . .

The Palestinians are more numerous than the Israeli Jews and will determine the character of the State.

Shafiq al-Ḥūt: *First, how can Farid (al-Khatib) think that the Jews and Zionists who came to set up an empire in our* *country have the privilege to express their democratic right in the Palestinian State? Second, how can he claim that it is difficult to convince Jewish citizens to join the liberation movement?*

Farīd al-Khatīb: *I think that most of the Jews living in Palestine are groups of people who were deceived by the Zionist movement and the world imperialist movement. And the Jew, as a man, has the right to express his opinion in a democratic manner regarding his future life after the collapse of the Zionist State, which is opposed to the Democratic State insofar as it discriminates between the Eastern Jew and the Western Jew and the Circassian Jew.*

The second point: The greatest ambition of the revolution is to draw the Jews of the Zionist State into the ranks of the resistance movement. . . . But what I wanted to say is that it is difficult to persuade the Jews to join the resistance movement because its immediate objective is to dissolve the Zionist contradiction within the Zionist State . . . .

Representative of the Democratic Front: *It seems to me that many of the disagreements that exist concerning this idea can be traced to some manner of misunderstanding or lack of communication. . . . This State is not bi-national in the sense that there would be two national States joined together in one form or another. This solution must be rejected, not only because it is inconsistent with our own desire, but also because it is not a true democratic solution. It is rather a solution that will represent the continuation of the national conflict which exists between the Jews and Arabs, not a solution of this conflict. It is impossible to speak of a democratic solution if it is powerless to eliminate the conflict between the different denominations and peoples within the Democratic State. When we speak of democracy it must be clear that we do not mean liberal democracy in the manner of "one man, one vote." We mean a people's democratic regime, which will put an end to the social basis upon which Zionism rests, and* *will consequently settle the class conflicts, and then those among the denominations and peoples.*

Representative of as-Sa'iqa: *The struggle is a protracted and very bitter one, and I think that adopting the slogan of the Democratic State at this early stage is premature, and that the Palestinian revolution should persevere in the way of the people's war of national liberation.*

Shafiq al-Ḥūt: *I agree with the representative of as-Sa'iqa, and I believe we are on the same wavelength.*

Representative of the Democratic Front: *I support what the representative of as-Sa'iqa says.*

Representative of the Liberal Front: *I agree with what the brother says.*

Farīd al-Khatīb: *I also.*

Thus the attempt to give positive contents to complement the hitherto negative nature of the Arab objective in the conflict calling for the liquidation of Israel became enmeshed in contradictions which frustrated the participants of the symposium themselves. They preferred to shelve the whole issue. Herein lies the gist of the weakness of the Arab position in the conflict. Furthermore, can the formulation of the final strategic objective of a political movement be simply deferred and brushed aside? Will it not have a feedback effect undermining the confidence and devotion of the followers of such a movement whose vision is thus blurred?

Lessons

When considering the possibility of an ideological change, we generally look to factors in external reality which may cause it. Indeed, in a clash between reality and ideology, reality prevails and ideology gives way, or is interpreted according to the exigencies of the time. But it seems that even the internal structure of a position and the content of an ideology may embody factors which necessitate a change: factors which condition the degree of receptivity to change, and others which condition its mode. For example, predicating the Arab position upon a rejection in principle of Israel's existence has made it less susceptible to gradual change and compromise of a quantitative modality, as in the case of a conflict between two states over a divisible portion of land. The Arab position has demanded elimination of Israel's sovereignty, not its partial elimination.

The call for politicide and the reduction of the Jewish community which it entails, makes the position difficult to maintain and impels its change. We see signs of this in the debate on the subject of the "Democratic State," for this slogan was adopted on account of the difficulty of adhering to the genocidal position of the previous formulation.

The representative of as-Sa'iqa declares that five years ago he contemplated slaughtering the Israelis, whereas now he cannot imagine such a deed. Has the trauma of the Six-Day War, the main event of the past five years, actually instilled in him moral refinement or compassion? It is more likely that the reason is rather that the Six-Day War and the events surrounding it revealed to him: 1) that the genocidal objective is impractical because the Israelis will not resign themselves to the slaughter; 2) the degree to which the Arabs lost the support of world public opinion because of rabid statements concerning slaughter of the Jews. The change in position was probably influenced by these factors.

If the Arabs must drop the objective of slaughtering the Jews, the question naturally arises: What is to be done with these Jews? This is not a matter of assessing what the Arabs would actually do if they won. The problem the Arabs face is that of defining their objective in the conflict. The form of guerrilla warfare requires more indoctrination of the soldier than conventional warfare, in which the individual merges more with his unit. It is for this reason also that the participants in the symposium stress the need for a clearly defined objective.

Old Illusions and New Awareness

If the number of Jews living in Israel is not reduced, then, on a national level their quantitative and qualitative weight will dilute the Arab character of the liberated state, and on a personal level there will not be sufficient room for these Jews as well as for the Palestinians who supposedly *all* desire to return. In order to evade these difficulties, the spokesmen in the symposium try to breathe life into old ideas: that the Jews brought to the country were misguided by Zionist deceit (Zionism therefore not being a vital need), and that they remain by coercion (criticism by Israelis of themselves and their state, in a manner unknown in Arab countries, is interpreted as a sign of hatred for the state and a desire to emigrate). On these grounds it is believed that the Jews would rejoice at the opportunity to leave. An interesting element of self-deception is added, that the Jews from Arab countries wish to return to their countries of origin. One may suspect that this illusion contains the psychological dimension of *amour-propre* and self-adulation: the Arabs are so good and were so kind to the Jews that it is inconceivable for the Jews not to desire ardently to return to live under their protection. However, along with these notions, there are signs of recognition that this is a false hope, and that the Jews have nowhere to return to, especially those born in the country, who will soon become the majority of the Jewish community. An attempt to grapple with these contradictory notions is most evident in the words of the as-Sa'iqa representative, who maintains at one and the same time that most Israeli Jews have nowhere to go, and yet that many will emigrate.

The spokesmen also try to evade this problem by claiming that the Israeli Jews are not a people. Their attachment to the country is therefore weak, and the hope that they will emigrate is reinforced. Moreover, in the clash between the Jewish group, whose cohesion is supposedly religious and not national, and the group whose cohesion is national, the latter will prevail, thereby determining the character of the country. Therefore, even if a considerable Jewish community remains there will be no such thing as a partnership between two homogeneous groups, creating a binational state. The Democratic Front, which stresses the Palestinianism of the Democratic State more than its Arab character, also regards membership in an Arab unity as inherent in the very idea of the Democratic State, while the Iraqi organization rejects the notion of the Palestinian State and regards it at best as a district within a unified state. (For this organization, the struggle in Palestine has the value of a catalyst for the rest of the changes in Arab countries, or a spark that will ignite a revolution that will spread to all of them.) Along with these hopes of reducing the number of Jews in the Democratic State there is the notion of tipping the population scales in the Arabs' favor by considering all Palestine Arabs, wherever they may live, as prospective citizens of the state according to an Arab Law of Return of sorts.

All the participants in the symposium agree that the Jews do not presently constitute a people. However, the recognition gnaws at some of them that nationalism is not something static but an evolution, and as time goes on, the Jews in Israel will become consolidated into a people and a nation. Hence the conclusion that this process must be forestalled by the founding of a Palestinian State. The temporal factor thus works against the idea that the Israelis are not a people, and against the possibility of founding a Palestinian State. It is no accident that Shafīq al-Ḥūt vigorously maintains the essential and permanent nature of the Jewish status as non-people and non-nation. According to the view presented by Arabs, only a people has the right of political self-determination and deserves a state of its own. If the Jews are indeed becoming a people, this means that they are in the process of acquiring these rights.

An Arab Pandora's Box

For most of the participants, the slogan "Democratic State" is merely tactical, the aim being to give the outside world a positive impression and to enchant the Israelis who, as the speaker who describes Fatah's views says, will only eventually discover its full meaning. For the Democratic Front this is presumably not merely a slogan, but a *principle* they sincerely hold as an implication of the progressivism they profess. However, even they wrestle with the slogan; they safeguard themselves by various qualifications or *hedges:* the state will be a member within an Arab federation, and the democracy will not be formal, nor expressed in numerical representation, but a "true" democracy of "the contents"—that is, its policy will represent progressiveness as expressed by "the Palestinian revolution." The final qualification is their insistence upon the precondition for establishing the Democratic State, that Israel be destroyed.

For those who regard the slogan "Democratic State" as merely a tactic, the problem arises that it is impossible to lead the public only by tactical slogans; one must present the objectives of a national vision. While the slogan "Democratic State" may be helpful externally, it is quite destructive internally, impairs the state's Arabism and undermines confidence in the feasibility of "returning" to the country, if it would not be evacuated. Shafīq al-Ḥūt states bluntly that acceptance of this slogan means abandoning the idea of Arabism. From the Arab viewpoint another two-fold question arises: 1) if the Jews are a people, it is doubtful whether they will consent to live in a non-Jewish state, and hence the expressed hope that they will emigrate; 2) since the Palestinians are a people, they will certainly be opposed to returning to a state which is not Arab.

It appears that the Palestinians and Arabs are beginning to sense the difficulty of their ideological position. In the past they could be content with the formulations "restoration of rights" and "restoration of the homeland," which were restricted to the meaning of the objective as bearing upon what would be given to the Arabs, and the implication concerning what would be taken away from the Jews was overlooked. Arab spokesmen in foreign countries are still striving to focus on the need to rectify the injustice inflicted on the Palestinians, while evading the implication of this rectification for the Jews. The necessity of defining the position in all its aspects and the debate concerning the Democratic Palestinian State undermine the Arab position. The slogan of a "Democratic State" seemed to be an escape from a genocidal position, but it was revealed as the first step of retreat, and the source of problems and bewilderment. I think it is no exaggeration to say that this slogan opened a Pandora's box for the Arab position in the conflict. Hence the deep apprehensions of all the participants in the discussion concerning this slogan, and the dramatic agreement of everyone at the end of it that the slogan "Democratic State" is premature, even though this contradicted the previous insistence by some on the need for a clear definition of the objective.

It appears that those who formulated the Palestinian Covenant of 1968 sensed the difficulties inherent in the Arab position and wished to anticipate them by nailing down the qualification that only a small Jewish minority (the descendants of those who came to the country before 1917) would be given citizenship in "the liberated state," thus assuring the Arab character of the country. If this stipulation manifests radicalization of the position, the reason was probably the apprehension that otherwise the ground would begin sliding beneath the Arab position.

The slogan of the "Democratic State" was offered as an escape from the odium that Article 6 of the 1968 Covenant brought upon the PLO stand, and as if the former superseded the latter, even without the formal act of amending the Covenant. It seems that the difficulties in which the idea of the Democratic State is enmeshed and the internal controversies it aroused, as expressed in this symposium, explain why Article 6 has not been amended, despite the fact that it damaged the Palestinian cause.

3. Postscript

The slogan of the "Democratic State" was hailed by Arab spokesmen as an all-important innovation demonstrating the liberal humanitarian nature of the Palestine movement. Yasser Arafat, to strengthen this impression, even said that its president can be Jewish. However, scrutiny shows that it is neither so liberal nor new.

The objective of setting up a Democratic Palestine was enshrined in the resolutions of the Eighth Palestinian National Assembly (March 1–5, 1971). The resolution was carefully formulated and it does not say, as Palestinian spokesmen purport to interpret the slogan, that *all* Israelis will be allowed to stay, but that the state will be based on equality of rights for all its citizens: "The future state in Palestine . . . will be Democratic, in which all will enjoy the same rights and obligations." This is quite compatible with the quantitative limitation included in the infamous Article 6 of the 1968 Covenant.

It is not new. All along the Palestinians have repeatedly declared that their state will be democratic. That is part of the spirit of the age, when even autocratic regimes call themselves democratic. For instance, the Congress, which set up the "All-Palestine Government" in Gaza and which unanimously elected the former Mufti of Jerusalem, Hajj Amin al-Husaini, as its president, proclaimed on October 1, 1948 "the establishment of a free and democratic sovereign state. In it the citizens will enjoy their liberties and their rights . . . ."

Even if the slogan of the "Democratic State" were free of inconsistency and insincerity it is not acceptable to the Israelis. The Israelis have no less a right to national self-determination than the Palestinian Arabs. They do not want to become Palestinians of Jewish faith; they intend to remain Israelis.

The difficulties for the Arabs inherent in the slogan of the "Democratic State" caused a decline in its discussion at subsequent Palestinian Congresses. This does not mean that it was discarded, as the alternative is to fall back on the brutality of the former, blatant, politicidal-genocidal position.

How to dispose of the Jews in Israel after Arab victory and turn the country into an Arab state is a problem which gives rise to gnawing doubts. One method is *statistical*—the tendency to inflate the number of Palestinians, presumably all awaiting to return to their homeland.

Dr. Nabīl Sha'ath (of the Planning Center of the PLO) estimates their number at 2.923 million (*The Journal of Palestine Studies*, Vol. 1, No. 2, Winter 1972). In a brochure *Palestine Illustrated Political History,* published by the PLO Department of Information and National Guidance, 1972, their figure went up to 3,270 million. No estimate is given as to how many of the Palestinians outside Palestine have been integrated in the societies where they live, consider their present residence permanent, and would not opt to go back to Palestine, even if given the choice.

Another method of reducing the number of Jews who would stay in the Democratic State is by *legal-economic* means. Palestinian spokesmen prefer not to delve into it. It is a forgone conclusion that all the Palestinians will have the right not only to return to Palestine, including Israel proper, but to regain their former lands. Thus the Israeli Jews would have to evacuate. Faced by such mass evictions the Jews would be forced, of their own volition, to leave the country. The complete destruction of Israel is thus a prerequisite for the establishment of the Palestinian Democratic State.

Indirectly, this issue came up in the discussions of the Political Committee of the Tenth National Assembly and Popular Congress. The Committee stated as part of the Political Program:

The Palestine Liberation Organization will define its tasks in the Palestinian arena: 1. Continuation of the struggle for the liberation of the entire territory of the Palestinian homeland and the setting up of the Palestinian democratic society *(mujtama')* in which all citizens will enjoy the right of work and honourable life. In it the interests will be safeguarded of all social groups which participated in the revolution, supported it, or even only contented themselves with sympathizing with it, without collaborating with the enemy or facilitating his task in occupying our territory and suppressing our compatriots; provided that these interests are not exploitative and do not transgress the interests of the toiling masses or serve as a limitation on the growth and rise of the standard of living and civilization of the toiling masses. In this society there will be full freedom of opinion, expression, gathering, demonstration, striking, the formation of national political institutions and syndicates, and the liberty of practice of all creeds, provided that the Palestinian democratic society will be part of the democratic general Arab society (Official Report in Arabic, P.L.O., *The Palestinian Popular Congress and Tenth Extraordinary Council,* 6–12 April 1972, pp. 83–84).

No doubt it is an intriguing compromise formulation. "Society" is used to overcome the problematic issue of statehood, as some fedayeen groups oppose increasing the number of Arab states. This "society" will be part of a "pan-Arab society." Its internal politics will be guided by an all-important principle: the interests of those who took part in the "revolution" or at least sympathized with it— supposedly including the Palestinians under Israel's control—will be safeguarded. This provision excludes the Israeli Jews who usually serve in Israel's forces and cannot be considered supporters of or sympathizers with the Arab struggle. The principle of equality in the Democratic state is cast to the winds. Thus Jews surviving an Arab victory will enjoy all the remaining civil rights with one decisive disability, i.e. in case of conflict of interests between them and Arabs, the Jews will have to give way. The rights of the Palestinians, as stressed in many Arab writings cannot, by any means, be put on the same footing as the rights of the newcomers, invading Jews or Zionists. Thus in a conflict between an Arab demanding his erstwhile property and a Jew living in it the Jew will have to quit. Preference will be given to Arab claims at the cost of the Jews.

No Need to Worry Now

Perhaps the most common attitude is to concentrate at this stage on the demand for "self-determination for the Palestinians in their homeland" and leave the rest. This demand is an objective that can be easily justified. Defining the final objective now, it is argued, is a waste of time, and only a source of bafflement. Political objectives should be set in a time sequence. The problem of reconciling the existence of a large Jewish community with the conversion of the country into a Palestinian state is one for the distant future and should not bother the Arabs and Palestinians now. Now they should exert all their efforts in the struggle against Israel and in attaining of their national and social objectives. The achievement of these and the return of the Palestinians will produce new conditions which may solve the entire problem.

This approach was already alluded to in the Symposium. It has been expressed with greater clarity by Alias Murqus in his book criticizing the platform of the Lebanese Communist Party (LCP) at its Second Congress in the summer of 1968. Murqus commends the LCP stand in defining that the "final solution to the Palestinian problem should be based on positions of principle, stemming from the inalienable right of the Palestinian Arabs in their land and homeland and hence their right to return there and achieve their self-determination . . . as the existence of the Jews in Palestine cannot impair the Palestinian natural and historical right in their homeland." He stresses that "the final solution to the Palestinian problem is Palestine as an Arab homeland," and as regard the future it calls for "the complete eradication of the State of Israel." He goes on:

How shall we reconcile the existence of two million Jews and two million Palestinian Arabs? This is not our task or yours now. Let us define our objective in principle and nothing more. Let us define the present way to the goal: The fighting and the falling of hundreds of thousands from the Arabs and the Jews (from the Arab more than from the Jews). With the victory of the Algerian revolution the majority of the French, young and old, went, returned to France. With Arab victory in the Near East (the battle will be longer, fiercer and with heavier casualties), it is possible that the Jews in great numbers will return whence they came—Baghdad, Allepo, Yemen, Morroco, Tunisia, Algeria, Egypt, Poland and other places, to France, or they will settle in Canada, the USA and Australia. This problem should not worry us, as its solution is by the struggle (*Marxism Leninism and the World and Arab Development in the Platform of the Lebanese Communist Party,* (Arabic) Dar al-Haqīqa, Beirut, 1970, pp. 362–363).

The circle is thus completed by returning to the point of departure.

5

The Weakness of the Fedayeen

Immediately after the Six-Day War some British, French and American visitors predicted that Israel would become a second Aden, a second Algeria or a second Vietnam. Such prophesies, it transpired, only reflected national traumas and had nothing to do with the local realities. Political and military situations cannot be evaluated by means of general categories abstracting the precise circumstances, especially with respect to guerrilla warfare in which the concrete conditions are of paramount importance.

Some spectacular victories of guerrilla war have influenced the cultural climate of our age, endowing the guerrillas with magical potentialities as an invincible instrument. These tendencies influenced people's judgment concerning the importance of fedayeen action against Israel. A more balanced evaluation may correct such impressionistic verdicts. Arab fedayeen action was a source of nuisance to Israel, yet, from a strategic point of view, it figured only secondarily in Israel's defense problems. Israel's main strategic concern has been its confrontation with the Arab armies. This does not mean that Israel treated terrorist activity with indifference, as nobody likes to be stung even if it is not fatal. Israel took vigorous action against the fedayeen not because their operations in themselves endangered Israel's existence, but in order to prevent the escalation of such activities.

Analysis of past failures of the fedayeen to achieve their objectives may throw light on their prospects.

The main prerequisite for the success of guerrilla warfare is that it becomes an internal war. This was stressed already by Clausewitz as regards a "people's war." The main achievements of a guerrilla war are due to its winning popular support. Guerrilla warfare is of minor or only ancillary significance in an external war. Guerrilla fighters should have an intimate relationship with the people, expressed by Mao Tse-tung as the relationship between fish and water. However, in this case, Arab fish could not endure in Jewish waters. So long as Israel's Jewish population did not rise against the Israeli Government, fedayeen action could not be considered an internal war. Even if more unrest were fomented in the occupied areas, these areas could be isolated. The fedayeen by calling their activities "Resistance" (*muqawama*) use a misnomer, as most of these attacks are from the outside. Their main problem is not how to subvert the regime in Israel, but how to enter the country.

Though fedayeen theoreticians philosophize at length on their warfare against Israel and have published prolifically, they have paid little attention to the dialectics between means and ends and the limitations imposed thereby. By means of guerrilla warfare France could be persuaded to give up Algeria, but no amount of guerrilla activities could bring the French to relinquish their sovereignty over France. A guerrilla war was instrumental in inducing the Americans to withdraw from Vietnam, but no guerrilla attrition could press the Americans to leave the USA. Thus no amount of fedayeen action could persuade the Israelis to relinquish sovereignty over Israel, or de-Judaize (alias de-Zionize) it. Fedayeen action cannot, by any means, accomplish the objective of the fedayeen organizations. This gap between means and ends has undermined their whole ideological structure, since they proclaim that their activities are not "tactics but a strategy," i.e., that guerrilla warfare is the main instrument of the struggle, and not an auxiliary arm.

The "balance of essentiality," i.e., the relative necessity of achieving the war aims, which in certain other cases of guerrilla successes has favored their side, in this instance favors Israel. For the people of Israel, it is more imperative that Israel exist, than it is important for the Arabs to destroy it; it is more vital for the Israelis not to lose their country, than it is for the Palestinians to regain it. This has had an important bearing on the conflict. The Israeli public has always taxed its efforts to the utmost, while the Arab publics' efforts have been half-hearted.

The fedayeen organizations failed to set up a network in the occupied areas. Most of their cells were discovered rapidly and dismantled. The local Arab population has acquitted itself by offering passive support, mainly of a declaratory nature, and is hesitant to support the fedayeen actively, to supply them, or to give them shelter. The fedayeen complained of such behavior in their writings, though apologetically they tried to explain it away by attributing it to Israel's alleged terrible repressive action. Life in the occupied areas has been normalized and the level of employment has been more or less satisfactory, these being important factors accounting for the lack of unrest in the areas. Furthermore, as explained by Challiand (interview in *Dirasat Arabiyah,* Beirut, July 1970), the majority of the population on the West Bank is of petit-bourgeois inclinations and there is no agrarian polarization between landlords and landless peasantry, which in many previous cases produced conditions for guerrilla warfare.

Failing to foment an internal resistance, the guerrillas have been pushed outside the present boundaries, and their operations have taken the form of shooting from the other side of the frontiers (sometimes using Katyusha rockets against built-up areas), or of superficial forays for the purpose of sabotage or killing.

Immediately after the Six-Day War the fedayeen organizations became an object of adoration by the Arab public, since after the defeat of the regular armies, they were the only element remaining to carry on the fight against Israel. Much was expected of them.

To close the gap between their pretentions and their deeds they have issued inflated communiqués. Though there was need in the Arab public to give credence to these communiqués, because of considerations of national dignity, people in the Arab world have become aware of the fedayeen distortions. They began to be criticized for their lack of success in transforming their war into an internal war, for their fabrications, and for their internal rivalries which became notorious.

The multiplicity of fedayeen organizations has no parallel in the history of guerrilla warfare. Attempts at unification until now have failed. Instead of "unification" they have resorted to some sort of "coordination" which paradoxically only perpetuates disunity. There has been a tendency among Palestinians and Arabs to attribute fedayeen failures to the proliferation of organizations and their inter-rivalries. Qadhāfi reckoned (in a speech on March 31, 1970) that 10 % of fedayeen energy was directed against Israel and that the remaining 90 % was wasted on internecine struggles. It seems that the explanation is the reverse. Lack of success in operations was an important factor reinforcing disunity, since the assignment of responsibility for their failures has become a major bone of contention among the different organizations, contributing to greater internal fragmentation. This is most apparent from the discussions after the September 1970 debacle in Jordan.

The weakness of the fedayeen organizations became very evident from their spectacular defeat in Jordan after only a few days of fighting. Their strategy was wrong, as they engaged in "positional warfare" in which guerrillas are usually at a disadvantage when facing a regular army.

The reasons for their defeat have been discussed at length in the Arab press. Fedayeen leaders scorchingly criticized their shortcomings and faults: exhibitionism, embourgeoisement of commanders, provocative slogans which irritated the Jordanian Government, factiousness, negligence in preparing a popular revolutionary base, braging, verbosity, etc. However, much of this self-criticism, it seems, was to some extent a cathartic exercise. The faults of the rival organization were described as strategic, while the critics' own mistakes were merely tactical errors. Shortcomings were explained as accidental or technical, so that their rectification became a question of will and decision, while in reality one may find their roots much deeper in the social fabric.

An important fact that emerged from the Jordanian events of September 1970 was that a considerable segment of the Palestinian population in Jordan did not support the fedayeen and aligned itself with the Jordanian establishment. These Palestinians have been integrated economically, socially and politically into Jordanian society and many of them belong to the grande or petite bourgeoisie. Despite their sympathies for the fedayeen, they became alienated from them because the fedayeen were regarded as the standard-bearers of social revolution in the Arab world. Though the fedayeen have promised to regain them their property in Israel, the fear of losing their present property in Jordan in such a revolution carried more weight.

Fedayeen organizations discuss at length the problem of the "united front" as preached by Mao Tse-tung for the purpose of gradualizing the confrontation, or mobilizing at each stage the widest possible support. The problems of the united front with the Arab states thus come to the fore. Fatah adheres to the view that in order to mobilize the efforts of all Arab countries and all segments of the Palestinian community the fedayeen should not brandish a social ideology. The radical organizations (Popular Front and Democratic Front) contend that collaboration with Arab regimes will be precarious and that eventually the contradictions will come to the fore, so long as basic attitudes have not been homogenized. Thus, for the sake of common action, a revolution has to be launched in all Arab countries, which will impose on them a socialist regime and bring about their unification and the mobilization of all efforts in a war à outrance against Israel.

The weakness of fedayeen action against Israel was not only on the strategic level but on the tactical level as well. Units were poorly trained and handled. In some cases officers stayed on the east bank of the Jordan, ordering their units to cross the river into action and danger. While in certain instances of comparable warfare the guerrilla side has enjoyed an advantage in intelligence, supplied by the local population, the Arab guerrillas lacked this assistance and were therefore unable to be selective in choosing weak targets in Israel. Manpower for the organizations still comes from the fringes of refugee society. Though students and intellectuals have declared their readiness to join the fedayeen, they have in many cases stayed behind in political and propaganda jobs. An inverse pyramid has been produced: a few operators writhing under the weight of a phalanx of administrative, political and propaganda personnel.

Previously, some people in Europe and the USA brushed aside the meagerness of fedayeen action on the grounds that in fighting a war of national liberation such signs of weakness are of transient importance. By definition, people fight such a war tenaciously; it may begin on a small scale but it is bound to spread and escalate. Today, their revealed weakness can no longer be overlooked, and this detracts from the stature of the fedayeen organizations in public opinion. Circles in the New Left ask themselves, in the light of the failure of the Palestinians, whether the fedayeen really fight a revolutionary war based on a mass revolutionary infra-structure. Now the manifestations of the weakness of the Palestinian action can no longer be overlooked, and this will induce people to question whether the Palestinians' operations really merit being defined as a war of national liberation, or a revolution. In large measure this weakness has throughout stemmed from the fact that the Palestinian organizations have not been fighting a war of survival whereas Israel has. They have, by virtue of their self-identifi-cation as Arabs, a territory and a homeland beyond Israel.

Fedayeen operations against Israel have declined consid-erably since their organizations were smashed by the Jorda-nian army. Their possibilities of action have been greatly curtailed. They may revert to a terrorist mode of operation in Europe and America, away from the area of direct con-frontation between Israel and the Arabs. Terrorist acts of this kind were initiated by the Popular Front and were then severely criticized by the other organizations as easy esca-pism from direct confrontation with Israel. Now they have become the main *modus operandi*. However, such actions are sporadic by nature. Big as they may be, they cannot defeat Israel and cannot change the general picture portrayed here. They may call the attention of the world to Pales-tinian fedayeen existence and their problem.

The Palestinians cannot by their terrorist action cause the redress of their problem, as their grievance is an unlim-ited one, one that cannot actually be satisfied. They aim not at exerting pressure on Israel to withdraw from the areas occupied in 1967, but at making Israel disappear. They will make themselves a nuisance to the world at large. Action will call for reprisals and measures of suppression from which, probably, they will be the main sufferers.

After September 1970, some of the fedayeen leaders stressed the need to lower the fedayeen profile and go under-ground. Others were afraid that such a move would lose the fedayeen their public standing. If a political settlement is reached with some of the the Arab states, the brunt of the actions of the fedayeen opposing such a settlement may then be directed against Arab societies. The fedayeen awareness of the lack of a rational solution to their problem may drive some of them to dreams of apocalyptic cataclysmic events as a means of solving their problems. Indications of such tendencies are already apparent in Dr. Habash's declared yearnings for a third world war as a way out of the impasse. The ideas of brutalization which the fedayeen and Arab states have preached to their young generation, though directing them outwardly, may yet rebound internally and take a heavy toll in Arab societies.

6
Fedayeen Consensus: The Agreement of May 6, 1970

The fedayeen organizations have been riven by personal, organizational, and—to some extent—ideological differences. There has been a general consensus, however, on the need for unity of action. This unity was not envisaged as the merger of all groups into one organization, but the creation of a common framework in which the organizations could meet and coordinate their efforts.

On Fatah's initiative, a number of groups held a conference in Cairo in January 1968. It was decided there that the communiqués of several organizations (some, in fact, fictitious) would be issued jointly in the name of the principal ones. The agreement stipulated that the meeting-ground of the organizations would be "on the battlefield," not within an institutional framework; however, steps would be taken to modify the composition and character of the Palestine Liberation Organization (PLO). Subsequently, the representation at the fourth session of the Palestinian National Assembly held in Cairo in July 1968 was changed. This Assembly, which amended the National Covenant, decided to set up a unified military command for the fedayeen forces. The decision was not implemented, but in March 1969 the "Command of Armed Struggle" was formed. Its headquarters was in Amman, and in due course eight organizations joined it. The Command of Armed Struggle limited its activities to issuing communiqués of the member organizations and arranging for a fedayeen military police, but it did not undertake coordination of policies or operations.

Yet its main drawback was that an activist organization like Dr. George Habash's Popular Front for the Liberation of Palestine (PFLP) did not take part in it.

A further step in the direction of unity was occasioned by King Hussein's abortive attempt a year later to impose restrictions on the freedom of action of the organizations in Jordan. As a rejoinder, on February 11, 1970 they created the "Unified Command," in which all organizations—including the PFLP—participated according to the "unified front principle," namely, equal representation (i.e., parity). This had been a constant demand of the PFLP, supported by the small organizations. It should be noted that the unified Command was set up *outside* the PLO framework. It assumed a policy role also, and a political committee was created within it headed by Dr. Habash. The very existence of the Unified Command was considered a spectacular achievement and a step in the direction of unity. The parties involved entered into deliberations to find a way of institutionalizing it, extending it beyond the emergency situation.

The seventh session of the Palestinian National Assembly, set for March 1970, was postponed until a solution could be found for the issues that divided the organizations, to enable all of them, especially the PFLP, to attend. The main controversy was between the "spinal column" principle prescribed by Fatah, according to which Fatah, as the oldest and largest organization, should be given preference in representation and influence, and the principle of "united front" representation, as advocated by the PFLP. More specifically, the issue was how to include the Unified Command within the framework of the PLO. Institutionalizing the Unified Command as a permanent body outside the framework of the PLO responsible for directing fedayeen action meant that the PLO would be emptied of real content, for the major Palestinian action would be conducted outside its framework. The bureaucracy of the PLO and Fatah opposed this. On the other hand, the incorporation of the Unified Command within the PLO called for concessions to Dr. Habash's organization in order to win its consent to join the PLO. The negotiations were protracted and tedious. Although as-Sā'iqa and the Popular Democratic Front (PDFLP) are closer in their social ideology to the PFLP than to Fatah, the latter was able to win their support against the PFLP, especially on the issue of representation. The organizational interests of these groups overshadowed their ideological affiliations and were decisive.

Finally, an agreement was reached on May 6, 1970. It should be noted that such a consensus among all the Palestinian organizations was unprecedented; hence its importance. According to the agreement, a *Central Committee* would be created as a body comprising: 1) the Unified Command, composed of ten organizations equally represented; 2) the Executive Committee of the PLO with its twelve members; 3) the commander of the Palestinian Army and the chairman of the National Council; 4) three independents. Thus, on the one hand, the demand of the PFLP was satisfied, and on the other, Fatah remained in actual control on the strength of its official representatives on the Executive Committee and its influence among the independents, as well as the support it could muster among the other organizations in cases of controversy with the PFLP. It should also be noted that in the formulation of the agreement there is a discernible tendency to comply with the ideological position of the PFLP without obliging Fatah to surrender its own.

It may be concluded that the radical organizations did not manage to overwhelm Fatah. It was precisely the most "establishment" organization, Fatah, which prevailed. However, the existence of the radical organizations radicalizes the establishment.

The agreement permitted the convening of the Palestinian National Assembly for its seventh session in Cairo (May 30 to June 4, 1970), this time with the participation of all the organizations (except the Communist group Quwwāt al-Anṣār (The Partisan Forces), which had announced its foundation in March 1970. This group was suspected by the others of inheriting the traditional position of the Arab Communist Parties, which supported the Partition Resolution of 1947, and of going along with the Soviet Union in its acceptance of Security Council Resolution 242). The PFLP participation was "symbolic"—a single delegate.

The agreement is a binding document like the National Covenant, hence the importance of being acquainted with it. It may assist us in understanding the Palestinians' program and the issues that occupy them. The English version cited here in italics is from *International Documents on Palestine 1970* (Walid Khadduri, general editor), The Institute for Palestine Studies, Beirut, and The University of Kuwait, 1973, pp. 795–796. It is a translation of the Arabic text in *Sawt Filastin* (Damascus), No. 29 (June 1970).

STATEMENT BY THE UNIFIED COMMAND OF THE PALESTINIAN RESISTANCE MOVEMENT DECLARING A FORMULA FOR NATIONAL UNITY AND A PROGRAM FOR POLITICAL AND MILITARY ACTION
Amman, May 6, 1970

All sections of the resistance represented in the Unified Command held a series of meetings after the crisis of February 10, 1970 [in Jordan] to discuss means of achieving integrated national unity linked with a program for political and military action, to constitute the minimum program that was agreed on in the debates of the Unified Command.

The Unified Command arrived at the following formula for national unity:

a. All sections of the resistance movement regard the Palestine Liberation movement as the broad framework for national unity.

At its inception the PLO claimed to represent and lead the Palestinian struggle. The PLO aspired to be, in its parlance, a "command"—not merely a "framework"—for all the Palestinians and their political actions. Until the fourth session of the Palestinian National Assembly in July 1968 Fatah refused to consider the PLO even as a framework. From the time it became the dominating force in the PLO, Fatah sponsored it as the umbrella organization of all the Palestinian groups.

After this session of the Assembly the PFLP withdrew from the PLO. It justified its non-participation on the ground of its accusations against the PLO: it was a bureaucratic organization unfit to conduct the revolutionary action of liberation struggle; its structure is defective since it is not based on the principle of equal representation; eighty percent of its budget is spent on administration rather than on the needs of the armed struggle; morcover it was equivocal on basic questions such as the attitude toward the reactionary Arab regimes and the principle of the independence of fedayeen action from the Arab countries, since its establishment by Arab kings and presidents produced a tendency to rely on them.

This article stipulated that the PLO henceforth would constitute a "framework" for the fedayeen organizations.

b. After long discussion the Palestinian resistance movement, as represented by the Unified Command, decided that the following points should be regarded as the broad outlines for joint political and military action, together with the

Palestinian National Covenant and the resolutions of the National Assemblies:

All the organizations thus endorsed the 1968 Palestinian National Covenant, the Resolutions of the Palestinian National Assemblies as well as the present agreement, as constituting a binding common political and military program.

1. The forces of the Palestinian revolution are the toiling Palestinian masses and all forces which have an interest in the stage of national liberation and the complete liberation of the soil of Palestine.

This article reflects the debate over the question concerning the identity of the forces which carry the main brunt of the struggle. The leaders of Fatah advocated the need to draw together all efforts by all Palestinians and all Arab states during the period of warfare against Israel, which is the crucial stage of "liberating the country." They thus stressed the need to refrain from commitment to any social ideology lest it cause the withdrawal from the battle of Palestinian and Arab groups that have a different social outlook. Preoccupation with a social theory would also divert attention from concentration on the struggle against Israel. Social ideological debate should be postponed, according to Fatah, to the second stage, which is that of "human liberation" after the complete victory over Israel. Furthermore, determining the regime of the liberated Palestinian state is premature at this stage and is "like selling the bear's hide before it is caught," in the words of Yasser Arafat.

The radicals—the PFLP and the PDFLP—contend that the national and social aspects should not be isolated. Mobilizing the masses' support for the struggle requires that the struggle be social as well as national. The issue

involved is not so much determining at present the future regime, but the definition as to which classes will play the main
role in the struggle. This must fall on the workers and peas-
ants, for they alone—having nothing to lose—are prepared
to commit themselves unreservedly to the task, and their
outlook, which stems from their class structure, is bound to
be revolutionary and correct. The debate boils down to
defining the role of the petty bourgeoisie. According to the
radicals' historiography, until 1948 leadership was in the
hands of the Palestinian and Arab grande bourgeoisie. It
was defeated in 1948. Leadership then passed to the petty
bourgeoisie (Nasser's regime, the Ba'th and the leadership
of the PLO), until the defeat in 1967 demonstrated the
bankruptcy of its class, which because of its outlook and
hankering for a comfortable life, cannot sustain the rigors
of a people's war. It is, therefore, no longer fit for leadership.
The PFLP brands the Fatah leadership as petty bourgeoisie.
Nevertheless, the radicals accept that the *national bourgeoisie*
can participate in the national struggle, but it must then be
at the base (*qā'ida*) and not in command (*qiyāda*).

The agreement is merely a verbal compromise. On the
one hand, to satisfy the radicals, the role of the workers as
bearers of the struggle is stressed; on the other, those who
have an interest in the struggle may participate, on condition
that they aim at the liberation of the entire territory, that is,
they reject the possibility of coexistence between a Palestinian
state and Israel.

*2. Palestinian struggle is based on belief that the people
in the Palestinian-Jordanian theater are one people, that
the people of Palestine are part of the Arab nation, and that
the territory of Palestine is part of Arab territory.*

The PFLP claimed that Jordanians should be permitted
to enlist in the fedayeen organizations and become members

of Palestinian unions and associations. This trend came to a head at the seventh session of the Assembly.

A Jordanian delegation headed by the veteran politician Sulaymān Nabulsi, Saʻid al-Mufti (chairman of the Senate) and ʻAqif al-Fāʼiz (chairman of the House of Representatives) proposed that unity of the Palestinian-Jordanian theater and its masses be proclaimed. The delegation asked that the Palestinian National Covenant be amended, as— according to the Covenant, or more specifically, the Fundamental Laws based upon it— only Palestinians are "natural members" of the PLO. The Assembly rejected this proposal. Instead, a vague declaration was made about unity of the Jordanian and Palestinian peoples, and it was decided that a committee be set up, composed of "the Jordanian national forces" and representatives of the PLO, to consider what such unity implied. It was also decided to amalgamate Palestinian and Jordanian associations—of women, students, etc.

The radical organizations have been hostile to Jordan because it is a monarchy and leans to the West, and they harbor opposition to its very existence. Though on the emblems of most fedayeen organizations Palestine is shown only as the area west of the Jordan, Palestinian circles presumably believe that Jordan will eventually disappear and be swallowed by Arab Palestine. Fatah circles may also lean to this view, the difference between them and the radicals being one of timing.

The objective of incorporating Jordan in Arab Palestine may be reflected in the somewhat inconsistent formulation of this article of the agreement. The article first deals with unity of the Palestinian and Jordanian peoples; then it proceeds to disregard the ʻJordanians and proclaims that the people of Palestine, not the united Palestinian-Jordanian people, is part of the Arab nation. It is likely that the phrases "the territory of Palestine" and "the people of Palestine" in the second part of the sentence subsume Jordan.

3. The Palestinian revolution is an indivisible part of the contemporary Arab revolutionary movement and an indivisible part of the worldwide national liberation movement against colonialism, imperialism and world Zionism.

This principle was taken from the ideological storehouse of the PFLP. Fatah used to stress the Palestinian aspect of the struggle. The Arab states and peoples play a role supportive to that of the Palestinians. Fatah spokesmen maintained that stressing Palestinianism did not mean neglect of Arabism. In Arafat's words, "The revolution has a Palestinian face and an Arab heart." The PFLP, on the other hand, emphasizes Arabism. It defines the struggle with Israel on the political and national level as part of the Arab social revolution.

4. The enemies of Palestinian national liberation are Zionism, the State of Israel, imperialism, and all subservient forces linked, dialectically and through their common interests, with imperialism and colonialism.

The PFLP, presenting itself as Marxist-Leninist, reiterates Lenin's slogan that without revolutionary theory there is no revolutionary movement. The theory begins, as with Mao Tse-tung, with a "scientific" definition of enemies and friends. Hitherto the failures of the Arabs, spokesmen of the PFLP expound, stemmed from an unprecise definition of enemies and friends, which led to fence-straddling and half-hearted war effort. The Palestinian leadership during the Mandatory period failed because it vacillated and could not make up its mind who was the main enemy: the British or the Jews. The PFLP defines the enemy as a fourfold coalition: Israel, Zionism, imperialism and Arab reactionary forces. There is no dispute concerning the first three, but Fatah declines explicitly and officially to list the Arab reactionaries among the enemies, lest a segment of the

Arabs be estranged from the campaign against Israel. Moreover, Fatah cultivates ties with the reactionary countries and enjoys their support. In this article the explicit designation of the reactionaries as enemies is avoided by means of the vague expression "all subservient forces linked . . . with imperialism and colonialism." For no Arab state, including Saudi Arabia and Jordan, will admit that this characterization befits it.

5. The object of Palestinian struggle is the liberation of the whole of Palestine in which all citizens will coexist with equal rights and obligations within the framework of the aspirations of the Arab nation to unity and progress.

The PDFLP raised the issue of the "Democratic State" in the negotiations that preceded the agreement. Since there was a difference of opinion on the subject, a formula was adopted which was acceptable to all: Liberation does not mean the establishment of a Palestinian state in part of the country but in its entirety; in the liberated state there will be no discrimination (this applies to the personal level); there is no recognition of the Jews as a group and the state will not be binational. The state will be Arab in the framework of Arab hopes for unity and progress. It should be noted that this article does not contradict Article 6 of the 1968 Covenant.

The establishment of a Palestinian state is not set forth as an objective in this article, for an organization such as the Arab Liberation Front opposes the very idea of a Palestinian state, which will increase the number of Arab states and thus hinder Arab unity.

6. Popular revolutionary war is the principal course to liberation of Palestine.

In the 1968 Covenant it is specified that "armed struggle is the only way to liberate Palestine." The change here lies in stressing the "revolutionary" character of the war, and reflects the thinking of the radical groups; however, it is not opposed by Fatah because it also identifies warfare against Israel with the "Palestinian Revolution." Nevertheless there is a basic difference: for Fatah, warfare against Israel is itself the revolution, whereas for the radicals warfare against Israel is the way to the revolution, defined more broadly as a social-political revolution.

7. *The people of Palestine and their national liberation movement are struggling for complete liberation and reject all peaceful solutions involving liquidation and surrender, including the reactionary and colonialist conspiracies to establish a state of Palestine in part of Palestinian territory, and the resolution involving liquidation adopted by the Security Council on November 22, 1967.*

The word *tasfiyya*, used here adjectivally, meaning "liquidation" (of an issue or problem), has taken on a pejorative connotation as something calculated to dispose of the Palestine issue without meeting the demands of the Palestinians. A compromise settlement would leave both sides to the conflict in existence, thereby implying a recognition of Israel, and is therefore rejected.

8. *Commando action regards the territory of the Arab countries which are Israel's neighbors as a legitimate field for Palestinian struggle, and considers that any effort to close any Arab country to the Palestinian resistance is treason to the goal of the people of Palestine and the Arab nation, which is the liberation of Palestine.*

This applies to Lebanon and Jordan. Use of their territory as a base for launching attacks against Israel is not a favor granted to the fedayeen organization but a national and legal right of the fedayeen.

9. *Commando action declares its complete independence*

*of all Arab regimes and rejects all attempts to encircle it,
impose tutelage on it, contain it or reduce it to subjection.*

A similar article is found in the National Covenant (of
1968, not 1964), except that in that document freedom of
action is presented in general terms, whereas here independence of "Arab regimes" is specified, in the spirit of
the PFLP. Regimes (*anzima*) has a pejorative valence and
is used synonymously with "states." The previous formula
opposed interference and patronage, whereas here there is
the further rejection of all restrictions placed on Palestinians
and their freedom of action. In the past patronage was
unbearable, whereas now all restriction on freedom of action
is intolerable.

*10. All sections of the resistance agree to the formation
of a unified military committee to develop the armed struggle
and ensure that it advances to a new stage of commando
action and people's war of liberation.*

*11. Action will be taken to arm the masses of the Palestin-
ian and Arab countries which are the neighbors of occupied
Palestine, to protect the resistance from efforts to strike at
and liquidate it, and to ensure effective combatant participation
in the confrontation of any Zionist-imperialist invasion of
Arab territories surrounding Palestine.*

This refers to raising a militia, as a popular organization
(*tanzīm sha'abī*) of armed citizens. The fighting force thus
comprises: a conventional army, fully mobilized fedayeen
and a militia of citizen formations. The militia constitutes
the fedayeen's rearguard, having as its primary mission
the warding off of attack against them on the part of Arab
states. Its secondary mission is to serve as an organization
of regional defense against Israel. Militia units were formed
in the refugee camps. They are a link in the theory shared
by all the fedayeen organizations that the battle should

be turned into a people's war. Syria espouses the theory of a people's war and formed a militia organization along with its conventional army.

A state's sovereignty over its territory is manifested by its exclusive monopoly of the employment of means of violence. The existence of fedayeen units impaired the sovereignty of Jordan and Lebanon. Whereas the fedayeen outfits could be justified as externally directed, the existence of a militia as an internal defense of the fedayeen is a much graver infringement of sovereignty. For this reason, Jordan and Lebanon resisted the formation of militias and this was a bone of contention between them and the fedayeen organizations. Furthermore, Article 11 states explicitly that this militia will not comprise Palestinians only but also Arabs (i.e., ordinary citizens of Arab states, whose allegiance will be divided between their state and the militia organization).

12. Israel, by virtue of its structure, is a closed racialist society linked with imperialism and, also by virtue of its structure, the limited progressive forces that exist in it are incapable of bringing about any radical change in the character of Israel as a Zionist racialist state linked with imperialism. Therefore the aim of the Palestinian revolution is to liquidate this entity in all its aspects, political, military, social, trade unions and cultural, and to liberate Palestine completely.

The aim of annihilating Israel engenders need to depict it as depraved, so that it warrants the death sentence. The evil in Israel is so inherent that there is no chance of changing it so long as Israel continues to exist. A decent Israel is a contradiction in terms. This outlook carries with it the notion that the evil in Israel is deeply rooted, inherent in the people who founded it, their history and culture.

Israel is so negative that a true revolutionary Left cannot arise within it. All its citizens benefit from the oppression and plunder of the Arabs, and it is therefore impossible to distinguish between Israelis and their government. Israel, as Arafat defines it, is like the East India Company. Hence, there has been a tendency to regard signs in Israel of a moderate position toward the Arabs as a deceptive plot to wrest recognition of Israel from the Arabs.

This article echoes the deliberations concerning the Israeli Left and the question whether it is capable of altering the nature of the state. Acceptance of this possibility would, by logical consistency, lead to acceptance of an Israel ruled by "the progressive forces." The possibility of progressive forces altering the character of Israel is rejected. The depravity of Israel cannot be altered because it is rooted in Israel's very foundation. This has bearing on the "depth" of the annihilation called for. It is not limited to the political existence of Israel but entails total eradication and obliteration of all its manifestations—even in the social and cultural spheres. The human aspect, sometimes included in the inventory of manifestations destined for annihilation, has been omitted from the list, apparently to avoid the accusation of genocide. The wiping out of trade unions reflects the condemnation of the Histadrut, described frequently in Arab writings as a sham and a tool in the hands of the Zionist ruling clique to tame the workers.

c. All sections shall adhere unanimously to matters on which agreement has been reached; matters on which agreement has not yet been reached may be dealt with by each section in conformity with its own individual views; all matters touching the security of the revolution shall be adhered to unanimously.

Freedom of action in the case of issues that have not been agreed upon, is preserved. Differences of opinion remained, for example, concerning the policy to be adopted vis-à-vis the reactionary regimes. There also remained disagreement over operational matters. The PFLP advocates attacking targets outside Israel (e.g., plane hijacking), since the struggle is regarded as world-embracing, as well as Western interests in Arab countries, even if this adversely affects Arab interests (blowing up the Tapline, for example). Fatah is opposed to this.

This freedom of action is limited by the general obligation to ward off attempts by the Arab states to impose restrictions upon the fedayeen groups. In these matters all must accept collective responsibility. This probably implies a demand to avoid independent provocation of governments (especially the Jordanian and Lebanese).

d. All sections shall be represented in the forthcoming Palestinian National Assembly and in the organizations affiliated to the Palestine Liberation Organization, and the extent of the representation of the organizations in the National Assembly shall not be discussed by the commando organizations.

In accordance with this resolution, all the fedayeen organizations participated in the seventh session of the National Assembly (May 30–June 4, 1969). The negotiations on the size of representation did not reach an agreed conclusion. Therefore the *Popular Front for the Liberation of Palestine*, the *Popular Organization for the Liberation of Palestine*, the *Arab Liberation Front*, and the *Executive Committee for the Liberation of Palestine* participated by sending one observer.

e. A Central Committee, in which all sections of the resistance will be represented, shall be formed by a resolution of the National Assembly, to act as the command of the resistance movement. The Central Committee appointed by the National Assembly shall take the place of the present Unified Command. This Central Committee will consist of the Executive Com-

mittee of the Palestine Liberation Organization, representatives of all the commando organizations, the President of the Palestinian National Assembly and the Commander of the Palestine Liberation Army.

The Central Committee (composed of 27 members) has a hybrid status. On the one hand, it has to supervise general activities; on the other, it was stipulated at the Seventh National Assembly that its competence would be defined by the Executive Committee. Another difference has to do with continuity. Whereas the Executive Committee is a permanent body, the Central Committee was to be convened occasionally.

Signed:
  The Palestinian National Liberation Movement (Fatah)
  The Democratic Popular Front for the Liberation of Palestine
  The Popular Front for the Liberation of Palestine
  The Popular Front for the Liberation of Palestine (General Command)
  The Palestine Liberation Army
  The Palestine Popular Struggle Front
  The Vanguards of the Popular War of Liberation (as-Sā'iqa)
  The Popular Liberation Forces
  The Arab Liberation Front
  The Arab Palestine Organization
  The Action Group for the Liberation of Palestine
  The Popular Organization for the Liberation of Palestine
  The Executive Committee of the Palestine Liberation Organization

7

Resolutions of the Eighth Palestinian National Council, March 1971

An examination of Arab basic policy documents, such as national covenants and resolutions passed by congresses, may provide insight into the problems which preoccupied their authors. While such documents need not be regarded as operative programs, they at least depict the state of mind, controversies and aspirations of their formulators. This is true of the resolutions of the 8th convention of the Palestinian Assembly which took place in Cairo on March 1–5, 1971.

This was the first congress to convene after two important events: the fedayeen defeat in Jordan in September 1970 and the UAR's declared readiness to reach a peace agreement. Such events posed a grave challenge to the Palestinian organizations, calling for a reappraisal of their policy. Owing to the divergencies between the various groups, most of the resolutions of the congress tended to restate the old familiar positions over which there is a consensus. However, there are parts of the resolutions which introduce new elements and deserve attention. A section of particular interest deals with the contradiction between Egypt's acceptance in principle of a peace settlement and its rejection by the Palestinians.

Another interesting section deals with the question of unity of the Palestinians and the Jordanians, which implies that the Palestinian organizations reject the Palestinian distinctiveness. This is clearly of great significance in the debate in Israel and abroad concerning the Palestinian entity.

The following is the full text (in italics) of the resolutions as published in the Lebanese newspaper *al-Anwar* on March 5, 1971 (subheadings as given in the original).

THE POLITICAL PROGRAM OF THE REVOLUTION

Ever since the vanguard of our struggling people set off in 1965 to ignite the armed revolution against the Zionist political entity which exists by aggression in Palestine, this vanguard and after it the Arab masses and all the freedom-loving people in the world, have been convinced that the armed struggle is the sole inevitable way to achieve the liberation of the entire territory of Palestine.

Fatah began its operations in January 1965. Its meagre operations of that period are described as a spectacular historical event which "ignited" a revolution. There is also the pretension to asserting that all the progressive forces in the world supported the struggle against Israel. It should be noted that reference is made to the liberation of all of Palestine including all Israel, which cannot be achieved by peaceful means.

At the present time the Palestinian revolution traverses a grave and critical phase in its struggle against a malicious campaign of liquidation in which the September 1970 massacre in Jordan accorded with the extermination and brutalities in the occupied homeland.

This malicious conspiracy no longer aims at liquidating the Palestinian revolution, or the Palestinian problem. Its aim is the actual liquidation of the Palestinian people itself, taking into consideration that the Palestinian people constitutes the driving force, as well as the instrument and the objective of the revolution. Therefore it was agreed collectively by an international imperialist power, world Zionism together with the occupying Zionist state and the counter-revolutionary forces in the Arab world, that the time had come to initiate the vicious campaign of liquidation. They recognized the dangers implicit in the escalated Palestinian revolution and its expansion throughout the Arab homeland, as it is bound to sweep away all the hostile interests which stand in its path, and must inevitably culminate in destroying their [imperialism and its partners] common interests in this part of the world.

The description of the events in Jordan as stemming from an imperialist conspiracy to which Israel is a partner serves to brand the Jordanian authorities as stooges of imperialism and Israel. Jordan's action against the fedayeen and Israel's policy in the occupied areas are described as parts of a single plot to liquidate the Palestinian people. Imperialism is portrayed as apprehensive of the possibility that the struggle against Israel would launch a revolution which would encompass the entire world and hurt its interests and investments.

In addition, the explosion of the situation in Indochina and the continued progress in Laos and Cambodia, as well as the proliferation of successes of the Vietnamese revolution, have prompted the American ruling circles to seek ways to pacify the region [M.E.] by consolidating the military gains made by the enemy in the 1967 war.

It would appear that the purpose of associating the September 1970 events in Jordan with the war in Vietnam is to magnify the importance of the Palestinian movement, presenting it as a sector in a worldwide struggle between the forces of progress and the forces of reaction. America's desire for peace in the Middle East is prompted by its difficulties in Vietnam. This supposed connection between the Middle Eastern and South-East Asian fronts suggests that thwarting the efforts to achieve a settlement in the M.E. would be a blow to the U.S. which would assist the North Vietnamese and Vietcong in their struggle.

THE DANGEROUS NEW CIRCUMSTANCES

In face of the dangerous new circumstances, the various groups of the Palestinian revolution and its forces together agreed to announce a phased political program according to the principles mentioned below, which are intended to answer clearly all the questions of the [present] phase. This program would serve as a blueprint for advancing the revolution, for increasing its organized force and for attracting broader strata of the Palestinian and Arab masses to advance the cause of the triumphant revolution.

The executive Committee of the PLO and Yasser Arafat had been criticized for failing to present the Assembly with a political program, contenting themselves with an organizational plan for the unification of the organizations under the leadership of Fatah.

The difficulty in modifying the stand of the fedayeen organization to fit in with the position of Arab states such as Egypt and Jordan regarding a political solution, prevented them from agreeing on a common political program. Nevertheless, in view of the solemnity of the occasion it was appropriate for them to appear as if they had arrived at a common policy.

ON THE PALESTINIAN LEVEL

The Palestinian Liberation Organization is the sole representative of the Palestinian Arab people in its various organizations, military and political, and of the bodies and unions, regardless of their directions and ideologies, provided they solemnly undertake to adhere to the principles of the Palestine Covenant, the resolutions of the legal and the executive bodies, the political and military plans, the internal regulation of the Organization, and also provided thay they commit themselves to the concept of the struggle for the liberation of the entire Palestinian territory and the restoration of the Palestinian people to its homeland. Under no circumstances may any individual or group who are members of the Organization be expelled, except for damage to the security of the revolution, or deviation from the principles of the Palestinian National Covenant, and pursuant to a decision by the Central Committee or the National Council during its convention.

This paragraph refers to the problem which had been dealt with extensively, namely, the nature of the Palestine Liberation Organization. The agreement of May 6, 1970 stipulated that the PLO was a "framework" encompassing all the Palestinian organizations. Here it is stated that it is "the sole representative." It is true that the Palestinian organizations frequently engage in fine semantic debates. However, there does not appear to be a fundamental distinction between the two versions.

The all-inclusive nature of the PLO is given emphasis, apparently as a critique of the position of the radical organizations, which tend to stress the class aspect of the struggle, and view the working class as its standard-bearers. It is precisely the setbacks suffered by the fedayeen which make the inclusion of all Palestinian groups imperative. The authority to expel from the PLO is not invested in the Executive Council, but in the Central Committee.

The complete liberation of the occupied Palestinian homeland is the central and fundamental goal of the Palestinian revolution. This is to be achieved by revolutionarily mobilizing the Palestinian masses, politically, militarily and doctrinarily, by englobing them all in the struggle for liberation, by advancing the armed struggle against the enemy, and by unifying all forces of the Palestinian masses inside the occupied homeland and outside for this purpose.

A National Liberation Movement

THE NATURE OF THE PALESTINIAN REVOLUTION

The Palestinian revolution is a movement for national liberation. Because of this it coordinates its tactics and strategy with other movements for national liberation in the world, since they represent the movement of all the masses struggling against foreign occupation, and believe in the necessity of freedom and are willing to be enlisted for the struggle for its realization. This means that the Palestinian people, with all its classes, bodies, organizations and unions, with all their various opinions and principles, is being called upon to form a united front in our armed national revolution.

The Palestinian revolution represents the progressive movement in the Palestinian Arab society by virtue of the following:

1) Its struggle against the settling-racist occupation which is a part of the dark forces opposing the trend of history;

2) Its struggle against international imperialism led by the United States, the protector of the Zionist occupation which thwarts our people's rights and aspirations;

3) Its intention to construct a Palestinian Arab society dominated by the principles of democracy, peace, justice, freedom and equality, which will respect all the ideologies and faiths, protect all the rights and freedoms, and which will firmly reject feudal rule, a reactionary socially backward relationship and religious and racial discrimination.

All the above is meant to substantiate the progressive nature of the Palestinian organizations.

THE PRINCIPAL FORM OF THE STRUGGLE

The armed struggle, kindled at the beginning of 1965 by the revolutionary vanguards of the Palestinian people, i.e., the guerrilla war which is evolving into an extensive war of national liberation, is the principal form of the struggle for the liberation *of Palestine. Similarly, the merging in the armed struggle between the regular armed forces and the popular forces is considered as the most effective way of realizing the triumphant popular revolution. Moreover, all other forms of the struggle must sincerely and persistently conform with the line of the armed struggle.*

The Palestinian National Covenant stipulated that "the armed struggle is the only way to liberate Palestine. Thus it is a strategy, not a tactic," (Ariticle 9). Further on (Article 10) it is mentioned that: "Fedayeen action constitutes the nucleus of the Palestinian popular war." In the May 6, 1970 Agreement it was stipulated that "the way of revolutionary people's war is the basic way for liberating Palestine" (Article 6). The position formulated here is slightly more moderate. While guerrilla warfare is described as the *principal* form of the struggle, and it is anticipated to evolve into a popular war, the possibility of other forms of struggle is hinted at, which may be an allusion to political methods and in particular to Egypt's acceptance of a political settlement. However, these methods must conform with, and serve the purpose of, the armed struggle. The armed struggle is not the continuation of the political way, but the other ways, including the political one, are the continuation of the armed struggle. Action will reach its culmination by combining the regular forces with those of the guerrilla's; whereas in the past the accent was on the guerrilla forces and the regular forces were viewed by the fedayeen as a supporting factor, rather than as a partner.

THE REJECTION OF THE CREATION OF A PALESTINIAN "MINI-STATE"

The only solution for the Palestine problem is the liberation of the entire Palestinian territory by the force of the armed struggle. Therefore the liquidation solution [of the Arab cause] or any other solution which violates the natural and his-

torical rights of the Palestinian people in its entire homeland, is
fundamentally unacceptable. The Palestinian revolution hereby
declares its commitment in principle to the following:

1) An unremitting struggle against any attempts, efforts,
schemes and forces which aim at arresting the progress of the
revolution, obstructing it, or deviating it from its goals, and
against any liquidation plans, in whatever form. This requires
that the Palestinian revolution be developed and made more
efficient in all its aspects;

2) A firm stand against the creation of a Palestinian mini-
state as a form of liquidating the Palestine problem.

A liquidating solution is a compromise solution aimed at
"liquidating" the conflict. The Arabic term "mini-state"
(duwaila) is a diminutive term with disparaging overtones.
The term *Palestinistan* is used in the same vein.

THE DEMOCRATIC STATE

The armed Palestinian struggle is not a racial or a religious
struggle against the Jews; therefore, the future state in
Palestine, liberated from Zionist colonialism, will be the
democratic Palestinian state in which those wishing to live
peacefully in it would enjoy the same rights and obligations,
within the framework of the aspiration of the arab nation for
a national liberation, and general unity with the accent on the
unity of the people on both banks of the Jordan.

It should be noted that the resolutions of the Congress
are binding and are, therefore, in the nature of appendices
to the Covenant. But the present version does not necessarily
contradict Article 6 of the Covenant, since it does not
abrogate the limitation concerning the Israelis who would
be permitted to remain. It resembles the corresponding
Article in the May 6, 1970 Agreement, which states: "The
aim of the Palestinian struggle is the liberation of the entire
territory of Palestine, in which all citizens will live together

having equal rights and obligations, within the framework of the Arab nations' aspiration for unity and progress" (Article 5). It does not say that all Jews living in Israel now would be allowed to remain and live in the new democratic state, but that all its citizens will have equality of rights. Moreover, aside from being a democratic state, the state of Palestine is emphatically projected as a part of the Arab unity, which would serve to ensure the *Arab character* of the state, by reducing the relative weight of the Jewish minority. Moreover, the Arab character of the state would also be strengthened by unifying Jordan and Palestine.

THE UNITY OF THE PALESTINIAN AND JORDANIAN MASSES

There is a national association between Jordan and Palestine and a territorial unity shaped by history, culture and language since ancient times. The establishment of separate political entities in Palestine and Jordan is not supported by any legality nor by any constituents that form an entity. They were a product of the dismembering policy by which colonialism after World War I sought to tear asunder the unity of the Arab nation and the Arab homeland. Nevertheless, this division could not prevent the masses east and west of the river from feeling that they were one people, faced with a plot by colonialism and Zionism.

The Palestinian revolution, which raised the slogan of Palestine and posed the issue of the Palestinian revolution, did not intend to separate the eastern bank from the western, and did not believe that the struggle of the people of Palestine could be waged apart from the struggle of the Jordanian masses. The requirements of a specific historical phase demanded concentration of all efforts toward Palestine, so as to make its issue prominent for the Palestinians, the Arabs and internationally. Our preservation of the unity of the Palestinian and Jordanian masses, our awareness of the role

which they can play in the development of the battle of libera-
tion, affirm our belief in the following:

1) The unity of Palestine and Transjordan as a territorial
unity which we are called upon to preserve and strengthen,
resisting all efforts to weaken and dismember it;

2) This territorial unity can be realized in a unified struggle
by setting up a National Jordanian Front, whose primary
function would be the establishment of a national government
in Jordan, which will participate in the liberation of Palestine
and support, by all the means at its disposal, the combatting
Palestinian force, since it is a part of the struggle of the
Arab nation for its liberation and unity.

The definition of Palestine in the text of the National
Covenant published by Shukeiry on February 24, 1964,
and copied in the 1964 and 1968 versions of the Palestinian
National Covenants, was ambiguous: "Palestine with the
boundaries it had during the British Mandate is an integral
territorial unit."

The boundaries of the Mandate changed—initially they
included Jordan, which was set apart only in 1922. The PLO
emphasized from the beginning that it was not conspiring
to take Jordan over, and indeed in the emblems of the various
organizations Palestine was represented as including all
the area west of the Jordan River but not the eastern part.

The Agreement of May 6, 1970 expressed the trend toward a Palestinian-Jordanian unity by proclaiming the
principle of "the unity of the people in the Palestinian-
Jordanian arena" (Article 2). The present resolutions add an
historical argumentation that the separation of the eastern
bank from the western bank of the Jordan, and the establishment of the Transjordanian emirate, were a colonialist plot
to dismember the Arab countries. This political act was
contrary to the sentiment of the people concerning its unity.
It would appear that this historical description implies

giving precedence to Palestine over Jordan, since it was Jordan which was torn apart from Palestine.

In declaring the unity of the Palestinians and Jordanians the Palestinians are actually following King Hussein for whom the slogan of the "Jordanian family," consisting of Jordanians and Palestinians, has been a basic tenet of his political philosophy. Jordan considered itself the successor to Palestine and shortly after the 1948 War promulgated its own "laws of return" granting Jordanian citizenship to the Palestinians: at first, in February 16, 1954, to those residing in the Hashemite Kingdom and who "used to have the Palestinian Nationality before May 1948, excluding Jews" and then, on February 4, 1960, to all Palestinians living abroad who wished to acquire it. The difference between Hussein and the Palestinians apparently lies in the question which of the twins is senior.

The demand that the Jordanian-Palestinian unity be emphasized was raised by the Popular Front for the Liberation of Palestine (PFLP) during the discussions which preceded the May 6, 1970 Agreement. At that time the topic of opening membership in the PLO to Jordanians was discussed, as the fundamental law of the PLO limited membership to Palestinians only. The PFLP demanded that the fundamental law and the National Covenant be amended accordingly. The problem was raised again at the Seventh Congress (August 1970). It was decided not to amend the Covenant, but to allow leaders of organizations who were not of Palestinian origin (such as Ḥawatmeh, Jam'ani, Razaz and Za'rur) to be members of the Central Committee.

Presumably, a number of factors led to the present resolution of the Assembly, providing a basis for the Palestinian claims to a say in Jordanian politics and government, since such a unity means that Jordan is their homeland as well. It is possible that it was precisely the reverses suffered by the organizations in Jordan and their consequent weakness which reinforced the need to vindicate that Jordan was their land as well. The emphasis on this point could also be a result of rumors about the setting up of a Palestinian state on the West Bank, an idea which has always been rejected both by the Palestinian organizations and the Jordanian authorities, since, if Jordan and Palestine are indeed one entity, there is no room for a separate Palestinian state on the West Bank. It is also possible that the fear among some circles within the fedayeen organizations that a political solution was on its way may have led to the declaration of unity as a claim to Jordan, after their forfeiting the territory of Israel, to prevent being left with nothing. However, for them a united state would only be the "state of confrontation," for the sake of continuing the struggle.

Moreover, the events of September 1970 have resulted in an interesting phenomenon in Jordan, in the form of an accentuation of its Jordanian identification. For the Jordanian establishment, the struggle against the fedayeen was a war of survival, which is not true of the struggle against Israel. They feared that strengthening the fedayeen would seal their personal fate. Not only would they be deprived of their position in the government, but their very lives would be endangered. Therefore, they mobilized all their strength and were not deterred from spilling Arab blood. The very fact of the Jordanian victory over the Palestinians strengthened the Jordanian identification.

Naif Hawatmeh, who is himself a Jordanian and whose leftist tendencies made him perceptive of social matters, summarizes the lessons of the war: "The body of Jordanian-Palestinian society has split vertically and the problem is no longer one of the unity of all classes and national forces against the forces of imperialism and reactionary classes, but since September, a Jordanian society was created opposed to the Palestinian society, the army against the resistance" (*al-Nahar*, March 7, 1971). Further on, he explains that in this way a "popular basis" was created for the present Jordanian government. (A similar analysis is included in a memorandum submitted to the Central Committee by the PFLP, the text of which was published in *al-Hadaf* of December 26, 1970: "The Jordanian regime used the battle (of September 1970) in order to create an abyss between the Palestinian and Jordanian peoples so as to crystallize a social force on which it could rely in attacking the resistance.") Hawatmeh blamed Fatah for helping this development by stressing the Palestinian character of the struggle against Israel. It seems that one can go further than Hawatmeh and assert that Jordan's ascendency has also manifested itself in the fact that many Palestinians, who have integrated into Jordan, have become supporters of the Hashemite Kingdom against the revolutionary fedayeen organizations acting as the standard-bearer of the revolutionary trends. These Palestinian circles are bourgeois or petty bourgeois and they fear a social revolution. Thus, at present, these Palestinians are undergoing a process of Jordanization to a greater extent than Jordan is being Palestinized.

This development is of significance too as regards the idea of a Palestinian state on the West Bank. In the final analysis, a mini-state of this nature will have to rely either on Jordanian or on Israeli support. Although many of the inhabitants of Judea and Samaria are hostile toward the Hashemite Kingdom, they certainly will not desire to remain with Israel. If pushed to choose between Israel and Jordan they will prefer to go back to Jordan. Their tragedy is that this would mean affiliation to Jordan at the very time that its Jordanian identity has been accentuated.

The situation is somewhat paradoxical, even for the Jordanian government. Although, the fedayeen organizations were not able to overthrow the Jordanian regime, the return of the West Bank to Jordan will strengthen the Palestinians there. This is likely to undermine the Jordanian regime, unless it can miraculously gain control over this populace by all kinds of manipulations. This populace's acquaintance with the Israeli administration is likely to increase its claims as to what the administration should be and make it restive. It will be an ironic twist of fate if this population, which under our government was rather quiescent, will become rebellious under an Arab government. Often, people cannot prevent the fatalistic unfolding of events, even though they may have some forebodings of their approach. Government circles in Jordan demand the return of the West Bank, but it is precisely the return of the West Bank that will seal their fate. The return of the West Bank to Jordan may in the long run reverse the present trend and bring about the Palestinization of Jordan. The idea of transforming Jordan into a Palestinian state will find supporters elsewhere, for example, in Egypt, which has always been hostile toward the Hashemite regime. It is also possible that this is how Egypt intends to compensate the Palestinians, should a political solution with Israel be achieved.

This tendency to emphasize Palestinian and Jordanian unity has significant implications which should be pointed out. If the Jordanians and the Palestinians constitute a single entity, then Jordan is also the homeland of the Palestinians, and the Palestinians do not lack a homeland. Their war is therefore not directed at acquiring a homeland, but rather at expanding their present homeland.

8

The Palestinians and Egypt's Acceptance of a Political Settlement

Egypt's acceptance of a possible political solution and a peace settlement contradicted the basic position of the Palestinian organizations and presented them with a dilemma. Some, like Fatah, reluctantly granted that Egypt had the right to act as it did. The radical organizations attacked the Egyptian move, but nevertheless Sadat was invited to address the first session of the Eighth Congress and was given an ovation. There is a parallel contradiction in Egypt's position, which at one and the same time accepts a peace settlement and declares its support for the fedayeen and its partnership with them which, according to Sadat's statement at the Congress, will continue "until and after the victory," notwithstanding their principled rejection of any settlement. Furthermore, Sadat recognized the Palestinians right to continue the struggle despite a settlement to which Arab states would be parties.

The two sides have been making efforts to control and even reconcile their differences. Indeed, if a political peace settlement signifies the end of the struggle, the contradiction exists; on the other hand, if such a settlement is viewed as temporary expediency, intended to further the cause of the struggle, then there is no contradiction. A resolution of the Eighth Palestinian National Assembly stipulated that "all other forms of the struggle must sincerely and persistently conform with the line of the armed struggle." The "sincerety" requirement is to ensure that such a settlement, accepted as a temporary tactic, will not evolve into a strategic and final settlement. "All other forms of the struggle" may signify political ones, including those by the means of a settlement. The "persistency" requirement may signify that the resumption of the struggle will not be indefinitely postponed.

The tendency not to regard the political settlement as the termination of the Arab-Israel conflict can also be discerned in the Egyptian statements. Egypt has been determined "to eliminate the traces of the 1967 aggression," even if it took a peace settlement to achieve it, because the *status quo* has been intolerable. But this did not mean that its goal was a final settlement. The ideological monthly of the Arab Socialist Union, *al-Kātib,* opened its March 1971 issue with an article by Ahmed Nabīl al-Hilāli, entitled: "The Arab Left vis-à-vis its Historical Responsibilities." The article states: "If the political efforts succeed and some sort of a political solution is found which will eliminate the traces of aggression, this would by no means bring an end to our struggle against Zionism and imperialism, and will by no means bring a happy conclusion to our fateful battle against the United States and Israel, because no political settlement whatsoever could eliminate the basic contradiction which exists—and will continue to exist—between the Arab nation on the one hand and American imperialism and Zionism on the other. . . . An Israeli acceptance of a political settlement with the Arabs will not alter its character of a forward base of American imperialism, undo its nature as an instrument of aggression, much less cause it to shed its expansionist ambitions to establish a greater Israel. As long as the racist colonialist entity continues to burden the usurped land of Palestine, there will be a "focus" for threat, expansion and aggression, a "center" for counter-revolution, and a "broadcasting station" for psychological warfare. Thus a political solution cannot by any means bring an end to the battle against the enemy" (11th Year, No. 120, March 1971, p. 3).

According to the above analysis, which is repeated by Egyptian spokesmen, the settlement will not last long yet the breaking of the peace and the resumption of the conflict will not emanate from the Arabs, but from the intrinsically evil nature of Israel. The Arab side is exonerated of any intention to continue the struggle. All blame is placed on Israel which is incapable of adhering to peace and will break it, even if the Super Powers guarantee it. Its expansionist and aggressive characteristics are inherent in its nature and cannot change so long as Israel exists. Its very existence is that of a foreign base, so that it must inevitably harm its neighbors, and cannot become a part of the region. Thus the chasm between Israel and the Arabs is presented as so profound and fundamental that no political settlement can bridge over it. Moreover, Israel's bid to strengthen itself by some territorial gains is not the consequence of Arab hostility and threats, but is their cause. Israel's terms for a political settlement are seen as confirming the traits attributed to it, representing its expansionist ambitions. Such an analysis serves to justify the fact that, despite the declared preparedness to make peace, Arab expressions of hostility toward Israel continue unabated, since this hostility stems not from the Arabs but from the nature of Israel. Egypt on the one hand proclaims its willingness to make peace while on the other hand, its broadcasts, official spokesmen and press, continue to heap abuse upon Israel. For example, Israel is regularly represented as racist, Nazi and "an enemy of mankind." But if Israel is so depraved surely the continuation of the conflict and not peace is mandatory. Therefore, the settlement is to be strictly on the diplomatic level, as a *force majeure,* a tactical maneuver in the conflict, whereas the hostility remains on the national level.

On the other hand, this interpretation is needed to mollify

those Arabs who are critical of Egypt's move, fearing that it may be pushed into a position which will lead not only to a peace settlement, but to a final conclusion of the conflict. Palestinian leaders are apprehensive that the postponement *sine die* of the continuation of the conflict with Israel may imply its eventual termination. In a conversation with journalists in Tunis, Yasser Arafat explained:

> It is possible that this generation will not be fortunate to see the complete liberation of the Palestinian territory. But it would be a double crime of this generation if, in addition to failing to liberate Palestine, it decrees non-liberation on future generations. In my opinion if we, the present generation, cannot achieve the liberation, we must not sign on behalf of future generations but we had better leave them the possibility of liberation (*The Palestinian Revolution,* No. 31, January 1971, p. 13).

Thus the road to the resumption of the conflict should be left open.

The Egyptians retort by paradoxically making Israel the guarantor for the continuation of the conflict.

These explanations that, because of the circumstances of the conflict and the nature of Israel, any settlement will perforce be a temporary tactical move, may seem to the foreign observer a casuistry, ideological verbal acrobatics and a rationalization of Egypt's deviation from the national position. But even if there is an element of apologetics in these explanations, it does not mean that they do not represent an historical view held by the Egyptian leadership.

Some Arab spokesmen differentiate between *suluḥ,* a peace of reconciliation or a real peace, and *salām,* a peace in form that does not end a conflict. This distinction was borne out by Col. Qadhāfi in an interview with Eric Rouleau (*Le Monde,* May 6, 1971).

ROULEAU: Don't you pursue, Mr. President, an opposite

course to that of Egypt which formally accepted the principle of recognizing the State of Israel?

QADHĀFI: No, because Egypt has never said that it would conclude a peace treaty *(suluḥ)* but only peace agreement *(salām)*. This distinction is fundamental.

ROULEAU: Supposing Israel withdraws to the 1967 frontiers and that, in exchange, Cairo accepts to reach a settlement according to the terms of Resolution 242, will Libya accede to such an agreement?

QADHĀFI: Egypt is free to do what it wishes. As regards ourselves, Allah is great.

Actually this differentiation between *suluḥ* and *salām* is not a fundamental one stemming from Islamic jurisprudence. The main difference is that *suluḥ* is the act of making peace, while *salām* is the condition or state resulting therefrom. The meaning given to these terms by Qadhāfi is new. Its importance is in the intention that peace with Israel should not be definitive.

It is possible that peace has its own dynamics and that once it is achieved or even a partial settlement is attained, a process of institutionalization would start to strengthen the settlement. In other words, Israel is the enemy of mankind so long as there is no settlement, and when peace comes this concept will disappear. This is possible. It is not, however, the way that many of the Arab spokesmen envisage peace with Israel and its consequences. Their way of seeing the conflict cannot be dismissed as irrelevant, and may also be a factor in its future development. Of course, a nation's behavior is influenced more by its "national interest" than by ideological rationalizations, and should be evaluated accordingly. However, "national interest" is not an objective datum but is defined by a political élite, whose views may be colored by their ideology. Moreover, given the instability in the Arab countries, and the fact that some Arabs are opposed to and agitate against any peace settlement, it is not unreasonable to consider that the more extreme positions may persist. The extremism on the fringes of the Arab public may still move to the center.

Israel must take into consideration the manner in which Arab ruling circles interpret the settlement of the conflict. So long as the settlement remains exclusively on the diplomatic level, while on the national level the attitude has not changed, the conflict may continue. It is impossible for Israel to regard a political settlement as an end to the conflict and a durable peace, if many Arabs treat it as a mere lull in the fighting. True, the strategic positions Israel demands may become in the future a source of irredentism and trouble. Our own predicament is that very serious considerations impelled Israel to demand them. The Egyptian leaders' statements regarding the peace settlement and its expected consequences, the contradiction between their agreement to make peace and their support for the fedayeen who oppose the peace—these are the convincing arguments for the Israeli demands in respect of the settlement.

The continuation of the conflict without a settlement is a nightmare haunting many Israelis. In order to reach a compromise one must no doubt venture to make risky concessions. Nevertheless, Israel's behavior may be influenced by the consideration that it is preferable for it to lead a dangerous existence, with the conflict, rather than to weaken its ability to defend itself by giving up some strategic asset. Furthermore, if the settlement does not take root, such concessions might incur the dangers of war in more difficult conditions and threaten Israel's very existence.

Israel's insistence on controlling some strategic positions was motivated basically by the desire to ensure that the Arabs would not revert to their belligerent stand, or in other words, that a peace agreement concluded—as far as the Arabs were concerned—as a tactical expediency would become a lasting peace that ends the conflict.

9

The Problem of the Palestinians

The Palestinian Arabs and their problem undoubtedly play an important role in the Arab-Israel conflict. However, the Palestinians cannot nowadays be considered as constituting one single factor in the conflict.

The Palestinian Arabs (besides the Israeli Arabs) are divided, geographically and, at the same time, more or less politically, into three main groups:

1. The Palestinian Arabs in Judea, Samaria ("The West Bank"), and the Gaza Strip.
2. The Palestinian Arabs in Jordan.
   Many of these Palestinians in Jordan have been integrated in Jordan economically, socially and politically. They are distinguished as Palestinians by the memory of their origin and an emotional attachment which have, practically, lost much of their political significance. Even if part of this group probably does not wholeheartedly support either the King or the Palestine Liberation Organization (PLO), in present circumstances, such a stance of neutrality means, for practical purposes, an attitude toward the *status quo* and the present regime which varies between favor and acquiescene.
3. The Palestinians elsewhere.
   Among this group the PLO, though constituting only a minority, has assumed a leading position and pretends to represent them. The PLO categorically has

rejected any settlement involving coexistence with Israel. From time to time, it is true, there have been rumors of changes in this stance, but they have always proved to be without foundation. Refusal to accept the existence of a Jewish state is for them a central tenet in their ideology, and they have shown no sign of being ready to give it up.[1]

The Political Problem of the Arabs in the West Bank

Among the Palestinian Arabs in Judea and Samaria—though even they are not all of one opinion—there is, it seems, a prevalent recognition of the need to arrive at a settlement with Israel. They have been affected by the consciousness that the Palestinians have always been the victims of the conflict, by the glaring contrast between the inadequacies of the Arab world and Israel's achievements in economic development and social progress, by the unexpected liberality of Israeli rule, by the failures of the fedayeen and—last but not least—by the brutal suppression of the Fedayeen in Jordan in September 1970 and thereafter.

The question is whether these Palestinian Arabs in Judea and Samaria can assume responsibility for a political settlement. Are they capable of reaching a settlement with Israel against the opposition of the Arab states? That would be the acid test of a title to be regarded as an autonomous factor of political significance. The test would reveal their serious weakness as a political factor in the conflict.

Let us examine the possibilities of a "Palestinian solution" even without taking into account Israel's position and the need for her consent.

An Independent Palestinian Arab State in the West Bank

Such a state is not viable, not because of its small size or economic limitations but because of political realities. Economically anything can be made viable by external aid, at least temporarily. It is landlocked and is dependent for an outlet on Jordan or Israel. If it were established in the teeth of opposition from Jordan—and there are no signs that Jordan is inclined to tolerate such a state—Jordan could isolate it from the Arab world and sever the ties between its people and their relatives in other Arab countries, with all the economic, political and social consequences of such an isolation for the new state and its citizens. The attitude of the other Arab countries would be no less hostile. [2]

For the potential citizens of a Palestinian state, the very idea of the ostracism that would be imposed on them by the Arab countries and the Palestinians outside is a nightmare, a powerful deterrent to the notion of a separate settlement with Israel. Any such settlement would leave them with no alternative but to rely upon Israel as their main market and sole outlet—which would further aggravate the hostility of the Arab world. Thus, the realities of the situation endow Jordan with what amounts to a *de facto* veto against the establishment of a Palestinian state in the West Bank.

Another possibility is to rejoin Jordan in accordance with King Hussein's scheme of March 15, 1972. The return to Hashemite rule, even if the name of the dynasty is symbolically excised from the title of Hussein's United Arab Kingdom, is not a cheerful prospect for many of these Palestinians, although they continue to keep their Jordanian citizenship—some willingly and others for lack of an alternative. Immediately after the bloody suppression of the Palestinian organizations in Jordan in September 1970, many West-Bankers condemned Jordan in the severest terms and vowed not to return to it. However, the mood has changed in the meantime. The realities and the recognition of Jordan's power over them prevail. This change was manifested in the procession of leaders from the West Bank and the Gaza Strip in the summer of 1972 to offer their condolences to the King after his father's death. But the scheme for a federated kingdom still meets with some opposition from West-Bankers.

If an independent Palestinian state in the West Bank is impossible, and adhesion to Jordan is undesirable and to Israel even less, the Palestinians find themselves enmeshed in ambivalent attitudes. In this situation, it seems that most of them tend to resign themselves to the *status quo* as the least of all possible evils. By defining it as temporary, they make submission to it easier. Some of them, it is true, envisage the possibility of a Palestinian state under the supervision of the United Nations for several years, to be followed by a plebiscite to decide their future, in the hope that their state would thus win acceptance from the Arab countries. This idea, however, does not extricate them from their fundamental dilemmas; at most, it postpones the decision. A plebiscite is an expedient for deciding between possibilities, it cannot create a new possibility.

In the past, some of the West-Bankers solved the problem cavalierly by assuming that in the course of time, with the reinforcement of its Palestinian element, Jordan as a whole would become a Palestinian state. For the time being, no such process is evident. The Palestinians as individuals may be more advanced and better educated than the Jordanians; the Jordanians, however, by interacting with a center—such as the kingdom—became more cohesive. The Palestinians always have lacked a center and thus are proverbially fragmented. One is tempted to generalize that, in a showdown between a more intellectual group and a more cohesive one, the latter will probably prevail, as was witnessed in September 1970. It appears, in fact, that politically the Jordanian factor is more serious than the Palestinian one, even for the very prosaic reason that the Jordanians possess an effective army obeying one center of command.

In any case, the impracticability of converting Jordan into a Palestinian state has become so obvious that even those Israelis who used to be fervently in favor of it have recently been quiescent. Some Israelis have been sensitive to the claims of the "Palestinian entity" yet strangely indifferent to the "Jordanian entity," which they volunteered to offer up as a sacrifice on the Palestinian altar. But there is no reason to regard the Jordanians as any less entitled to their political identity than the Palestinians—and they have defended their claim with deeds.

A settlement between Jordan and Israel may and probably will in the long run bring about the Palestinization of Jordan by the sheer numerical preponderance of the Palestinians, augmented by the West-Bankers. But a settlement cannot start by the Palestinization of Jordan. This distinction cannot be overstressed.

The Palestinian Arabs as a whole may be an important factor in the final stage of a settlement, but until then their importance for a formal *political* settlement of the dispute is in doubt—and it is the present stage that really counts now, for it will have to be traversed in order to get to the final stage. Without the Palestinians a peace settlement would not be complete; without the Arab states it cannot start. The Palestinians claim that they must have a say in the settlement. The claim is sound. The question is whether today the West-Bankers have anything to say of their own that is of substantial political significance.[3] The problem is not that the Palestinians have not been recognized as a people or nation, but that they are unable to translate such a recognition into reality. That is why a formal recognition of the Palestinians as a people, no matter how justified, has been barren of tangible political consequences.

That is the essence of the tragic situation in which they are placed. The Arab states can conclude arrangements without the Palestinian Arabs, but the Palestinians cannot do so without the Arab states. Hence, a "Palestinian" political solution of the conflict is hardly foreseeable.

The argument that the Palestinians could effectively sabotage a settlement between Israel and the Arab states is exaggerated, as events in Jordan have shown: what Jordan has done could be done by the other Arab countries with less drastic measures of repression. Even if Palestinian underground groups were from time to time to perpetrate terrorist acts of more sophisticated nature than the previous ones, that would not change the picture.

Can a Political Settlement Grow Out of Practical Arrangements?

In the absence of a settlement with the Palestinians in the West Bank, the present situation in the West Bank will continue. The prophecy that Israel would be unable to maintain the *status quo* even temporarily in this area has not come true. Such learned predictions, based on historical analogies and sociological theories, of increasingly acute civil resistance and insurgence, have been refuted. The five years that have elapsed cannot be dismissed as merely a provisional truce. Of course, military occupation cannot last indefinitely. However, so far, there are no indications that the patience of the population is becoming exhausted; on the contrary, it seems to be growing. One reason for this is the improvement in the economic situation; another is the dilemma which it faces, as described above. A man does not revolt if he knows what he does not want but is unable to choose between existing alternatives or create new ones.

In the meantime, many of the West-Bank Palestinians are preoccupied with the new opportunities for improving their standard of living and many shrug off the problem of their political future as a matter for politicians—especially those in the Arab states—to grapple with. This tendency, which may be called, with no disparagement, *self-depolitization*, is a further testimony to, and an admission of, their weakness as a political factor.

Israelis and foreigners are not conscious of how embarrassing are their relentless inquisitions of West-Bankers about their views on their role in a political settlement and how such interrogations, notwithstanding their good intentions, virtually amount to exercises in political sadism.

Since a "Palestinian" political settlement is beyond the capacity of the West-Bank and Gaza Arabs, they cannot, in the near future, be partners with Israel in a political settlement. They can, however, be Israel's partners in *practical* arrangements, which at present take the form of joint economic activities, but go further. Israel's policy to minimize intervention in the life of the areas and allow a great amount of internal autonomy may continue. A cumulative process of such *de facto* practical arrangements may contribute to a *de jure* political settlement in the more distant future. However, since these Palestinians are not autonomous politically, the possibility of such a result transcends the subsystem of relations between Israel and the Palestinians under its rule: it depends on the development in the relations between Israel and the Arab world, as well as on possible internal changes in that world.

The Palestinian Establishment Perpetuating the Conflict

The importance of the third goup of Palestinian Arabs, who are organized under the aegis of the PLO, has declined after their failures in the fight against Israel, and later, their defeat in Jordan. Nevertheless, it would be wrong to let these things tempt us to underrate their importance. Most of the Arab countries still regard them as the representatives and standard-bearers of the Palestinians.[4] At their head stands "the Palestinian establishment": the bureaucracy of the PLO, leaders and officials of Palestinian military groups and trade unions and other associations, and a gathering of Palestinian intellectuals—writers and journalists for whom the Arab-Israel conflict is a vocation and a source of livelihood. All these "professional Palestinians" depend for their positions and their livings not only on the conflict in general, but on the conflict in its present form, which is expressed in the demand for "the liberation of Palestine." It is the liberation of Palestine—namely, the liquidation of Israel—that is to transform their lives and make of them the leadership, administration and bureaucracy of the liberated land. For the time being, they have no other occupation. In the past, these people could find openings in the Arab countries, but an indigenous intelligentsia has arisen in the meantime which has displaced them.

The paradox is that, while they experience difficulty in finding employment in the Arab countries, and they are unwanted there, the same Arab countries are willing to allot sufficient money to maintain this extensive Palestinian establishment and enable its personnel to occupy themselves with "the liberation of Palestine." This applies particularly to the more distant Arab countries, like Libya, Kuwait, Algeria, Saudi Arabia and Iraq, which are not burdened by the continuance of the conflict and are prepared to perpetuate it with their subsidies.

The conflict plays a particularly important role for the leftist Arab radicals, who expect it to be a major factor in fomenting social revolution in the Arab countries. Arab leftists are seriously hampered in their revolutionary theorizing by the absence of a proletariat or a revolutionary peasantry, which excludes the possibility of following either the orthodox Marxist or the Maoist schemes for revolution. In this predicament, aggravated by the militarization of the regimes which makes social revolutions difficult, many of the radicals cling to the hope of finding salvation in the Arab-Israel conflict as a means of creating the "revolutionary situation" by the heat which it generates as a catalyst that will precipitate the revolution.[5]

At the other extreme, Islamic radicals like Qadhāfi are prepared to inflame Arab fervor for the restoration of the lost lands as a means of reviving Arabism, injecting new life into the idea of Arab unity and intensifying devotion to Islam.

Thus, the Palestinian establishment receives the support of both varieties of Arab radicals—leftist and Islamic. In the absence of any progress on the political front, the future of the Palestinian establishment is, therefore, assured for the time being as having the mission of keeping up tension and making sure that the flame of the conflict will not flicker and die.

A Palestinian Region, not a Palestinian State

A Palestinian state can rise either on the ruins of Jordan or on the ruins of Israel. Neither country shows any enthusiasm for its own destruction in order to fulfill the aspirations of the Palestinians. Thus the members of the Palestinian establishment are correct in their belief that, so long as Israel or Jordan exists—and all the more so if both of them do—they cannot achieve national self-determination and national independence in their own state according to their definition. The idea of a Palestinian state is squeezed between the sheer facts of Jordan and Israel. This is a pragmatic conclusion derived from studying the historical realities and not an expression of an ideological approach. It is an irony of history that the Israeli government, Jordan, the PLO and the fedayeen organizations have been unanimous in rejecting the idea of a Palestine state as a third state between Jordan and Israel. This broad front of rivals in agreement is not accidental, it is the outcome of the situation: the unfeasibility of such a Palestinian state.

What is left is the possibility of a "Palestinian region," which could arise in cooperation with Israel, in cooperation with Jordan, or, more probably, *through a twofold settlement with both of them*. The configurations of the last possibility are not clear, but it could grow out of *practical* arrangements with Israel and the realities that are thus created and a *political* settlement between Jordan and Israel. Thus the Palestinian region may maintain an economic relationship with Israel, even if politically it reverts to being part of Jordan, or more probably becomes a region in a federation with Jordan. However, the establishment of such a federation would in all likelihood mean the ascendancy of the Jordanian element over the Palestinian one, at least in the first phase or even so long as the present regime lasts. It may, too, set a seal on the Jordanian character of the East Bank, for the Palestinians living in the Jordanian region will in the course of time be stamped as Jordanians. Paradoxically, the longer the present separation between the two Banks lasts, the more the Jordanian character of Jordan is consolidated.

On the other hand, the longer the association of the West Bank with Israel, the more marked will be its effects on the economic and social development of the West Bank. Apprehensions in Jordan that disparities in development between the two Banks would hamper their reunion may interject an element of competition between the two Banks and induce greater exertions for development in the East Bank.

A "Palestinian region" is not the vision to which fedayeen organizations and many other Palestinians have aspired; it is not the realization of their collective aim and the expression of their self-determination. One can understand them. History is sometimes cruel. But if the Palestinians cannot transform either Jordan or Israel into Palestine, a region is all that is left. Such a settlement will certainly seem unjust to the Palestinians abroad and their sympathizers, but there is no guarantee that a "just solution," which will give every party "what it justly deserves," is always possible. The slogan "just solution" is fine; the problem is to prove that it is feasible, and that the "just" solution would be regarded as just by both parties, for it is precisely a dispute over the nature of a "just solution" that is usually the cause of conflicts.

One may sympathize with the Palestinians, whose hopes have come to this; we may consider it a tragedy, but any alternative can only be an illusion, courting further suffering, especially for these Palestinians themselves, until they resign themselves to the limitations of reality. A Palestinian region may not be the realization of full justice, but at least it is a step forward as "practical justice."[6]

Will the Palestinian Movement Decline?

Toward the end of the 1950s and during the 1960s, the

idea of Palestinian nationalism and activism arose. The Palestinians were called upon to take the initiative and lead the Arab world in the dispute; they must become a fighting people, the vanguard of the Arab camp. There was talk of a "new Zionism"; hope flared up in weary hearts and the prestige of the Palestinians soared sky-high. Analogies were drawn between the "liberation" of Palestine, which was glorified as the "Palestinian Revolution," and such world-shaking events as the Communist revolution in China, the wars of Indo-China and Vietnam, the liberation of Algeria and the Cuban revolution. The image of the Palestinian movement grew to gigantic proportions to fit it for the role of a link in these momentous developments.

It was an impressive picture. Palestine would be liberated and the Palestinians would return to their homeland as victors, cleansed in the crucible of exile and the purgatory of the struggle. Their exploits would be a source of inspiration, a symbol of Arab renascence and the starting point for a mighty tide of national renewal which would burst forth from the very country that lies, as has often been said, at the "heart" of the Arab world, and would flood all the Arab countries.

I believe it is growing clearer that the goal was much too pretentious. The Palestinians will not be the godfathers of an Arab renascence.[7] All that they can hope for is not a state, but a "region," unless there is a radical change in the character of Jordan. If this development is not yet generally recognized among them, the understanding of it may begin to percolate, despite the grievous disappointment that it involves. It is true that national movements do not rapidly despair of their aims and irredentism has a long expecation of life. In this case, moreover, the refusal to accept the existence of the Jewish state is also nourished by the disproportion between the rivals and the faith that the Arabs are basically stronger because of their numerical superiority over Israel, whose past victories were described as transient anomalies, and that they will eventually prevail.[8]

In the "Palestinian region," Palestinianism will continue to be a sign of collective identity, but its fervor will decline, and perhaps has already begun to do so. During the past decade, there has been a widespread impression that Palestinianism is bound up with the idea of the "liberation" and belligerency, but it could become a symbol of identity without this bellicose component, as we find among many Israeli Arabs who identify themselves as both Palestinians and Israelis at the same time.

The decline of the Palestinian idea will facilitate the absorption and assimilation of the Palestinian Diaspora in the Arab countries. A "Palestinian region" cannot continue to be a source of inspiration for the Palestinians outside of it and retain their hopes and loyalty. In fact, many of the Palestinian Arabs have actually been absorbed in the Arab communities. The ambivalence among the Palestinians regarding their Palestinian and Arab identities may also facilitate the process.

There has already been a considerable devaluation in the status of the Palestinian idea in the Arab countries. The hopes that kindled the imagination of radical Arab leftists—that the pan-Arab revolution would grow out of the conflict and that it was the historic mission of the Palestinians to ignite it by their heroic struggle—have begun to languish. Dissatisfaction with the Palestinians is common in the Arab countries, there was criticism of the feebleness of their national struggle ever since the beginning of the Mandate, their factiousness, the collaboration of many of them with Israel and the Jews, and charges of responsibility for the tribulations of the Arabs as a result of the conflict with Israel. In the course of time, these trends may reinforce the tendency among Arabs to accept, or even justify, the Palestinians' fate.

Palestinian prestige has also declined in some previously sympathetic circles abroad, with a consequent effect on the prevalent ideas about the nature of the Arab-Israel conflict. The character of the conflict has already changed; in a sense it is becoming once again what it was during the period 1949–1965, an Arab-Israel confrontation, after the attempts that were made in the 1960s to present it as a Palestinian-Israel dispute and, paradoxically, thereby to inflate it. The Palestinians have already lost their central position in the conflict—a development that lessens its gravity, without as yet ensuring a settlement.

The members of the Palestinian establishment will not want to submit to the shrinking of their ideal from a state to a region, especially with a dual status between Israel and Jordan. They will, no doubt, revolt against this prospect, which cannot settle the personal problems of this active, well-educated côterie. It will not be surprising if they stick to the old ideal; and, if they cannot see a logical way to realize it, they may take refuge in apocalyptic visions of wars and catastrophes in the Middle East as an escape from their distress.

Indeed, a change in the trend of the Palestinians' decline could come about as the result of war, but, if that does not happen, and there are no radical transformations in the situation, such as a revolution in Jordan, it seems probable that the trend may continue, even if it is long-drawn-out. It is true that the activity of the Palestinian leaders will counteract and even slow down the trend, but their heroic image has been tarnished in the Arab world. Sooner or later, they and their successors will have to draw in their horns and be content with more modest positions than those to which they looked forward as leaders and ministers of state in a liberated Palestine and pioneers of the pan-Arab revolution.

The future, of course, is subject to unpredictable changes,

and no forecast can claim to be completely reliable. Any attempt at long-term political prediction contains elements of guesswork, imagination and hope. That is inevitable. Accountants and bankers are entitled to write E & OE in the margin of their accounts, though they can be accurately checked and mechanically tested. This is all the more legitimate in social and political forecasting.

Notes

1 These Palestinians do their best to eschew the use of the old slogans calling for the destruction of the State of Israel. The slogan-in-trade is "the liberation of Palestine from the Zionist entity," as if the purpose is not negative and destructive; only some plastic operation to remove a blemish from the face of the state. Such a quibble makes no difference, as basically it implies that Israel as a state will exist no more.

The Palestinian organizations justify their position on the ground that it follows from the principle of self-determination for the Palestinian Arab people. Their definition of their self-determination, which is based on the idea that the Palestinians as "the people of Palestine" should be its masters, excludes the continued existence of Israel. The Political Committee at the Tenth Popular Palestinian Congress stated in its Political Program: "The right of self-determination as regards the Palestinian people means [the right of] liberating the entire homeland and the establishment of the national Palestinian state. This is the scientific and legal meaning of the right of self-determination" (Official Report in Arabic, PLO, *The Palestinian Popular Congress and Tenth Extraordinary Council*, April 6–12, 1972, p. 105).

Thus, according to this definition, endowing the Palestinians with the right of self-determination does not mean allowing them to develop their national personality but authorizing them to destroy Israel. Such a definition enmeshes Israelis, who would like to recognize the Palestinians as a people possessing the right of self-determination, in the complexity of their own self-negation, i.e., consenting to their own political disappearance. No wonder that Israelis cannot accept it and no wonder that there is instinctive opposition among the public in Israel to the very notion of a Palestinian entity. Furthermore, Prime Minister Meir's announcement that Israelis, too, are Palestinians, is intended to underline that Israel too has a claim to Palestine and cannot entirely be excluded from it. The task of defining Palestinian self-determination in a fashion that unequivocally allows coexistence with Israel awaits moderate Palestinians.

The attitude inherent in the PLO definition is not accidental but a basic tenet in the PLO position. Ibrahim al-Abid, citing Professor Fayez Sayegh, explained why a compromise settlement of the conflict is impossible: "The call for a compromise solution in the case of the Palestine problem is not permissible. . . . In the light of these principles we say 'no' to Israel because we say 'yes' to Palestine" (I. al-Abid, *A Handbook to the Palestine Question*, PLO Research Center, Beirut, First Edition, October 1969, Second Edition, August 1971, pp. 173–174). Saying 'yes' to Palestine and to Israel is proscribed. Only the Palestinians have the right of national self-determination. Such a claim on Israel's behalf is emphatically rejected by the Palestinian National Covenant.

Paradoxical as it may seem, the degree of importance that some, especially moderate, Israelis attach to Israel's recognition of the Palestinians may arouse suspicion of some pretentiousness. It is as though by our recognition we instill life in the Palestinians as a people. Palestinians siezed upon this issue as a means of denigrating Israel, as if by reluctance to accord recognition to a Palestinian entity, Israel maliciously bereaved them of their collectivity. However, it should be realized that a people is constituted by its own internal cohesion and not by foreign recognition.

Since the issue of recognizing the Palestinians has been artifiicially inflated (with the aid of some Israeli circles), it seems that prudence dictates declaration of Israel's preparedness to recognize them. It should be stressed that no practical results will follow from such a gesture. We may chant the hymn of recognition day and night, but Israel cannot withdraw from the West Bank without a political settlement and such recognition can neither bring about such a settlement, nor even shorten the road to it. It will have a single merit, namely the preemption of one argument against Israel.

2 The Palestinian organizations have repeatedly condemned most blatantly the idea of a Palestinian state in the West Bank or Gaza. They described it as an Israeli ruse to overcome Arab rejection of coexistence with Israel. They have coined several pejorative appellations for it, such as *"duwaila"* (mini-state), *"Filastinistan"* or *"al-kian al-hazil"* (the emaciated entity).

3 In the present stage their main political importance resides in the pressure that they exercise on Jordan, even unwittingly by their sheer existence, not to forsake interest in a political settlement, counteracting those circles in the inner core of the Jordanian establishment who wonder whether Jordan should exert itself to get the West Bank back with its troublesome Palestinian population. Thus the less interested Jordan is in a settlement with Israel, the less ready it may become to offer concessions in order to meet Israel's security sensitivities and demands and reach a settlement.

Jordan may manipulate measures lessening its connections with the West Bank, such as imposing limitations on the traffic of people and commerce or even closing the bridges. Such measures may have destabilizing effects on the West Bank. However, their impact on Jordan may be fateful. They may condemn Jordan to a mini-kingdom, an idea which the King is far from cherishing. Furthermore, severance of connections with Jordan may force the West-Bankers toward acceptance of a separate entity despite their opposition to this idea in the present circumstances. Such a development may be destabilizing for Jordan, even jeopardizing its existence. The Jordanian establishment may prefer to have the West-Bank Palestinians under its control and fear a territorial political entity of the Palestinians competing for the loyalty of the Palestinians who now constitute half the population of Jordan. An aggravating factor in Jordanian considerations may be that in such an eventuality the Jordanians would not be in a position to control the West Bank as during the years 1949–1967.

4 Recognition of the PLO as the sole representative of the Palestinians was explicitly stated by President Sadat in his speech on April 6, 1972. Such collective Arab recognition is implied by the nomination of Yasser Arafat as head of the PLO Executive Committee, by the Arab League Council at its fifty-first session on March 12, 1969, to be the "Representative of Palestine" in the meetings of the Council. In this capacity he participates in the League's deliberations. This appointment is according to the annex to the Pact of the Arab League of March 1945, which stipulates that until Palestine achieves independence the League will select a representative of Palestine in its Council.

It seems that there is a general tendency in international public opinion to think of the PLO and the fedayeen when discussing the Palestinian problem and the Palestinians. One reason for it, perhaps the more obvious, is that the PLO and fedayeen organizations have gained prominence abroad by their activities, publications, propaganda and even terrorism. Thus the other Palestinians, those in the West Bank and the Gaza Strip who constitute the majority of the Palestinians, are pushed to the background. Another reason is that the problem of the PLO's Palestinians is more acute. Whereas the majority of the Palestinians under Israel's control, apart from the problem of occupation, live more or less their normal lives in their houses and on their land, the PLO's Palestinians do not want to or cannot settle where they are, and consider themselves and are considered by many other Arabs as aliens.

5 Such an expectation has been expressed, for instance, in the following: "If the Resistance movement will be saved for a long period from the solution by peaceful means, it is destined to fulfill the mission of a basic historical lever which will push the Arab national liberation movement to a decisive confrontation with Zionism, imperialism and the local reactionary classes. These are class developments in the Arab region which the reactionary-bureaucratic-bourgeois-military regimes would

not be able to resist for long" (*Limādhā Munazzamat al-Ishtirakiyīn al-Arabiyyīn?* (What of the Organization of Arab Socialists?), Introduction by Muhsin Ibrahim, Dar at-Tali'a, Beirut 1970, p. 142).

Professor L. Abu-Lughud of Northwestern University charges the Palestinian movement with the mission of bringing revolution to the Arab world: "This revolution [the Palestinian] must be general; not to revolutionize the Palestinians but to revolutionize the Arab society as a whole. The Resistance despite its local identity constitutes a revolutionary vanguard to Arab society" (*Shu'un Filastiniyya*, No. 11, July 1972, p. 55).

The Popular Front for the Liberation of Palestine goes even further in describing the war against Israel as the spectacular event that will usher the Arabs into the modern age and will uplift them from backwardness. In its basic document "The Political, Organizational and Military Report," the PFLP stated: "Lastly the Palestinian war will be, as far as the Palestinian and Arab people are concerned, an introduction of the Arabs into the civilization of the age and a transition from the state of under-development to the requirements of modern life" (L. S. Kadi (ed.), *Basic Political Documents of the Armed Palestinian Resistance Movement*, PLO, Research Center, Beirut 1969, p. 225).

6 One may speculate on or draw analogies between the Palestinians and other ethnic groups which could not achieve political separateness, for instance the Bretons or the Kurds. In some such cases, there are even differences in so important a factor as language, which does not apply to the case of the Palestinians. Furthermore, their secondary status in Jordan may eventually change.

7 There has been sharp criticism of overcharging the Palestinian movement as the moving factor toward general revolution. For example, see the writings of Alias Murqus, such as his *Al-Muqawama al-Filastiniyya wa-al-Mauqif al-Rāhin* (Palestine Resistance and the Present Situation), Dar al-Haqīqa, Beirut 1971.

The Arab sociologist Professor Halim Barkat includes the Arab-Israel conflict in his list of the main factors hampering the cause of revolution in Arab societies: "The clash with the exterior generates a strong will to ignore the internal disputes and to set up an internal cohesive front. Arab struggle against the outside diverts the Arab's attention from the struggle against the interior. It is probably correct to conclude that the clash with the external induces the Arab to resort to the traditional institutions and relationships, upholding and clinging to them" (his article "Alienation and Revolution in Arab Life," *Mawāqif*, No 5, July-August 1969, p. 41). Thus the Arab-Israel conflict is described as counter-revolutionary.

8 The idea that eventually the Arabs will achieve their purpose in their conflict with Israel is expressed, for instance, by Professor Hisham Sharabi: "The Zionist edifice is not eternal and its smashing is not only within the bounds of reason but is an historical imperative, considering the potentialities of Arab transformation and of Colonialism's disintegration. It is possible to persist without a solution on the contradiction between the Zionist state and its Arab environment by the continuation of Arab paralysis (the continuation of disunity and social and political backwardness) and by strengthening the domination by Zionism and Neo-imperialism. It is an historical folly [to suppose] that 2 percent of the region's total population and its area—that is the percentage of Israel in the Arab world—can extend their domination over the other 98 percent (as though Hong-Kong dominated China), even with the support of the richest imperialist power in the world" (*Shu'un Filastiniyya*, No 14, October 1972, p. 23). In such an analysis Israel's coexistence with the Arab states is described as the outcome of Israel's domination. Thus, as Israel's existence in the teeth of Arab opposition is an act of coercion against the Arabs, such an existence implies domination over them.

10
Reflections on Israel's Policy in the Conflict

It is an accepted practice to differentiate sharply between the functions of analyzing the behavior of an opponent state and the circumstances—in short, evaluating a situation—and that of political or operational planning. Otherwise one may jumble the two, and instead of basing policy upon the facts of reality one may form images of reality that conform to one's policy planning.

Mao Tse-tung has warned against the tendency which he terms "subjectivism"—viewing reality through the lenses of wishful thinking, desires, hopes, or anxieties. An individual who indulges in such a tendency determines the data of the problem through himself and not through reality. Thus the way to a solution is made easy in an almost cavalier fashion, though the solution is biased and distorted. It is as though the analyst-planner were playing chess with himself.

The tensions of a prolonged conflict are likely to increase such tendencies toward "subjectivism." Indeed, it sometimes seems that not a few Israelis have attained impressive achievements in this regard.

My own concern has been with the study of the conflict, not with elaborating policy prescriptions. However, as a byproduct of studying the conflict, some thoughts and criticisms concerning Israeli approaches to the problem arise. There is no guarantee that my view of the problem's nature and solution is correct; still I venture to think that at least I am conscious of the pitfalls of subjectivism.

There is within Israel a wide range, an entire panoply, of ideas and opinions concerning the Arab-Israel conflict. But it is convenient to divide this spectrum into two poles, as the two ends of a continuum: a soft, moderate, "dovish" approach, and a hard, radical, "hawkish" approach. Paradoxically, in my view, both approaches tend to make the same mistake in their evaluation of the Arab position— they both assume that a settlement can be brought about if Israel makes territorial concessions.

Briefly stated, the two positions are as follows:

The extremists are apprehensive that if Israel announces its readiness for concessions and withdrawal in exchange for peace, the Arabs would grab at the bargain and, under the influence and pressure of the Big Powers, would conclude a settlement with us. As a consequence, we would not only forfeit an opportunity to broaden the base of our existence. Our withdrawal—and this is the paramount component within the hard-line position—would invite eventual disaster, since such a reconciliation with us would be merely a tactical step from the point of view of the Arab states, for in the not very distant future, the Arabs would again open war while our strategic posture would have been worsened seriously by our territorial withdrawal.

Correspondingly, the moderates believe that if the State of Israel were to adopt a more conciliatory position, a thawing process would set in, a de-escalation that eventually would lead to the conflict's settlement. They conclude that the Arabs, presently hard-pressed, wish deep within their hearts to be rid of the conflict—to reach a settlement, or at least to hope that the Big Powers will impose one upon them. According to this view, only Israel's excessively rigid stance compels the Arabs to stick to their official position. Although, it is ceded, there is no guarantee that the Arabs will refrain from renewing hostilities, the chance for a settlement terminating the conflict is such that it is worth taking that risk.

Thus, both conceptions are based on the assumption that a settlement will come about as a reaction to concessions by Israel, the difference being in the assessments of that settlement's stability.

In my view, both approaches are mistaken. At this stage of the conflict, no concession on our part will make the Arabs acquiesce in *Israel as a sovereign state*. The spokesmen of the Palestinian organizations, including the fedayeen groups, declare that they will not agree to a political solution come what may, not even one based on the borders of the 1947 UN Partition Resolution. Despite the many divergences of opinion among the organizations, there is a consensus on this score, and the Palestinians' position has recently acquired great weight within Arab circles. Their declaration is by no means mere window dressing; it is a political stand and a national vision. Creation of a Palestinian state, even within the 1947 borders, is seen as a Zionist plot calculated to confer surreptitiously a kind of legitimacy upon the State of Israel, however diminutive. Nasser employed double-talk. He demanded Israeli retreat to the pre-1967 borders and support for the rights of "the people of Palestine" in gaining sovereignty over their "homeland." Thus he coupled readiness to make peace with Israel with the demand that Israel should cease to exist. Let us have no illusions concerning Yasser Arafat's statement that he is ready "to go to Evian"—at Evian France relinquished sovereignty over all of Algeria. This is precisely what Arafat seeks, elimination of Israeli sovereignty.

Arab Opposition Is Not Psychological

Although interest in and knowledge of the Arab-Israel conflict has grown within Israel, Israelis still have difficulty in understanding the nature of Arab opposition to them. The

Arabs' staunch refusal to accept Jewish statehood does not stem from hatred, but rather from a national conception that unfortunately has become part of the collective Arab ego. This is not an eternal position, nor is the collective Arab ego monolithic. The hostility will eventually pass, but at the present stage, this opposition to our existence is powerful.

Another important factor must be considered, namely that the model of this conflict differs from most others, in which one state or coalition is pitted against another state or coalition. In this conflict there is one actor (Israel) against many actors (states and organizations) which do not constitute a cohesive coalition. This lack of cohesion has paradoxical results. The many actors experienced difficulties in coordinating warfare against Israel and their military efficiency was consequently impaired. On the other hand, it is more difficult for them to reach a consensus on a settlement because some radical actor will always remain opposed to any agreement, brand it as national betrayal, and attempt to subvert it.

We have wrestled a land from the Arabs, a territory they regard as part of their national inheritance. A restive Palestinian people exists which has not found a solution for itself. We have routed the Arab armies more than once. It should come as no surprise to us that they are in no hurry to make peace with us. Their bitterness is understandable. The blow to the Arabs has not been merely psychological, and their position in the conflict does not stem from a certain mentality or from a psychological or social flaw. Arab psychological and social characteristics are expressed in their behavior in the conflict and less in their basic opposition to Israel.

The idea that the conflict is psychological appears often in Israel because it has a psychological role for us—to mitigate the severity of Arab antagonism to us. Dr. Nahum

Goldmann wrote in his second article of the series published in *Ha-Aretz:* "The true character and the true difficulty in the Arab-Israel conflict is first and foremost psychological . . . The Arabs are people guided much more by emotions than by reason." This may imply that when God distributed reason to mankind the Arabs were somehow absent. Since man's pre-eminent superiority over animals lies in his ability to reason, Dr. Goldmann unwittingly places Arabs on a lower level than the rest of mankind. Thus, the Arabs require a nursemaid to care for them. This is a typical 19th-century colonialist attitude; Europeans then regarded the colonized peoples as children guided by emotion. And the colonized peoples bitterly resented this attitude.

If in the Arabs' behavior—as in the behavior of others—there are emotional factors, this does not mean that their opposition to Israel is only emotional. The problem also exists on the practical level: it is not only a clash over territory they think was taken from then unjustly; they also claim that Israel's existence threatens them and prevents them from achieving their other national goals. Dr. Goldmann's point of departure, that "with good will it would be possible to solve most of the political problems in the world," certainly does not apply to serious international conflicts. Both sides to a conflict may have good will, but their interpretations differ and their conclusions diverge. All peoples have envisioned peace as their ultimate goal, but since their images of peace differed, wars erupted. The idea that "good will" is the key to the solution of human problems is a shallow world-view, in which all the tragedy of human existence, all disputes and wars, become merely matters of irrationality. If "good will" means an inclination to compromise, the explanation is tautological, since conflict exists precisely because the adversaries are not inclined to compromise.

Advantages for Israel of an Initial Moderate Position

The prevailing tendency in Arab countries to refuse to make peace with us and to reject our very existence as a nation has not yet changed. Nevertheless, I think, Israel would be wise to declare openly its readiness to withdraw as part of a peace settlement. Israel could also attach a temporary condition to such an offer, to the effect that the occupied areas do not constitute a sacred trust that we intend to keep intact for the Arabs for an unlimited period. Arab unreadiness for a settlement, if it should continue, proves that their grievance is unlimited and that they cannot be satisfied as long as Israel exits. Significantly, expressions like "liquidation of the conflict" or "liquidating solution" have taken on a pejorative connotation in Arab parlance, implying an act of national betrayal. Arab rejection of direct negotiations is not based on a preference for some other procedure of settlement; they have rejected any procedure for terminating the conflict. They have rejected every gradual or staged settlement unless an opening is left for them to revert to their fundamental position advocating the liquidation of Israel. As long as the Arabs reject negotiations so totally, Israel has no choice but to attend to its security and consolidate its hold over the occupied territories in the light of its strategic requirements.

Many people within Israel and in the world at large probably assume that since Israel seeks peace, it is prepared to withdraw for peace's sake and that the refusal to withdraw stems from the recalcitrant Arab position. This attitude has been articulated by some Israeli leaders, for example, Moshe Dayan when he said that he would be prepared to pay a lot for peace. However, the impression has been created in some circles that Israel's position has hardened. This impression may well be mistaken. If so, then not enough has been done to set things right, though Golda Meir's speech of May 26, 1970, in the Knesset (Israel Parliament) was a significant step in this direction.

Israel does not need to draw a map showing the lines to which it will withdraw, since the territorial arrangements should be based on the degree to which Arab hostility is modified. But Israel must demand not only practical peace arrangements; Israel must insist on Arab readiness to initiate changes in their national position. As long as Arab hostility persists and is sustained by communication media and institutions of propaganda and education, a diplomatic settlement is likely to be ephemeral. If peace arrangements are accepted but the Arab national position is not modified, an absurd situation will arise: there will be formal reconciliation on the *diplomatic* level and continued adherence to the idea of annihilating Israel on the *national* level. As long as there are Arab elements that have not agreed to peace with Israel—such as the Syrians and Palestinians—the probability of a renewal of hostilities is considerable. Thus, as long as change does not include all Arabs, Israel's need for territorial safeguards is greater.

Israel may derive a three-sided gain from adopting an initial dovish position—internally and externally, both in the international arena and among the Arabs.

Internally: Various groups in Israel harbor doubts as to whether official Israel really wants peace. These groups may be small but they should not be dismissed. Such notions are found among some of our youth, and such ideas may be translated into a suspicion that the older generation is callous about their sacrifices. These signs are appalling, but it must be realized that a situation of protracted conflict, with all its tensions, may produce wild growths. The tension of living in such a conflict situation may also produce a tendency to grasp at straws, to seize upon imaginary solutions—as though the conflict might have ended if some step or another had been taken. Complaints about the absence of peace may be lodged against the government, as though the government could have brought about peace and was somehow remiss since it did not do so. We won victory in 1967 because of our own general conviction of the justice of our cause. This conviction must not be shaken, not even at the fringes of the national camp. Precisely because ordeals may await us, standing morally erect is of such great value.

To be sure, Israel is not without fault. The constant menace of our neighbors and their frequent attacks sometimes force us to take steps incompatible with the criteria of absolute morality. But the tension of the conflict causes certain sectors of the population, particularly the youth, to be overly critical and to draw improper analogies between instances of wrongdoing by the two sides. They may be inclined to believe that the Arabs oppose Israel because it has faults, not because it exists. (However, one must not conclude that, since the Arabs' opposition to our existence as a state at this stage is independent of the quality of our conduct, we need not behave according to moral standards.) Although there is no way to prevent these tendencies toward excessive self-disparagement, an officially rigid extreme position presumably may foster them. Thus, even for internal reasons, we should adopt a moderate initial position, for it will be a factor in self-fortification and national consolidation.

Externally: In many quarters—including sections of Jewish youth abroad—Israel has become known as an expansionist state, not a seeker of peace. This blemishes our image both as a people and as a government. The Soviet Union's intervention in the Arab–Israel conflict increases the importance of support for us on the international level. Indeed, a more positive image might make it easier for the United States to support us and supply the arms we need. And changing our image might induce Jewish youth to immigrate to Israel in greater numbers.

In my view, there is no justification for the suspicion of Israeli extremists that the Big Powers will trap us with our own words—demanding that we withdraw forthwith without a peace settlement once we express our willingness to withdraw. Nor can the Powers call into being a change in the Arab national position. Moreover, a consensus among the Powers does not depend upon Israel's declaring its readiness to withdraw, and the United States' thinking, for example, assumes Israeli withdrawal. The real barrier to agreement among the Powers has been Arab refusal to commit themselves to peace and their insistence upon "withdrawal without peace."

Toward the Arabs: The Arabs reverse the order of events when they claim their refusal to make peace follows from our expansionism. The case is actually the opposite. Our expansion is a reaction to their intransigence and persistent call for our liquidation. Our adoption of a moderate initial position would not alter their position, but it would deny them the pretext that peace is impossible with "expansionist" Israel.

There are signs of soul-searching and reappraisal among the Arabs, a process which may eventually lead to their adoption of a softer position. Their awareness of the extent of the destructiveness of the conflict for them may induce them to reconsider their position, and Israel must not foreclose this possibility. We must not permit Arab leaders to represent pursuit of the conflict as a national imperative. Thus, even though an initial soft Israeli position will not yield immediate practical consequences, in the long run Arabs may grasp that our expansion was actually a reaction to their belligerency. If this comes to pass Arab consciousness of culpability will facilitate reconciliation with us.

Comparison of the Two Approaches

A comparison of the moderate and the extreme positions may elucidate our present political situation. The extreme position is correct strategically in its conclusion that since the Arabs are nonresponsive to us at this stage, security must be our chief concern. But it is mistaken tactically in not opening with a soft gambit.

In contrast, the moderate position is mistaken strategically in its assessment that the Arabs would consent to a settlement with us if we were to display readiness for withdrawal. But it is correct in advocating a generous initial proposal. Since proponents of this position believe that through a generous proposal it will be possible to attain peace, they regard the failure to make such a proposal as not merely a strategic error, but even a crime. From this stems the disparaging language of such circles when they criticize Israel's policy. In this they sin more than they err. The same description applies to those of this persuasion who, more cautiously, estimate that there is a slight chance—even if only a five-percent chance—that a conciliatory Israeli stance would bring about peace. A nation which, in fact, turns its back on an opportunity for peace—be that chance as meager as five percent—certainly deserves to be gravely censured.

If present official policy approximates the "hard" position, it would appear justifiable to draw the conclusion that Israeli policy was strategically right and tactically wrong. The seeming error may be only a matter of public relations, however, as noted before. It is not that we have missed an opportunity for peace. However, our political situation undoubtedly could be improved, and diplomatic flexibility would raise our stature.

It is conceivable that the two approaches could reach a common ground based on a soft initial position. For the moderates, the move will be strategic; for the extremists, tactical. Such a concession by partisans of the extreme position would be a valuable contribution to Israel, its cohesion, and its standing in the world. Their position contains additional national and historical elements which they would have to forgo, but I don't think they risk much by adopting the soft position. They will subsequently gain a firmer base for their national vindications.

At least some Arab countries can agree temporarily to practical and partial settlements which do not impinge upon their national position: to a settlement permitting free passage through the Straits of Tiran, for example, or even to a partial cessation of belligerency. But what Israel demands is a peace settlement, a liquidation of the conflict. Precisely because peace implies a change of their national position—not merely modification of some diplomatic stance—the Arabs have rejected it so relentlessly.

I assume that my proposal for the adoption of a moderate initial position is not new and is, in some form or other, the position of many Israeli decision-makers. Still, Israel would do well to explain it. Our position is not sufficiently clear, neither to the public at home nor to the large audience abroad.

Perseverance in the Conflict

For quite some time the Arabs have been searching for "contradictions" in our very existence; they have anticipated that signs of self-recrimination would appear among us. The "aggression" by which the state was founded, they rationalized, would necessarily produce disquiet, discontent, and division; thus our position would be undermined from within. Indeed, precisely because our coming was the cause of the conflict, because of the suffering caused to the Arabs, particularly the refugees, and even as a reaction to our 1967 victory feelings of guilt and of a need to atone might arise among us.

Perseverance in the conflict is not to be taken for granted. Official Israel has paid scant attention to the fact that the task of withstanding the conflict is not only military and political, but also educational and social: how to be psychologically and spiritually fortified to face the ordeals of the conflict, the weariness it brings, and the gloom it spreads. No committee of educators, psychologists and sociologists has been organized to analyze the consequences of protracted tensions and anxiety and to determine how to alleviate the effects.

In my view the study of the Arab position in the conflict would provide an important means of fortifying our spirit. Such a study can produce an understanding of this position without necessarily leading us to approve of it. On the contrary, the student will discover the depth and obduracy of the Arab stance and will become familiar with its uglier features. The counterclaim that such a study may be disheartening—even counterproductive—when the student comes to understand the difficulty involved in altering the Arab position has some merit. But on the other hand, it will produce an internal strength of spirit and resilience on the part of Israelis. Understanding that the conflict may be protracted will prevent the nerve-wracking oscillations of mood that come over our community, the false hopes and the disappointments that come in their wake. Moreover, the viewing of this particular international conflict against the broader background of relations between states may teach us that conflicts do eventually come to an end, even if no clear prescription for their resolution is presently at hand.

Study of the Arab position must include all its shades according to their relative importance. However, the rabid features will stand out, for they predominate. It is not accidental that no detailed surveys of indications of moderation in the Arab position have been published in the wake of my book *Arab Attitudes to Israel,* in which the vehemence of the Arab stance was elaborated. There has been little moderation to latch onto. The desire to highlight signs of moderation is certainly natural, but exaggeration of the value of these signs may produce intellectual distortion and may even impair morale. For if there really are significant signs of moderation among Arab governments and the mood that dominates Arab political behavior is not one of utter rejection and negation, then Israel's failure to attain peace, one might suspect, is due to its lack of trying to do so or its neglect of taking chances for peace. If describing Arab extremism may produce obduracy and extremism in the Israeli public, weakening conciliatory tendencies, then exaggeration of the signs of Arab moderation may foster illusions, thus undermining self-confidence and determination.

Indeed, if there were readiness for compromise on the part of serious Arab circles, the contention that extremism on our part has thwarted peace would be justified. But if this is not the case, brandishing signs of Arab moderation, even with the best motives—to inculcate hope that the end of the conflict is at least in sight or to act with fairness toward the Arabs—may mislead those who are unfamiliar with the details of the conflict into finding moral fault with us.

Enduring an international conflict requires mature behavior based upon rational judgment and self-control. But the conflict itself may weaken the power of rational judgment, producing anger against the opponent, and error—or excessive self-reproach, and impotence. Both extremes are emotional: hatred for the enemy on the one hand, self-hatred on the other. Self-hatred may be focused on the "establishment," as that which represents us and conducts the government. Such hatred is in vogue throughout the world, and it may take root among us as well. Certainly there is room for criticism of the Israeli establishment—for complacency, for negligence and poverty of creative spirit. Such criticism could be a salubrious stimulus. But criticism insinuating that the government does not ardently desire peace is entirely different. It is not an indictment of human weakness and limitations, but subversion of the government's moral basis.

Such a slander is more an emotional release than a rational judgment, a wild growth spawned in the turbulence of the conflict. Unfortunately, various groups of Israelis, particularly intellectuals and academics, have overlooked the fact that their critical assessments often nurtured such growths. It is true that these groups were cautious not to blatantly deny the moral basis of the government's policy. But who knows whether or not the recent serious expressions of nonconfidence in our cause among youth groups are a vulgar translation of criticism of the Israeli stand and exaggerated descriptions of the Arabs' moderation and readiness for a settlement.

The Arabs watch us closely. Signs of fissures in the national front raise their hopes that we will disintegrate and collapse from within. Thus criticism leveled against the government, though intended to shorten the conflict, may actually prolong it.

In a study on "Guerrilla Warfare" by the Center for Planning of the Palestine Liberation Organization, headed by Professor Yusuf Sayegh, it is stated:

"Fedayeen actions will attempt to benefit from the dissension existing within the Zionist society, in order to encourage some groups within it to resist the occupation and mobilization, and thus the occupation government will dissipate considerable effort. We may here indicate the possibility of exploiting the position of certain organizations within Israel, such as Matzpen and Rakah—the Communist Party, the group of Wilner and Tubi—and some independent personalities—professors, lawyers, and others—who were opposed to the June War" (*Ṣawt Filasṭīn,* No. 27, April 1970, p. 26).

Official Israel has been late in explaining to the people that the conflict may be protracted, in order to prepare them for it. The reason was not negligence; it seems to have been more a matter of lack of knowledge and understanding. It was my impression that a certain ignorance of the basic issues of the conflict and of the Arab position prevails even among the government élite. I think that familiarity with the 1968 Palestinian National Covenant is essential in analyzing the conflict. I wonder how many of our government ministers have read the Palestinian Covenant, how many are acquainted with its principles, and how long they have known about it.

Preparation for a Long Conflict

National leaders must be a source of hope, and there is certainly justification for the consideration that it is best not to stress the conflict's severity, especially in order to attract immigration. But we must also consider the opposite possibility, that spreading false hopes may court disappointment. To take one example: a few weeks ago a government minister announced that he had information indicating that peace is closer than people generally think. I have no way of knowing to what confidential information he referred. But if peace does not come, and there are even signs of the situation's aggravation, do the minister's words not jeopardize his credibility? The matter is even more serious, for such an announcement implies that Arab refusal to make peace with us is not outright; if this is so, then why hasn't Israel acted to bring about peace? This minister, instead of fortifying the spirit, weakens it.

In a conflict situation the choice is not between good and bad, but between bad and worse. It seems reasonable to conjecture that statements about the length and persistence of the conflict and the sacrifices to be made, may be disheartening. Between the two poles—that of somber prophecies concerning the perpetuity of the conflict and that of rosy predictions of peace already on the wing—there is a broad intermediate range, namely, assessing the situation as it is or appears to be rather than according to the impression one wishes to create. A cool analysis of our situation will reveal that, despite its menace, it is not so bad as it is sometimes described. We can point to many achievements, and this can be a source of pride. We are now virtually a "power" in the Middle East, and we are scarcely aware of this development. To paraphrase Mao Tse-tung: "Just as a long course is a test of a horse, so a protracted conflict is a test of a leadership and a people." We are capable of meeting the test. It is true that the Soviet involvement is a serious threat, but we must not unnecessarily intimidate ourselves because of it. A long conflict is still not eternal. Developments, even unexpected ones, may shorten the conflict. But linguistic gyrations—such as the advice one of our leaders gave me to avoid saying that the conflict may be protracted, and instead use the euphemism "peace does not appear to be on the horizon"—do not improve matters. The people, including the youths in the army, are sufficiently mature to understand our predicament. Furthermore, understanding that the conflict may be drawn out is not equivalent to despairing of peace. It is, rather, a realistic view of the nature of international relations.

Our hesitation to declare that the conflict may be protracted, lest foreigners think it chronic and slacken their support for Israel, merely underestimates their power of comprehension. There are many chronic conflicts spread over the world. It is not that the Big Powers fail to impose a settlement because they are unaware of the severity of the conflict; their inaction is due to their difficulty in reaching a common decision so long as the Soviet Union represents the side demanding that there be withdrawal without peace.

Many predict that if the present situation lasts a militarization of Israel may take place, and it will become a "garrison state" or a modern-day Sparta. There are some who argue thus in order to spur us to settle the conflict, as though without this fear we would slacken in our efforts. If there is a danger of internal militarization, let us be conscious of it and thus exert ourselves to avert it. No clear signs of this process are yet apparent, despite the learned prognoses. Indeed there are indications of an opposite trend: the kind of criticism we often hear, the fact that the Minister of Education found it necessary to meet with protesting Jerusalem high school students, the fact that the bitingly satirical revue, "The Queen of the Bathtub," was permitted on the boards—all this shows that our social fabric is still wholesome. These phenomena may also be a salutary catharsis of pent-up tensions.

Ideological Warfare

We should not minimize the degree of our failure in the arena of world opinion. The adoption of a moderate initial position would certainly have improved the situation. Still, it often appears that Israel cooperates with Arab propaganda, for Israel has refrained from openly presenting the malice and vilification that are virtually organic within the Arab position. From a politicidal demand—to destroy the political entity of Israel—the Arab position has been driven by force of its inner logic to depict the State of Israel as a monstrosity deserving a death sentence. Hence, this state's depravity is deep and inherent in the people who built it, their history and their culture. Thus it is not accidental that, despite the attempts of Fatah and the Palestine Liberation Organization to refrain from anti-Semitic themes, their hostility has impeled them in some cases to transcend these bounds—as in the recent instance of the broadcast accusation that Jews suck the blood of Arab children and discard their bodies. Such accusations have long appeared in Arab government-published literature.

While Israel has exposed the ugly anti-Semitic cartoons and texts featured in Arab elementary schoolbooks, it has never openly protested against other anti-Semitic incitement, such as the publication of *The Protocols of the Elders of Zion* and dissemination of other offensive literature by Arab governments. Such manifestations have not even been given the publicity accorded to publication of a single book of similar content in the Soviet Union. The No. 1 book on the best-seller list of the weekly supplement of the Beirut newspaper *al-Anwar* (March 8, 1970) was an Arabic translation of *The Protocols,* by Muhammad Khalīfa, under the title *The Jewish Peril (al-Khaṭar al-Yahūdī).* It is inconceivable that *The Protocols of the Elders of Zion* would appear at the top of a best-seller list anywhere else in the world. If a private individual somewhere reviles our people and culture, the government of Israel need not react; but when a state or governmental body does so, I think Israel is neglecting its duty toward the Jewish people when it keeps silent. It is true that there are anti-Semitic circles which would not be repelled by these manifestations. But among circles of foreign intellectuals, who often criticize us, such instances of vulgar Arab anti-Semitism, though literary and not social, are bound to arouse reprehension.

Moreover, our silence harms our own position. The Arabs attempt to portray their position as moderate, and foreign groups tend to seize upon these moderate words, for this makes it easier to propose a settlement demanding concessions only from us. Fedayeen actions are represented as the natural reaction and resistance of a people to a foreign conqueror—as though the objective of the Palestine Liberation Organization is merely to drive us from the occupied territories.

Why are we not prepared to withdraw in the absence of a settlement which will assure our security? Why do we have some territorial claims? Because we know the Arabs have malicious intentions toward us which may force them to exploit our withdrawal. But since we do not present the malicious nature of the Arab position, a "representation gap" arises between our explanations and our behavior. An information policy which does not conform to behavior is not convincing and is doomed from the outset.

The Arab position and all its features must be studied in Israeli schools. If Israel's youth knew of the invectives constantly directed against us, they would be in a better position to understand the situation. Some of their criticism of the government's policy would thus be forestalled. These criticisms surfaced recently, but they have been fermenting for some time. We need not arouse hatred for the Arabs among our young people, but neither should we embellish the Arab position, as we do when we fail to present these anti-Semitic manifestations.

It is claimed that if we stress these malicious features we compel the Arabs to adhere to their position. I think exactly the opposite is true. Precisely when expressions of Arab vilification were publicized Arabs began to indulge in apologetics and even self-criticism. It is difficult for Israelis to realize how convinced Arabs are of the moral superiority of their position in the conflict. Indeed, this is one of the principal factors prolonging the conflict. There are those who suffer from a guilt complex. Arabs in the conflict have a "non-guilt" complex. Strange as it may seem, pointing out the unsavory features of their position may help them recognize that they are not altogether innocent, and this may make it easier for them to resign themselves to our existence. This is one of the means we have—and such means are not numerous—of persuading them of the need for a peace settlement.

Acknowledgment that the conflict may continue well into the future appears, perhaps, somewhat pessimistic. However, this acknowledgment is coupled with optimism concerning Israel's capacity to persevere. Only those who are intoxicated with their own greatness are certain in their "subjectivism" that the opponent cannot withstand the impact of their "peace offensive." Israel can only act within the framework of reality. We should not desist from our efforts to convince the opponent of our desire for peace, and we should stress this also to the world at large. We should seek ways to break the present stalemate and smooth the way for the opponent to be reconciled with us. At the same time, we must consider that he, too, has ideals, a national vision, grievances, traumas of catastrophe, and hopes.

When I consider what we have achieved in many areas— the dedication, talent, and resourcefulness of the people—I am filled with admiration and confidence in our ability to overcome difficulties. International reality has always been bleak and menacing. Many of the world's societies are in a process of disintegration and a state of bewilderment; problems that appear both chronic and insoluble are increasing and widespread. To be sure, a conflict cannot be exhilarating, but we can be gratified when we see that we are behaving properly in the conflict, managing to withstand its ordeals. For the end of this conflict, too, will surely come— even if at present we cannot point to its exact time.

11

Prudence in Situations of Conflict

A short time after the Six-Day War Y. Harkabi published a booklet: *The Indoctrination against Israel in UAR Armed Forces* (Israel Defense Forces, Chief Education Officer, November 1967, 135 pages). It contained annotated extracts translated into Hebrew from material issued by the Egyptian "Directorate for Guidance and Moral Orientation" for the purpose of teaching the Egyptian troops about Israel and preparing them for war. Prominent in this material is a lecture by Dr. Ḥasan Ṣabri al-Khūlī who bore, both under Nasser and Sadat, the prestigious title "The Personal Representative of the President of the Republic." This lecture is rabid in its sacrilegious language and anti-Semitic themes.

To counterbalance the impact of such a publication on the Israeli troops Y. H. tried to provide in his introduction some guidelines of so-called "wisdom" or "prudence" in the conflict, emphasizing the need for moderation.

> In the international arena, which is one of clashes between states, we must behave prudently. But what does this mean?
> Prudence is behavior in accordance with our own interests without forgetting that the opponent has interests as well; faith in and devotion to our national ideals without ignoring that the rival, too, has ideals, tribulations and dreams; a sober evaluation of the reality and of the opponent's stance, but also of our own.

Prudence lies in the awareness that there are limits to our power, but that the capabilities of the opponent are also limited and even the great powers are not free to do exactly as they like.

Prudence lies in the distinction between the desirable and the possible, and the recognition that aspirations alone are not sufficient for the achievements of aims.

Prudence means not to rely on miracles, but to take into account the possibility that a miracle may sometimes happen if propitious conditions exist in the world of reality.

Prudence means exploiting opportunities for consolidating and strengthening one's position, without neglecting any opportunity for appeasement and reconciliation.

Prudence means knowing when to learn from past events and draw analogies, and when not.

Prudence is the capacity to choose between incompatible goals.

Prudence is the knowledge that we are destined to live side by side with our opponents for an indefinite period of time, and that therefore we must think beyond the antagonisms of the present.

Prudence is not to regard the opponent as a criminal, to whom we may do whatever we like because he is an enemy, but to realize that there is no absolute justice on either side, and each has its truths.

Prudence is not to treat the opponent as a hopelessly unregenerate aggressor, or to regard him self-conceitedly as naive.

Prudence is to adopt an attitude of appeasement toward an enemy who should and can be appeased, and an attitude of unflinching determination against an irreconcilable aggressor.

Prudence is neither relaxation of preparedness, which is liable to invite attack, nor provocation increasing hostility.

Prudence is the capacity sometimes to forgive an opponent for abuse and scurrility against us, without succumbing to the illusion that these invectives do not represent his attitude.

Prudence is neither intoxication with short-term success, while forgetting the long term, nor the contemplation of distant prospects, while stumbling over the first obstacle.

Prudence means not treating political situations as immutably fixed, and at the same time understanding that they are not so plastic and malleable that we can mold and manipulate them to our heart's desire. If we are not the prisoners of history, we are certainly not its warders.

Prudence lies in the knowledge that in most cases what comes to pass is not so bad as we fear, and not so good as we hope.

Prudence is not to ignore incovenient facts or those that are incompatible with a chosen line of action. Prudence lies in seeing the facts without adornment and without illusions : neither ideological sanctimoniousness, nor realistic cynicism, nor idealistic naivete.

Prudence lies in the recognition of the importance of prudence and the awareness of its limitations.

12

Obstacles in the Way of a Settlement

When one has been dealing with a particular subject for too many years—as I have been dealing with the Arab-Israel conflict—one must speak with some hesitancy, lest commitment to certain views lead to the disregarding of contradictory evidence. Though I try to exercise self-criticism, I am apprehensive that the "blindness of involvement" will impair openness, perceptiveness, and flexibility. The danger of such blindness is exacerbated by the fact that many of my views on the harsh nature of this conflict and the rabidness of the Arab position—initially vehemently resisted by some circles in Israel—have been borne out by subsequent developments; nothing is more blinding than success.

No doubt the validity of my diagnosis will one day expire. I eagerly await this change, and hope to adjust my analysis in time to accord with the new reality. However, there is also an inverse danger, one that is more common in Israel—that of seeing a change prematurely, before it has actually taken place. Hope can distort our vision that we perceive what we are looking for as an established fact. The whole history of the conflict from the Israeli side can be summarized as a series of predictions of changes that somehow failed to come about. The error of unwarranted optimism, or running ahead of history, has been more common than the error of sober pessimism, or lagging behind history. Let us not overlearn this lesson. Yet let us not herald Messiah before He really comes.

It is difficult for many Israelis to comprehend Arab rejection of Israel, and to understand the nature and depth of Arab hostility. Consequently, they have underrated the difficulties of settling the conflict. For some, self-adoration was an obstacle to the understanding of Arab resistance: "How can they oppose people as nice as we are?" As though we had done them a favor by establishing Israel! Many Israelis treated Arab statements of their position in the conflict in a cavalier way, insisting that the Arabs are victims of their beautiful language, which makes them say what they do not mean—as opposed to other peoples, for whom language is an instrument. Yet what the Arabs said, even if it was not indicative of their immediate intentions, was a faithful projection of their wishes, their dreams, and their attitudes. If Arab pronouncements were not always translated into daily political action, they did reflect their *meta-political* level which, though it does not influence every step, imparts a sense to the general orientation.

It must be acknowledged that Arab rejection of Israel is not just an expression of malice. People express their humanity by rebelling against what they consider to be unjust. It is the grandeur of man sometimes to say *No*, and to persist in it. German hostility to the Jews, blaming them for stabbing Germany in the back, was artificial, the figment of sick imaginations. The Arabs' suffering as a consequence of Israel's emergence, their defeats and agony, are real—and so is their urge for vengeance.

I shall undertake the unpleasant task of describing some of the specific difficulties lying in the way of settling this conflict, some of the factors that have contributed to its obduracy. These factors are not necessarily insurmountable; they do not enjoin eternity on the conflict, and may someday disappear. However, as long as they are operative they constitute constraints on the mellowing of the conflict and on its resolution, and any attempt to resolve the conflict must tackle them first and foremost. They are some of the Gordian knots that have to be cut.

My presentation is limited to an analysis of the current situation and does not involve policy recommendations. It is not my intention to preach to any of the protagonists, to demonstrate to them what their position should be or to criticize them. Criticism is leveled only in case of refusal to see the consequences of assumed positions.

It is easy to construct models of how the Arab-Israel conflict may be resolved; it is more difficult to contrive how to harness history into such models and induce it to move submissively in the right direction. Other conflicts are sometimes manipulated and their lessons twisted in order to make the Arab-Israel conflict appear more malleable. Some political scientists, historians and specialists in international relations prescribe methods to end the conflict that are based on generalizations from analogies drawn from other conflicts, as if they were patent medicines for all conflicts; these scholars act as if the wisdom distilled in their learning is sufficient to ordain them as general practitioners and healers, and that it absolves them from the need to learn the specifics of the case in hand. Some hasten to offer detailed prognoses without tarrying on the diagnosis, as though this was a superfluous technical detail. Conferences and symposia called for the purpose of analyzing the Arab-Israel conflict tend to veer elegantly to discussions of the general nature of conflicts. Such discussion is much easier and requires few qualifications. I venture to suggest that what is needed instead is a thorough examination of the specifics of this conflict.

I would first like to dispose of one issue, namely that of "the Arab position." Some people deny the existence of any such position, on the grounds that there are many Arab positions. The old argumentations of what philosophers called "nominalism" are very belatedly revived: There is no such thing as "table," only "tables." Of course the term "Arab position" is a conceptualization, but it is a necessary one. We call the conflict "Arab-Israeli," thus juxtaposing two positions. Certainly the Arabs consist of different groups holding different positions. There is no need to impose uniformity where it does not exist. Nevertheless, there is some Arab communality. Even if it is only a fiction, it derives practical importance from the fact that the Arabs devote so much effort to maintain it, that they maintain an Arab League under the auspices of which they meet, even frequently quarrel, and try to coordinate their action, though often unsuccessfully. Why should Israelis demand perfect unison as a sign of the constitution of an entity when dissonance is rampant in their own ranks? Who predicted the dispatch of Moroccan troops to Syria? Of course, one can comfortably explain it away by asserting that King Hassan wanted to get rid of the troops, or that it was a gesture to gain popularity. That may be true, but it signifies that sending troops to Syria to confront Israel, and not elsewhere, is popular and can confer popularity.

The Arab position perhaps has a rather thin and emaciated common denominator. It is what influences and reflects their collective behavior. In the context of the conflict, before the Six-Day War of 1967, it boiled down to the rejection of Israel.

The only way to grasp the Arab position is to *refer to them*, to see what *they* say about it and the way they act. Arabs interpret their position copiously, and their elaborations of it are always superior to foreign, including Israeli, expositions. These latter constructs are frequently motivated by the desire to render the Arab position more palatable or reassuring. Thus the Arab position is not reproduced but fancifully created. Well-wishing Israelis were not thus aware of how much their versions of the Arab position and interests—drawn up in disregard of what the Arabs said—implied contempt, as if saying: The Arabs are only talking; we know better what they really mean.

As we deal with political behavior of collectivities, we must refer to the pronouncements by their leaders as decision-makers, and their entourages. The leaders wish to mobilize public support, hence they must expound their views to their people. Arab leaders do sometimes express themselves to foreigners in terms that are more moderate than the language they use when they speak to their own peoples. But I have learned that many times such discrepancies are smaller than is commonly held. Foreigners may be misled by the cryptic semantics used for private audiences or diplomatic exchanges, by attributing moderate connotation to expressions that have other meanings. At any rate, had the moderate views whispered into foreign ears been a true indicator of the Arab position, peace would have been achieved many years ago. The merit of Arab ideological writings and public speeches has been that they explain Arab rejection of Israel. Thus in the last score of years, Arab ideology has been a better guide to the *main thrust* of Arab behavior in the Arab-Israel conflict than have their diplomatic exchanges. Diplomatic transactions seemingly portending a change in the Arab position were like ripples on the main tide of rejection of Israel that was portrayed in their ideology: they did not affect the mainstream. Repeatedly, it transpired that the change was only verbal. Chancelleries and diplomats (including Israelis) were reluctant to acknowledge it, presumably as it seemed to downgrade their art.

A common misunderstanding of the Arab position arose from the Arab vilifications, in which Israel was accused of being expansionist, aggressive, oppressive toward its Arab minority, an alien of foreign culture in the Middle East, annexationist, disobeying UN decisions, and so forth. The impression formed in some circles was that it was these specific qualities that made Israel obnoxious and that a purified Israel would be acceptable. However, that was not at all the Arab intention. The great variety of terms of abuse heaped on Israel were intended to buttress the Arab "politicidal" stand (calling for the destruction of Israel); they did not motivate it. These qualities were described as inherent in Israel. Israel was rejected not so much for any fault in its behavior, as for its basic fault—its existence as a Jewish state. Mistakenly people may hail Arab's expressing readiness to live peacefully with Jews or Israelis as a sign of change of heart. However, such an expression usually means rejection of coexistence with Israel, and readiness to live with the Israelis surviving the destruction of their state. It is a kind of peace not with Israel but without it.

The Gap between the Contestants

As a result of the Six-Day War there has been a move on the Arab side toward acceptance of Israel. But if the gap was slightly closed from the Arab side, Israel's demands for territorial changes, notwithstanding their justification, enlarged it. In order to be in a position to evaluate the gap it is necessary to analyse the present positions of the rivals.

Arab positions

Four trends or schools of thought are discernible among the Arab positions on the conflict.[1]

(a) *Peace school.* Those who would like to conclude a peace agreement with Israel.

This school is found in the *public level* in Egypt and Lebanon, and among the Palestinians in the West Bank. Politically more significant is the fact that this school is represented in *governmental circles* in Jordan.

The question posed is: What is the political importance

of the *public circles* in Egypt that advocate peace as the termination of the conflict? We know about their existence partly from occasional sentences in which they express themselves, but most of our information is derived indirectly, from criticism leveled against them by the press; this criticism reflects the rejection of their stand by the government. These voices, it should be stressed, have not reached the stage of the Samizdat (underground literature) found in the Soviet Union. As the United States cannot base its policy toward the Soviet Union on the Samizdat and must relate to the position of the decision-making élite, so Israel cannot base its policy on these faint dissident voices. If we deal with this phenomenon in a political and not in a folklorist fashion, its importance, for the time being, is marginal. These circles will be important when they are influential within the Egyptian government. Israel cannot enthrone them, enhance their status, or nourish their growth, largely because of the gap between their position and Israel's.

Moderate Arabs demand that Israel withdraw to the 1949–1967 lines. They consider that such a withdrawal would not be a concession for which the Arabs would have to pay in some territorial terms, but simply a fulfilment of an international injunction for which Israel would be handsomely remunerated by the very conclusion of a peace agreement. They deny any justification for the satisfaction of Israel's security sensitivities. Had moderate attitudes been prevalent among the Arabs, perhaps Israel's security needs could be more limited. The existence of important extremist circles and states which call for the liquidation of Israel will loom heavily on any settlement with a moderate state. Israel will not be able to treat a settlement with one of its neighbors as if it had been made with all of them. The possibility of renewal of hostilities with the unreconciled parts of the Arab world (which may draw the moderates into the cauldron) limits Israeli readiness to forgo territorial strategic advantages for the sake of satisfying the reconciled sectors.

Israel is thus caught in a grave dilemma. The need to take into consideration the attitudes and actions of Arab extremists may impose on Israel a policy which may nip in the bud the moderate circles, and even push them toward the extremist ranks.

The possibility that the Jordanian position of desiring peace could lead to a settlement seems rather tenuous. It is hardly conceivable that Jordan could venture a separate peace with Israel, and her spokesmen repeated acceptance of Security Council Resolution 242 in an "Arab framework." [2] Israel's demands of Jordan are considerable and clash with Jordan's need to present a political settlement as a victory.

(b) *Tactical school.* These Arabs advocate announcing acceptance of the Resolution 242 as a public relations gesture. The Arabs, they reason, do not run the risk of having to recognize Israel and conclude peace with her, since Israel cannot permit herself to accept the resolution, and will obstruct its implementation.

(c) *Strategic school.* This school is prevalent in the position of the Egyptian government. These circles contend that it is the Arab interest that Resolution 242 be implemented, but they do not consider that a peace settlement will terminate the conflict. They tend to differentiate sharply, on the one hand, between a "peaceful settlement of the Middle East Crisis" (an expression they frequently use to designate what should be done, and which mostly means a return "peacefully" to the pre-1967 situation), or even "peace," and, on the other hand, the "historical conflict" which will continue. They argue that the chasm between Israel and the Arabs is so wide and basic that no peace or settlement can conjure it out of existence. In the long run, coexistence between Israel and the Arabs is impossible. Thus, inevitably the conflict will re-erupt. Nevertheless, implementation of Resolution 242 will improve the Arab strategic posture.

They argue that states have to be flexible in the international arena, and must sometimes acquiesce temporarily to undesired courses of action, evoking the French forgoing of Alsace-Lorraine in 1871, and Lenin's concessions in the Treaty of Brest Litovsk. Resolution 242 is the best the Arabs could get, as it represents not the actual balance of power but a balance tilted in the Arabs' favor by the pressure of the Big Powers. By their own might the Arabs cannot induce Israel to withdraw: only through acceptance of the resolution can a withdrawal be achieved. The obligations that Resolution 242 imposes on the Arab side are invidious; still, it is more than worthwhile assuming them to force Israel's withdrawal. Otherwise Israel will stay on the present cease-fire lines, which may become permanent as did the armistice lines of 1949.

Furthermore, in Resolution 242 there is the stipulation of "justice for the refugees," which the Egyptians interpret as "justice to the Palestinian people" or "the return of the rights to the Palestinian people." The basic meaning of these expressions used to be to grant the Palestinians sovereignty over their country, since that is their "natural right." In the new Arab parlance it is also called "the historical rights of the Palestinian people."[3] These expressions are based on the idea that if a country and people bear the same name, the people are masters of that country. The enitre country of France belongs to the French, and the entirety of Palestine should revert to the Palestinians. Thus, full implementation of Resolution 242 is made dependent on the fulfilment of a provision that, as a result of maneuvers, would subvert the whole notion of peace with Israel and ensure that the Arabs do not forsake the basic stance of rejecting Israel.

Another Arab interpretation of the meaning of "justice" for the Palestinians follows a positive law approach. Justice is the fulfilment of their "rights" as stipulated by UN resolutions, in particular that of November 1947. This is a more diplomatically presentable position. Israel is to withdraw to the 1947 Partition lines, and thus more room will be made for the Palestinians now outside the country. The demand for Israel to withdraw to the 1947 lines is nothing new. The 1947 lines are the acceptable "secure and recognized boundaries," according to Egypt's reply of March 27, 1969, to the Jarring questionnaire. For Israel this demand is almost synonymous with its destruction. The Arabs know this and, in part, this is why they made the demand.

(d) *"Rejecting any settlement" school.* This school proscribes as a matter of principle any settlement with Israel. Any settlement even partially acknowledging the right of Israel in Palestine abrogates the principle that the Palestinians are the sole "people of Palestine." The Palestinians' right to Palestine is indivisible. Thus a partial settlement is total as far as the Palestinians are concerned. The unqualified rejection of Israel, whatever its size, is a national imperative. The Arab objective cannot be achieved by phases as suggested by the *Strategic school.* Phased or salami tactics are feasible when there is continuity between the phases. Tactics and strategy should form a harmonious unity. However, the policy of temporary acceptance of Israel in order subsequently to subvert its existence is contradictory and will prove self-defeating. A conciliatory tactical stance will court national disaster. Once a settlement with Israel is achieved it may take root, as painful memories may deter the Arabs from risking a renewal of the conflict. The world order has become rigid, and to revert to war is a tenuous option. Israel and the big powers will ensure that it will be blocked.

Followers of this school argue that the Arabs should keep the conflict ablaze. A settlement will take the wind out of Arab sails. The liquidation of Israel is a central tenet of the Arab national vision, and a national vision cannot be treated as the subject of political maneuvering. Time is on the Arab side and the Arabs should not be disheartened by Israel's victories. Perseverance *(sumūd)* is a national characteristic of the Arabs. Eventually the Arabs will close the technological gap which enabled Israel to achieve victory. The quantitative variable favoring the Arabs is constant, while the qualitative variable which favored Israel is changeable. A Luxembourg cannot be a China, but a China can develop sophisticated industry like Luxembourg. Numbers and superiority in resources (oil) will ultimately prevail, provided the option of a final showdown is not foreclosed by a settlement.

Comparison of the last two schools shows that ultimately both reject coexistence with Israel, though they labor under different fears. While the *Strategic school* is afraid that the present lines will congeal, the *Rejecting school* is afraid that peace itself may congeal. Paradoxically, the *Strategic school,* which is more moderate, considers lasting coexistence an impossibility. Thus it is moderate in the short term and radical in the long term, while the *Rejecting school,* though more radical in the short term, is moderate in the long term, for it considers that there is no inherent incompatibility between Israel and the Arabs and peace may become permanent.

In stressing the passing nature of conflict, the *Rejecting school* is, I believe, more realistic. Conflicts are basically men's handiwork, depending on human approaches and tastes. What was unacceptable to one generation may become acceptable to its successor.

However, Israel cannot mortgage her national security on the opinion of the *Rejecting school* and the assumption that *any* settlement closes the door to its reversal. The road from peace to war is two-way. Thus Israel demands strategic territorial assets which would make the launching of war by the Arabs more difficult or make it easier for Israel to fight back. The *Strategic school* envisages only an armistice and demands that Israel pay for it as if it were perfect peace. With this demand Israel cannot comply.

My guess is that the center of gravity among the Arabs lies with the (third) *Strategic school*, especially as it is supported by the Egyptian establishment.

Israeli positions

The spectrum of positions in Israel is known to this audience and it would be tedious to detail it. It ranges from holding the present lines to, at most, readiness to return to the 1949–1967 lines. Motivation varies from emotional, historical, and religious considerations to the more pragmatic considerations of security. One cannot belittle the importance of religious-nationalist vindication rooted in the anxieties prevalent on the eve of the war, the sudden exhilaration of victory, and the frustrations of the aftermath. However, when the chips are down, it seems to me, security considerations will predominate. Thus, the central majority of Israeli public opinion and, what is more important, the governmental position calls for significant changes in the boundaries as dictated by security considerations. This is the factor that enlarges the gap I referred to.

One comment must be made on an important aspect of Israel's strategic and political thinking that is often overlooked. Israel's sensitivity to its security has stemmed not only from the urge to ensure its existence, but also to ensure the continuance of its being a "success story." Other states may exist if they are not successful. For Israel, as the pole of attraction for immigration and capital, success has so far been an existential imperative. No doubt it shows weakness. One can criticize, ridicule or condemn it. However, it is a conviction of Israel's leaders and people and has constituted an operative factor of utmost importance. It has been a factor during Israel's formative period, and may lapse when the formative period comes to its conclusion. Furthermore, this factor can be abused as a pretext for an extreme stance and a cover for vindication of such a stance. That is a danger we must be conscious of. Yet without undue emphasis this factor limits Israel's latitude for concessions.

The Arabs are well aware of this factor. It underlies their notion that what the Arabs need is one mini-victory that will turn the tide.

The Territorial Divergencies

The political gap can be illustrated through some concrete examples which yet do not exhaust the whole range:

Israel's claim to the *Golan,* or at least the strip of the Golan Heights dominating the settlements in the Hula Valley, seems natural—almost self-explanatory—to the great majority in Israel, including the moderates. Many foreign visitors have confirmed that geography proscribes Israel giving it up. But the Syrians—if they eventually come around to agree to a settlement with Israel—may consider the Golan rise as the only military obstacle on the road to Damascus. There is no sign whatsoever that Syria will be ready to give up the Golan. Egypt, too, as an ally of Syria, refuses to consider a settlement that returns Sinai but not the Golan. Egyptian statesmen have been very assertive on this point, deliberately specifying that Israel should withdraw from *all Arab* lands, and that there cannot be a separate solution with Egypt (Sadat's speech of May 1, 1973).

Jerusalem is a very difficult bone of contention. The position which commands a wide consensus in Israel, i.e., united Jerusalem under Israel sovereignty, is unacceptable to Jordan and the other Arab states.

Many moderates in Israel delude themselves in thinking that a peace can be achieved on their terms, and that it is only the vindications of the government of Israel and the majority of the Israeli public that thwart peace. But a settlement tolerable to moderate Arabs is not acceptable to most Israeli moderates. This hard fact should not be swept under any carpet. The Israeli doves should be aware that the Israeli hawks feast on a corpse that the doves have slaughtered. If a dove is he whose conditions are acceptable to the opponent, Sadat is correct in his assertion that in Israel there are only hawks: Israel's self-styled doves are only hawks who are unconscious of their hawkishness. The irony is that the Arab position, including Sadat's declarations, makes it extremely difficult for Israelis to maintain what Sadat would consider to be a dovish position—unless of course one chooses, as some do, to ignore the Arab position. The rationality of this attitude is of course questionable.

We are in the land of resurrection, and what I called figuratively "a corpse" may revive one day. Then the difference between moderates and extremists in Israel could be significant.

The interpretations of Resolution 242 as regards territory range between the demand for a *complete* withdrawal to the pre-war lines, as a *sine qua non* condition for a settlement by the more lenient sectors of Arab opinion, to readiness for a *partial* withdrawal—Israel's official position. Israel is haunted by a grave dilemma: Without withdrawal peace cannot be achieved, yet with a complete withdrawal Israel may eventually have to fight without the strategic advantages of the present lines—and will tragically regret its withdrawal. Some Israelis argue that Israel should not fear the results of a complete withdrawal, as its proven military superiority would deter the Arabs from war, whatever the borders. Furthermore, even if there are risks in a complete withdrawal it is worthwhile taking them in order to escape the present deadlock with its dangers of no peace and a new conflagration.

This argument overlooks one important aspect. A withdrawal to the previous lines, after the diplomatic bickering and wrangling of the last five years, will be hailed by the Arabs as a tremendous victory that may arouse in them an impetuous aggressive stance that in turn might eventually lead them to war. What makes such a contingency more probable is the nature of the Arab position, its rabidness, the seething urge for vengeance, and the recurrent cultural, social, and political crises in Arab societies. Thus the only way, which also is not totally devoid of risks, is to persist in the demand for retention of certain strategic positions.

When faced with the hard facts of the gap between the majority position of the two sides, one may dismiss the opponent's claims that upset the possibility of an imminent settlement on the grounds that they are only a tactical gambit and that a compromise will be struck mostly by the opponent's retreat. Such hopes may be self-gratifying but also self-defeating. I do not believe that Israel's demands for Jerusalem and the Golan are merely a gambit. The Arab counterclaims are no less adamant.

Once the Arab position is described as being more moderate than realities warrant, one falls into a stance of putting the blame for the deadlock on Israel. History is then caricatured as a procession of opportunities missed by Israel. The Arab leaders' faint and most ambiguous expressions of a change and acquiescence to genuine coexistence with Israel—as Egypt's truncated acceptance of the Jarring letter is alleged to be—are described as momentary openings of the heavens at Pentecost (Shavuot) midnight which, according to Jewish folklore, closes instantly unless grasped.

However, the seriousness of a political position is attested by its steadfastness. A fleeting mumble, assuming for the sake of argument that it took place, proves only its triviality.

I do not claim impeccable correctness for the behavior of the Zionist movement and Israel in the conflict. Far from it. I acknowledge that the Arabs may be justified from their standpoint in considering Israel as bearing the original sin for this conflict. However, by the same token Israelis may be justified in seeing subsequent Arab sins, in the way the Arabs reacted, as graver than their own sin. I do not pretend at all that Israeli policies and diplomacy have always been moral, wise, and adept. But unfortunately, I have come to the sour conclusion that, even had Israel been a paragon of wisdom, this basically would not have changed the substance of the Arab stand. Only those who are intoxicated with their own wisdom and virtue consider that the rival cannot withstand the impact of their persuasiveness, nor resist the nobleness of their political ingenuity.

There is a vogue in Israel for proclaiming that once negotiations start, all difficulties will be overcome. The day negotiations start will indeed be a great occasion for celebration. Yet let us remember the lessons psychologists teach— that direct contacts between human groups do not always draw them together, but may make them realize how far apart they are and thus lead to further estrangement. In addition to being beneficial, negotiations may also demonstrate to the parties the width of the gulf and generate greater acrimony. Perhaps the state of expectancy on both sides that diplomacy or negotiations may produce results, or that the other side may give way, is better as a temporary palliative than negotiations followed by a deadlock and a break.

A Structural Difficulty

Most conflicts have been between two entities, be they two states or two coalitions. The structure of this conflict is rather unusual: one entity (the State of Israel) against a multiplicity of entities (the Arab states and the Palestinians). This structure produces paradoxical results. In times of war it has made it difficult for the Arabs to coordinate their actions, and thus efficiency was impaired. It also makes it difficult to achieve peace, as there will always be extremist actors who would oppose peace and incite against it.

The conflict is a burden only on a minority of the Arab actors—the states contiguous to Israel and the Palestinians. The rest, and especially such states as Algeria, Kuwait, Saudi Arabia, Libya, and Iraq, even derive benefits from the continuation of the conflict, for it serves as a means of draining the internal discontent. For some states (such as Saudi Arabia) the conflict serves as an insurance against attempts by other states (such as Egypt) to foment revolution. The states which have no interest in the termination of the conflict—though they are not directly involved in the conflict—exercise pressure on the other states not to make peace, and they are ready to subsidize the conflict as long as it does not run wild and jeopardize their own interests (such as oil).

It is hardly thinkable that Egypt can reach a settlement with Israel against the opposition of Libya and Syria. In fact, Egypt, in the Treaty of Federations (August 20, 1971), accepted the obligation that important issues like peace, war, and sovereignty (over territory) should be determined by a unanimous vote of the three presidents (Article 14 A'2). Syria and Libya have until now opposed a peace settlement with Israel. Perhaps they would tolerate a settlement with Israel only if it were transitory and seriously prejudicial to Israel's interests. Perhaps this is why they do not oppose outright Egypt's acceptance of Resolution 242 and it is, presumably, the way Egypt justifies her dissidence to them. Needless to say, such an eventuality will be opposed by Israel. Thus there is a factor of *indivisibility of peace* as far as the Arab actors are concerned. One Arab actor may find it risky to face general Arab condemnation for "doing it alone."

Asymmetry Protracts the Conflict

A small state beaten by a big one will tend to resign itself to the results of the showdown as a final verdict of history. A big state defeated by a small one may rebel. Despite their rivalries, the Arabs consider themselves as constituting a communality, greater than Israel in area, manpower, resources, religion, allies and supporters, and the justice of their cause. History, many of them argue, will eventually vindicate their cause and the balance of power will be reversed. Israel's victories, though impressive, are not such that they leave the Arabs no alternative but to seek peace. The Arabs can absorb defeats, while Israel cannot. They soothe their worries and self-reproach by insisting that the 1967 defeat was only a temporary setback (*naksa*), a battle lost even as the war goes on.

The Arabs can sustain the stance of "no peace–no war" for a long time. Furthermore, the United Nations and the Big Powers have shielded them from the necessity to choose between these alternatives. The case has been made that the present world order not only contributes to the resolution of conflicts, but to their perpetuation as well.

For most Arab actors the present situation of no solution is not at all intolerable, so that they may not feel a compulsion to seek a settlement. True, for Egypt the termination of the present situation has become an obsession. Golan is not less important to Syria than Sinai to Egypt. Still, Syria is not so preoccupied with "the battle to regain the lost territories" as Egypt is. Egypt may try to lower the importance of Sinai in national priorities, i.e., act deliberately to Golanize (alias Taiwanize) Sinai and thus allow the present situation to go on.

The Palestinians

The Palestinian problem is also a major obstacle to a settlement. I have dealt with it in detail in the chapter "The Problem of the Palestinians."

I shall limit myself here to recapitulating some of the main theses:

(a) The main bone of contention between Israel and the Palestinians is not simply the demand addressed to Israel to recognize the Palestinians as a political entity that should be allowed to develop its personality, but the implications of such a recognition. The Palestine Liberation Organization (PLO), now including all the fedayeen groups, has laid down that such recognition means that Palestine should by definition belong to the "People of Palestine," i.e., the Palestinians. The PLO, representing the Palestinian problem in its gravest form, i.e., of the Palestinians abroad, sees no other possibility of their absorption unless the whole country reverts to the Palestinians. Thus it is adamant in its opposition to a Palestinian state confined to the West Bank or even in the 1947 configuration. The Palestinians do not want a declaratory gesture but what they consider their homeland.

(b) The antagonism between the PLO and Israel is head on and irreconcilable as it involves two core values or two basic tenets: Israel cannot give up the idea of Jewish statehood whatever its size; while the non-acceptability of a Jewish state whatever its size and the demand that it should be superseded by a Palestinian state is the central idea of the PLO.

(c) A final solution of the conflict is impossible without the Palestinians. Yet it cannot start with them but only with the Arab states.

(d) The Palestinians in the West Bank are not a political autonomous factor with whom a settlement can be achieved.

They cannot defy the wishes of the Arab states, especially Jordan, lest they be cut off from their kin in the Arab countries and disowned by the mainstream of Arab nationalism. These threats are sufficient to force them to keep step with the Arab states. In the present stage they may be partners with Israel in practical arrangements which, in a long, cumulative way, could assume political significance.

(e) Some Israelis, who were sensitive to the Palestinian entity but callous to the Jordanian one, magnanimously proposed to sacrifice Jordan on the altar of Palestine and offer it to the Palestinians. This great design evaporated in September 1970. So long as the army supports the Hashemite regime, it is impossible to subvert it and "Palestinize" Jordan. The army is devoted to the King and the regime. Once peace is achieved, Jordan may be Palestinized in an historical process, but peace cannot be achieved by the Palestinization of Jordan.

(f) A Palestinian state can be established on the ruins of either Israel or Jordan, or both. However, neither country shows enthusiasm for its own destruction in order to gratify the Palestinians. What is left is only a "Palestinian region" between Israel and Jordan and with ties with both. Thus the Palestine idea or Palestine nationalism is squeezed between the existence of Jordan and Israel. A Palestinian region can be a solution for its inhabitants but not for the Palestinians abroad. It cannot serve as a source of inspiration as did formerly the ideal of a model Palestinian state. Recognition of this hard fact may cause a decline of Palestinian nationalism. The Palestinians abroad, despairing of their national vindication, may tend to settle where they are. This is a very long-term prognostication.

(g) The PLO will resist the shrinkage of their idea and will constitute a hard core of irredentism, fighting back with terrorism.

Israel is faced with the serious problem of what to do with

the West Bank. The debate in Israel over the West Bank is inconsequential if the issue of aims—what should be done with the West Bank—is not treated along with the issue of means—how to achieve the aim. In the present stage of deadlock the problem is not whether it is desirable to annex the West Bank, but whether is it possible to dispense with it, or rather, what to do in the meantime, until the achievement of a general settlement which will include the solution of the political problem of the West Bank, a prospect which does not appear imminent.

Radicalization in Arab Societies

Considering that peace is not an *event* but a *process* it will be affected by developments in the region and especially in Arab societies. Arab societies are in the throes of a grave crisis which is political, social, and cultural at the same time—a general malaise. All expectations of political, social and cultural achievements have been disappointed. Internal disintegration, frustration, alienation, nihilism, a feeling of collective inadequacy, are rife. As a prominent Arab poet bewailed: "The basis of our difficulties, it seems to me, is that we are consumers of civilization not its producers."[4] This malaise drives Arabs to look for remedy in a total revolution and toward radicalization, which is evident in the young generation.[5] Frustration begets greater radicalization in a vicious circle.

Hottinger sees radicalization taking one direction, toward the left; in his opinion it will even sweep over the conservative regimes and subvert them. It seems to me that radicalization may take a polarized form—on the one hand, social, leftist, anti-Islamic; and on the other, Islamic social radicalization, as epitomized by Qadhāfī. The strife between these two tendencies may mold developments in the Arab countries. These trends do not mean that completely new ideologies will emerge. There is no need for that. For both brands of radicalization, the conflict and the hostility to Israel are important weapons. This does not mean that the Arab-Israel conflict is their main cause. South Yemen is politically the most radicalized Arab state, but its radicalization cannot be attributed to this conflict.

For lack of a proletariat with class consciousness and a revolutionary peasantry, many left-leaning radicals, realizing that they cannot engineer a revolution on the Marxist or Maoist models, hope that the regional conflict, by the heat it generates, will usher in a revolutionary situation. Thus, they need the conflict as a main agent and a catalyst of salvation, beyond the narrower confines of Jews versus Arabs. One can argue that the conflict has been more counter-revolutionary than revolutionary, as the external emergency it produces diverts attention and pressures for internal change. However, most Arab radicals differ. Furthermore, their opposition to Israel is vehement, as they consider that the struggle against her is of class nature as well, between Arab toilers and Arab states which are by nature proletarian and Israel, which is by nature bourgeois and capitalist, organically linked to imperialism and foreign domination.

Islamic radicalization injects new life into the anti-Jewish elements in Islam, and for these circles the conflict serves as a means to galvanize the Arabs under the banner of Islam and Arabism.

Radicalization may give rise to countervailing forces, as evident in Sadat's Egypt. Yet balancing the possible eventualities, it seems that these trends, even if they do not culminate in revolutions and change, may produce *instability,* which, it can be surmised, is not conducive to the conciliatory mood needed for a settlement of the conflict.

Another hypothesis on the future development in Arab societies is offered in Israel. This view holds that a period of stagnation will set in, marked by the following manifestations: Arab national élan and messianic nationalism have petered out; ideological movements have exhausted themselves; the public is weary and suspicious of the nationalistic frenzy of Nasser's times; in most Arab countries present regimes lean toward greater moderation; and all leftist coups in recent years miscarried.

The Depth of the Conflict

Though the conflict is originally political—as a contention over land—it has spilled over into cultural, psychological, ideological fields. The great efforts by Arabs to ideologize the conflict have consolidated and reinforced their position. The Arab position in the conflict is not limited to the political, diplomatic level, but has seeped into the national level and is now enshrined in national writs and in the educational system. True, Israel is not the sole concern of the Arabs, yet they have forged their national thought on the anvil of the conflict to a greater extent than could have been expected. Thus a real change toward permanent, as distinct from transitory, acceptance of coexistence with Israel is not a diplomatic or political act, but a national transformation; not a change of norm but of a value.[6]

Changing the Arabs' demonological imagery of Israel, though important in itself, does not necessarily impinge on their political stance. Arabs did not reject Israel because of a depraved image of the Jews and hatred of Jews. They first and foremost rejected Israel, and that influenced their emotions and conceptions of Israel and the Jews. Thus a change in the image of Israel, starting in the West Bank and spreading elsewhere by Arab visitors, has not affected the political position, for example, of Libya or Egypt. It does not touch upon the nub of the conflict. If, previously, Arabs complained that "nasty Jews usurped the land," they, at most, may now concede that "nice Jews usurped the land."

The real grievance of usurping is not mitigated by the cognitive dissonance between the goodness of the perpetrators and the evilness of their act.

The Six-Day War has perhaps persuaded most Arabs that the liquidation of Israel is not on the order of the day. It has not convinced many of them that this hope must be given up altogether, or that they must make territorial concessions. Postponing the achievement of their objective may eschatologize it and eventually deprive it of practical importance. This is not the way that the *Strategic school*, which considers a settlement as transitory, sees it. There is no evidence that their pronouncements about the continuation of the conflict after a settlement are only a public relations device to throw dust in the eyes of their detractors.

The Arab position has started to change and will hopefully change even more in the future. The cumulative effect of failure to achieve their objective, exhausting all the methods they hoped would achieve it, may have the dialectical result of inducing them to forsake the objective altogether. It does not mean that the change is unilateral, only on their side, as Israel too has to contribute to it. My task was to describe the obstacles to a settlement; as there are also factors pressing for a settlement, the picture emerging in this article is one-sided. Nevertheless it seems that until now the forces operating against a settlement have outweighed those that militate for one. This is commonplace, as attested by the fact that no settlement has appeared. From 1949 to 1967 the main opposition to a settlement rose from the Arab side. Yet a fierce position from one contestant calls for greater harshness from its rival, even if his original position was milder. A very good case can be made that in face of the barbarous Arab stand, the bloodthirstiness in their incessant invectives, anti-Semitism in their literature under official auspices, [7] Israel owes them nothing for having achieving victory and does not need to make concessions.

Though Israel's territorial vindications increase the gap, it seems to me that the obstacles to peace are still more on the Arab side, even if the opposition and rejection of Israel have become, in some Arab circles, more tempered and restrained.

The deep feeling of injustice the Arabs harbor induces an extremely pugnacious and obdurate position on their side. In its turn, it may produce an extreme unconsiderate, nationalistic position on the Israeli side. Symmetry will be redressed to Israel's moral loss. That, too, may produce a grave obstacle to peace. The way to combat such developments is not by facile prescriptions of solutions, nor by lighthearted prognostications of imminent peace which may court disappointment and the hardening of positions. Panegyrics of peace may gratify their singers and demonstrate their self-righteousness. Yet if peace does not come, two candidates for responsibility emerge: Israel and the Arabs. That may engender in Israel two undesirable, rather pathological, growths induced by the fatigue and tension of protracted conflict and expectations of its termination: excessive self-hatred among some intellectual circles, or excessive hatred of the Arabs among the people.

What is needed to fight against such developments is the dissemination of better knowledge of the realities of the conflict. The alternatives in this conflict were never so-called optimism versus pessimism, but sober description versus the cavalier giving of good tidings. Withstanding a conflict is not only a political or military affair, but one of education as well. People who do not understand the causes of the predicament in which they find themselves enmeshed may become alienated from their past, their present, and their fate. With all its inconveniences, the effort to understand this conflict with its tragic complexities is the first line of defense against the deformation, moral, social and political, that the conflict may cause.

Notes

1 For a detailed description, see my article in *Gesher* (The World Jewish Congress Quarterly, Nos. 72–73), December 1972.

2 King Hussein opening the Jordanian Parliament on 1.11.72: "All talk of partial settlements or individual arrangements are lies and nonsense."

3 Sadat and Arafat used this expression at the opening session of the Palestinian Tenth National Council on April 6, 1973.

4 Nizar Qūbani in *Mawaqif,* No. 16 (July–August 1971), p. 71.

5 A. Hottinger, "The Depth of Arab Radicalism," *Foreign Affairs,* April 1973; and my own analysis in *Arab Lessons from their Defeat* (Hebrew), Am Oved, Tel Aviv 1969. Affluence brought by oil may blunt social tensions and sooth the internal restiveness. It is difficult to envisage the revolutionary potentialities lurking in the new found richness.

6 Cultural and psychological factors may hamper reconciliation to Israel's existence. This line has been brilliantly propounded by H. W. Glidden in the *American Journal of Psychiatry,* **128,** 8, February 1972. Glidden stresses the factors of shame, seeking vengeance, fear, and the competition among Arabs for prestige and domination. I prefer to view the conflict in more concrete political terms. However, these cultural and psychological factors cannot be brushed aside.

7 See D. F. Greed (ed.), *Arab Theologians on Jews and Israel,* Editions de l'avenir, Geneve 1972.

13

Who is to Blame for the Persistence of the Arab-Israel Conflict?: Lessons from Five Explanations

The past few years have witnessed a growing tendency toward reconciliation, détente or, at least, relaxation of tension in international disputes. The Arab-Israel conflict appears to be a striking exception to this general trend. This raises the question: What factors have rendered this particular dispute so intractable?

The question is of vital importance not only because the answer to it is an intrinsic part of any effort to comprehend this conflict, but also because of its practical, political implications. The conflict now hinges not on the rivals jockeying to secure better conditions in a settlement but has become a polemic concerning who is responsible for perpetuating the conflict. Even when settlement negotiations get under way, the controversy over attribution of blame may play a role in the proceedings. Let us therefore examine the various answers offered to this key question.

1. The Arabs are to Blame Because of Their Refusal to Accept Israel's Existence

Such an explanation is incisively and brilliantly presented by Harold Glidden, an orientalist and former senior official of the U.S. State Department's Bureau of Intelligence and Research, in a lecture read at the 12th annual meeting of the

American Psychiatric Association, May 1971 (published by the *American Journal of Psychiatry,* February 1972).

Glidden does not link the origins of the conflict with its pertinacity. His explanation implies that any other community which had lost territory which it regarded as part of its homeland would have resigned itself to the new situation and would not, like the Arabs, have persisted in the demand that the *status quo ante* be restored. Thus the Arab behavior in this dispute is unique and derives, according to his analysis, from the cultural and psychological traits of Arab society, whose values were inherited from a tribal desert society and later consolidated in Islam.

This way of life engendered the desire for conformity within the tribal framework, a conformity which imparted to Arab culture its authoritative nature and created an other-directed personality. Thus, in contrast to Jewish and Christian culture, which are guilt-oriented (judgment coming from within the individual), Arab society has been characterized as a "shame society," in which greater importance is attached to judgment by others. Thus it is not so much the nature of the act which is decisive but its evaluation by others. (This shame-orientation of Arab society has been discussed by a number of writers, some of them Arab.) The links between the Arab individual and his group are much stronger than similar ties in Western society, and hence his greater sense of relatedness to the collective shame.

Another factor which has left its mark is the competition between tribes for prestige, as reflected in a power struggle. An effective weapon in this rivalry is the shaming of others in order to undermine their influence. On the other hand, shame is eliminated by revenge and thus Arab society is based on these two fundamental values—shame and revenge. Glidden cites statistical evidence of the drive for revenge in modern Arab society.

This value system finds expression at the individual, group

and national levels. The emphasis on group, rather than individual, orientation makes it impossible for individual Arab states to dissociate themselves from Arab collectivity. These states threw off the yoke of their colonial rulers but are not independent of one another. Their value system demands solidarity and because of the constant struggle for superiority or domination a tension is created between solidarity and rivalry.

The battle for prestige and domination has engendered a fierce power struggle characterizing inter-Arab politics, each leader exploiting every means, including the Arab-Israel conflict, in order to shame his rivals, and by suspicions that they in their turn will not hesitate to employ similar means against him. This breeds outward- and inward-directed suspicion, anxiety and "free-floating hostility" as well as readiness to employ subterfuge against one another.

All these manifestations have inhibited the Arabs from creating a real united front against Israel, and since shame prohibits admission of the internal hostility, they tend to externalize the blame for such failures and pin them on Israel and on Imperialism.

The crux of the anti-Israel struggle is not the restoration of territory to the Palestinians, an issue in which a compromise in the form of some territorial partition is possible, but the overriding need for elimination of collective shame which is not divisible. Westerners and Israelis err, Glidden implies, in assuming that Israeli victories could, rationally speaking, convince the Arabs of the need to make peace. Arab logic does not operate in this way, since objectivity is not a value in the Arab system. Defeat does not generate a desire for peace but rather a desire for revenge. Nor is peace a positive value since, in tribal society, strife was the normal state of affairs. In Islam, the ideal of peace was restricted to the community of Islam while outwardly, at best, there was a state of truce until the next round.

Islamic law never discussed the question of conduct in defeat since such a possibility was never considered. The Arab conception of time is also different from the Western one and the desire for revenge may endure for a very long time.

Glidden makes his point concisely and briefly and further summarization may distort his purport. Those who are acquainted with Arab Islamic culture will have taken note of several of the phenomena he discusses. (The view that it is not in the nature of the Arabs to make peace was also voiced by Glubb, former Commander of the Arab Legion.)

It seems to me that Glidden's theory, based as it is on *cultural determinism,* is only a partial explanation and could prove misleading if accepted as the whole picture. At the base of this conflict there are political factors which are of greater significance than the cultural ones. What is more, the political factors constitute the background against which the cultural ones can operate.

Glidden's remarks suggest that in Arab Islamic culture there are, on the one hand, elements which preclude coexistence with an external element which has caused shame and whose very existence is a reminder of this shame and intensifies it. On the other hand, the fundamental internal dissensions and the internal and outward-directed hostility are ravaging these societies. The conclusion as regards the Arab-Israel conflict is rather pessimistic since it is assumed that the Arab stance is culturally intransigent, so that peace does not depend on political steps, maps, negotiations or resignation to the existence of Israel because of its strength or the acknowledgment that it cannot be destroyed, but on a transmutation of Arab culture and its detachment from its roots—undoubtedly a protracted process.

2. Israel is to Blame—Its Very Existence Perpetuates the Conflict

This explanation is prevalent in Palestinian organizations and other Arab circles. Israel, it is said, was created as the result of a crime and of agression toward the Arabs, which is inherent in its Zionist nature. Continued Israeli existence perpetuates the injustice perpetrated against the Palestinians and the threat of Jewish expansion hanging over the heads of the Arab states. By definition and by force of "natural law" the Palestinians are "the people of Palestine," i.e., of all and not merely part of the country, and should therefore achieve their "natural" or "historical" and "national" rights, namely sovereignty over all Palestine. The self-interest of all Arabs dictates that they should rally to the support of the Palestinians, since as long as Israel exists, they face the threat of Israeli and imperialist expansionism and domination and will have no peace. The Arabs cannot accept Israel as long as it is a Zionist state, i.e., the Jewish state. Thus the blame for Arab refusal to accept the situation lies with Israel, and the conflict can be resolved only through changing Israel's character, abolishing it as an entity and transforming it into an Arab state—Palestine.

This Palestinian state will constitute one of the territorial units within the Arab world, and the Jewish minority which will be granted citizenship after agreeing to renounce its Zionist aspirations, will be obliged to adjust to an environment which, from the national point of view, will be Arab. The main manifestation of the cultural singularity of these Jews will be religious autonomy but, under no circumstances, a national one. Such a settlement of the present conflict is proposed as a fair compromise and exchange—the Arabs renouncing their intention of exterminating the Jews and the Jews waiving their rights to the country.

According to this viewpoint, Israel's existence is the cause of the persistence of the conflict. The proposed solution refers to peace with the *inhabitants* of the former State of Israel but not with their State. The change demanded here may resemble that described in the previous explanation, the difference being that in this case we are speaking not merely of a cultural change but of a fundamental transformation amounting to the elimination of the political entity.

3. Israel is to Blame—Israeli Intransigence Perpetuates the Conflict

This is essentially a political explanation: resolution of the dispute depends not on a change in the Israeli entity but on a political act on the part of Israel, ushering in a settlement by peaceful means. Satisfaction of two basic demands will bring about a settlement: 1) Israeli withdrawal to the pre-1967 borders; 2) a just solution of the Palestinian problem. The first demand is clear; the second calls for detailed definition.

The just solution of the Palestinian problem is envisaged not on the individual level, through monetary reparation or resettlement, but on the collective national level, as "restoration of national rights" or recognition of the Palestinian right to self-determination, since these alone can produce a settlement. One category of rights has already been specified, namely "natural rights" to sovereignty over their country. The second, legalistic and based on positive law, is that the rights of the Palestinians were explicitly formulated in UN resolutions, and primarily the Partition Resolution of November 1947 and the General Assembly Resolution of December 11, 1948, proclaiming the rights of Palestinian refugees to return to the area of Israel and to their property.

According to this theory, Israel must withdraw to the

Partition boundaries and offer the Palestinians the choice between return to their land and property and monetary compensation. There are therefore two dimensions to the territorial problem: Israeli withdrawal to the 1967 borders would satisfy the demands of the Arab states; and withdrawal to the 1947 Partition borders would provide a solution, however partial, to the Palestinian problem.

The demand for withdrawal to the 1947 configuration has also practical implications. The West Bank is not large enough to solve the Palestinian problem which is, essentially, the problem of those Palestinians now residing in the Arab countries who are unwilling or unable to assimilate there. Only if Israel were to evacuate such towns as Lydda, Ramleh, Jaffa and parts of Galilee would there be room to absorb some of them, besides those who would return to live in Israel itself.

The demand for implementation of the Partition Resolution is also depicted as a fair compromise. The Arabs may have refused to accept it in the past but they have now repented. This solution would create a truncated State of Israel, adjacent to a small Palestinian state, and would not give full satisfaction to either of them.

It can be assumed that those who advocate this approach know full well what fulfillment of their demands would mean for Israel. They perhaps concede that a decimated Israel, with a greatly increased Arab population, would be unable to hold its own, and that the eventual restoration of the 1947 borders and absorption of refugees would be synonymous with Israel's destruction. But they would rejoin that the Arabs are not to blame for this development, which is only a trenchant proof of the fact that the Zionist ideal was unreasonable from the start.

This explanation of the durability of the dispute, which attributes it to Israeli intractability, originated before 1967, took on final form after the Six-Day War, and has become a central tenet in the Arab camp. It has recently been expounded by the Egyptian Foreign Minister, Hassan al-Zayat, at the Security Council (June 6 and 14, 1973).

There are those who take comfort in the thought that these demands, and, particularly, the call for a return to the 1947 borders, are but the opening gambit and that the Arabs will concede to something closer to the 1967 lines. An Israeli may feel psychologically motivated to view the situation in this light, as a form of self-solace, but there are no indications that this evaluation is correct.

Of course, the Arabs may eventually back down from this demand, but this does not seem to be their present intention. We should avoid confusing final outcome with political intention, since it is the intention and not the result that shapes present political stances. The Arab insistence on return to the Partition borders is certainly a tactical move, but is not meant to be employed as an argument in the bargaining process but rather as a device for attributing the blame for the absence of a settlement to Israel.

4. Divided Blame—Israel is More Guilty

This view is prevalent in international political circles, some moderate Israeli circles and among moderate Arabs. Its Israeli proponents pretend to have a balanced view of the situation and to have risen above narrow nationalist considerations. Since there are varied possibilities of distributing the blame, this explanation has many versions but their common denominator is that the lion's share of the blame is attributed to Israel.

As regards the Arabs, it is claimed that under the impact of the Six-Day War there has been a qualitative change in their stance, and that they now recognize Israel's existence, although they may hesitate to proclaim the fact in unequivocal terms. One should avoid a static view of the dispute, it is argued, and must discern its dynamic characteristics. The validity of the "Khartoum Nos" has long since lapsed, the Arabs are now cognizant of Israel's strength and have renounced the aim of destroying it. They are anxious to extricate themselves from the conflict and its damaging effect on Arab countries, and are seeking a settlement which will not involve too great a loss of self-respect, enabling them to concentrate their energies on internal problems.

Israelis, it is said, should pay no heed to the violent pronouncements made from time to time by the Arabs. Some Israelis themselves have propounded the view that the Arabs are not serious in their statements as they are carried away by their own exuberance. It is necessary to comprehend the intensity of their feeling that the establishment of Israel was unjust to them; their extremist statements provide a healthy catharsis for these emotions and thus alleviate the need for revenge against Israel.

In any event the Arabs would be required to announce unequivocally that they are ready to recognize Israel and coexist with it, and that peace will spell the end of the dispute. They must also agree to a settlement entailing security guarantees, which will safeguard Israel and ensure that its withdrawal will not serve as the pretext for renewed aggression against it. This demand is directed at the Arabs. Among those who advocate this viewpoint there are some who believe that the statements of Arab leaders have already indicated readiness to fulfill these conditions. Hence, from their viewpoint most of the Arabs have already done what is demanded of them. At the most, their readiness needs to be given binding and authorized expression in an international document.

The attitude of the fedayeen organizations and the Palestine Liberation Organization (PLO), which reject the idea of a peace settlement, does not fit in with this explanation. In the not-so-distant past, the Israeli representatives of this outlook tended to regard these organizations as a rising force, and even claimed that they constitute the *interlocuteur valable* with whom Israel should negotiate. There were even those who were willing to believe that the struggle of these organizations was focused on merely obtaining Israel's recognition, for the purpose of negotiating with it.

The same Israeli circles now tend to denounce the fedayeen organizations, because of the modes of operation—terror—and deny them the right to representation in the Palestine problem. They take this view despite the fact that all the Arab states have officially recognized the PLO, that Yasser Arafat participates in meetings of the Arab League Council as "representative of Palestine," and that many other countries have accepted the PLO as "representative of the Palestinian struggle" (this was the formula used at the last conference of non-aligned countries held in Algeria in September 1973).

These circles assume that the Palestinians would be content with the West Bank and the Gaza Strip as their state and perhaps with the annexation of Jordan in due course, and that these would suffice to solve their problem and satisfy their demands, and this despite the fact that the Palestinian organizations themselves have rejected these solutions.

The State of Israel, they say, must withdraw to its former borders or boundaries close to them and as a first step proclaim its readiness to do so. Until Israel adopts such a policy, it is to blame for the perpetuation of the dispute. The international community has decreed against territorial expansion and Israel must hearken to world opinion on this matter and refrain from isolationism and from displaying a parochial and narrow-minded attitude to worldwide trends.

Israel must learn from the fact that most of the world is against it. The establishment of new settlements and annexation of territory are the main stumbling blocks in the way of peace, and deprive Israel of political support. It is wrong to draw analogies between what Zionism was permitted and able to do in the past, and the present situation. Nor is Israel in need of such strategic strongholds as Sharm al-Sheikh or settlements in the Jordan Valley, since it has demonstrated its military superiority and has no reason to fear that the Arabs might attempt to exploit a withdrawal for renewed aggression. True security depends on a peace settlement and peaceful neighborly relations and not on constant reliance on military force.

Israel must recognize the Palestinians and their political identity, and its refusal to do so is prolonging the dispute and giving it a bad name. Such recognition, according to this conviction, does not preclude the possibility of coexistence of the "Palestinian people" with Israel, because, in contradiction of the PLO definition, it is claimed that recognition of them does not imply that they are sovereign rulers of the *entire* country.

As for the question of the right of the Palestinians to return to Israel and regain the property they owned there prior to 1948, opinions are divided. Those Arabs who support the theory of divided blame (as do many West Bank Arabs) demand this right in full or almost fully. Among the Jewish proponents, there are those who have cavalierly decided that even if the Palestinians were permitted to return they would not do so (despite the fact that this theory is refuted by the evidence that many Arabs, for personal reasons, are willing to crowd in and live under Israeli rule on the West Bank). There are Israelis whose position is close to the official government standpoint, i.e., readiness to compensate the Palestinians as part of a peace settlement and to assist their economic consolidation outside the borders of Israel.

Since Israel has prevailed and is the stronger party, it is incumbent upon it to take political initiative for bringing about a détente. Israel should also display understanding of Arab psychological sensitivity. The Israeli representatives of this standpoint consider the concept of "political initiative" as a magic formula, but (with the exception of a declaration of willingness to withdraw) they usually offer no details of the nature of the proposed initiative and the way in which the Arabs are to be persuaded to accept their conditions.

The present stagnant situation is the fault of Israel, its territorial acquisitiveness and its intransigence on the Palestinian question. Israel should not wait until all the Arabs have declared their willingness to arrive at a settlement with it, but should read between the lines. If Syria is extremist in its stand, then the wall of hostility should be breached through Egypt or Jordan. Israel should not be suspicious of Arab declarations of intention to adopt the "method of stages" as preached by Bourguiba, since the Arabs resort to such statements simply to justify their change of stance. The important issue is the first stage of the settlement and this, with correct handling, could activate the dynamics of new relationships, thus preventing the second stage from being implemented.

Political situations are not historical decrees and can be manipulated and changed by human effort. To become resigned to the *status quo* and to believe that the political circumstances in which the conflict is enmeshed are the cause of its prolongation is to advocate a passive and fatalistic approach which is not commensurate with human dignity. Herzl's adage "If you will it, it is no legend" applies not only to the building of a state but also to the attainment of peace. Without daring and risk-taking there can be no achievements.

Diplomacy, it is claimed, is omnipotent as has recently been demonstrated by the achievements of diplomatic efforts in settling Great-Power disputes. Nor should Israel be apprehensive of agreeing to withdrawal. In the spirit of science and empiricism, the proponents of this theory say that it it is worth experimenting.

There is no problem which cannot be resolved between men of goodwill, and failure to find solutions indicates that the goodwill was lacking. This particular conflict, it is stated, is unresolved only because Israel is not sufficiently anxious to solve it. The present situation is convenient for Israel and has weakened its desire for peace. In order to reinforce this desire, these circles try to emphasize the dangers inherent in absence of peace, which are represented as internal more than external—the internal moral decadence that the perpetuation of the dispute and of Israeli domination of an Arab population could breed.

This explanation resembles the previous one with one principal difference that there the demand for withdrawal to the Partition borders is included, while this theory vindicates return to pre-Six-Day War lines. Israel's present grave situation in the international arena stems in part from the fact that this explanation has been accepted in many important political and public circles, even those not particularly sympathetic toward the Arabs.

The weakness inherent in this explanation is its acceptance of the moderate dissident Arab minority as representing the true predominant Arab stance. It is deluded by Arab tactical maneuvers, which sometimes find expression in diplomatic manipulations, without ascertaining their implications, since if it did so its weakness would become apparent.

For example, even those Arabs who deny the existence of Israel employ the device of attacking the establishment of new settlements as if they alone constituted the obstacle to peace. For the sake of appearances, it is more convenient for these circles to emphasize Israel's sin in creating settlements than their own sin in seeking its destruction. Concentration of the offensive on these settlements, however, does not imply acceptance of Israel without them. This approach also ignores the fact that if all Arab circles were moderate in their views, Israel might be able to relax its demands for strategic strongholds. Israel cannot regard a settlement with one moderate Arab element as tantamount to a settlement with all the Arab states.

The existence of Arab extremists forces Israel to vindicate more stringent conditions for a settlement even with a moderate Arab element. This approach also disregards the tenacity of the Arab stand and its roots in the Arab political, social and cultural world. It ignores the existing hiatus between moderate Arab views and the moderate Israeli stand. Extremist Israeli demands for territorial expansion constitute an obstacle to peace, but a prior obstacle are the conditions advocated by the Israeli moderates, which are also unacceptable to the Arabs. This is reflected in the central Arab demand that the settlement be based on the Partition boundaries.

5. Circumstances are the Cause— the Arabs Bear Heavier Blame

I myself favor the following explanation: the durability and intractability of the dispute derive from the gap between the positions of the two opponents, which are influenced by the circumstances in which they find themselves.

The Arab side

The desire to eradicate Israel does not stem from any aggressiveness or maliciousness inherent in the Arab character or culture, but from the Arabs' situation and their view of it. It is not the result of intoxication of senses but of an ideology; Israelis may belittle or denounce it but this does not detract from the force of its influence and persuasive impact on the Arabs.

This ideology depicts the establishment of Israel as the

greatest injustice perpetrated in human history, which must be set right through the annulment of Israeli existence. Israel is also envisaged as the main stumbling block preventing the Arabs from realizing their greatness and fulfilling their national objectives. The dispute with Israel has become the pivot of Arab nationalism. The Arabs believe that unity is the precondition for the attainment of all other national objectives, however long-term they may be.

It should not be deduced from their adherence to the idea of Arab unity that they will in fact realize it or are on the path to its fulfillment. But the intensity and impact of ideas should not necessarily be measured by the degree of their implementation. The frequency with which the Arabs mention this idea indicates its importance. If Arab leaders brandish the slogan of unity as a means of winning popularity, this fact indicates the popularity of the slogan. There is also a pragmatic aspect to the idea of unity, since in modern times national economic systems have become too narrow.

Israel, the Arabs emphasize, has split the Arab world and is an obstacle to the unification of its eastern and western regions. Its expansion and domination are also feared and can only be halted, Arab ideaologues contended, by its eradication. The irritation caused by the various Arab defeats, which have been as agonizing, is understandable, and even though a psychological factor was involved, this apprehension was not totally irrational.

The Arabs refused to accept Israel's victories as the judgment of history, impelling them to recognize its existence and to concede territory to it. Their refusal, more than it has been based on cultural reasons as explained by Glidden, derives from a rather sober assessment that these victories are not final.

Israel won its victories, they explained, because of technological superiority. It is not surprising that they refuse to reconcile themselves to a technological and scientific inferiority which implies human inferiority, and cherish the hope one day to abolish this disparity. Then, they say, their greatness in territory, manpower and resources will prevail.

The desire for revenge, as depicted by Glidden, certainly exists, but would wane and perhaps even disappear if it were thought to be a vain hope. What nurtures it is the Arab recognition of their latent greatness and potentialities which they believe can be realized. The two prevalent views among the Arabs, that which rejects any acceptance of Israel and that which advocates the "theory of stages," are based on confidence in their potential ability.

Another key factor influencing the Arab stance and behavior in the dispute is the structure of the conflict, reflected in the multiplicity of factors and states on the Arab side. Generally speaking, a state chooses to make the transition from conflict to peace when continuation of the struggle is intolerable. The Arab-Israel dispute imposes burdens on only some of the Arab states, Israel's direct neighbors, while it does not disturb most of the Arab countries. Their regimes even derive benefit from it and are ready to perpetuate it since it serves to canalize internal disaffection. These states, though not directly involved in the dispute, hamper any settlement because of that same inter-Arab rivalry and competitiveness which Glidden described so well.

A serious obstacle to any peace settlement is the Palestinian problem or to be more specific, not so much that of the Palestinians on the West Bank but of those in the Arab countries. There is a large stratum of educated Palestinians for whom it is now hard to find employment in Arab states, and the Palestinian students, whose number is increasing, will find it even more difficult to find work in the future. The Palestinian intelligentsia and their leaders believe that not only national, but also individual problems could be solved by the destruction of Israel and their absorption into the new state to be established.

There is nothing surprising in the fact that these Palestinians are convinced that solution of their problem is irreconcilable with the existence of Israel. The network of relationships in the Arab countries is marked by contradictions and a proliferation of ambivalent attitudes. Undoubtedly there are grave conflicts and mutual suspicions, even hostility between the Palestinians and the Arab states, but we should not underestimate the weight of the Arab committments to the Palestinian cause.

The Arab stand has never consisted of an unequivocal demand for Israel's destruction, and has always been accompanied by gnawing hesitations and doubts as to the feasibility of this aim. Just as there are varying degrees of confidence in the realizability of this objective, there are also different levels of acceptance of, or resignation to Israel's existence. After the Six-Day War the tendency to reconciliation with Israel increased even if this was tied to the acceptance by Israel of difficult conditions. Any analysis of the dispute must measure squarely this acceptance of Israel. Its significance should be neither exaggerated nor underestimated; its growth should not be prematurely hailed (as it has been by many Israelis) but neither should it be ignored.

In the face of the threats to Israel's existence, even though these are not immediate, the open Arab statement that even if a political settlement is attained it will not spell the end of the conflict, and of the maliciously anti-Israel and anti-Jewish pronouncements by Arab leaders and personalities, it is only natural that the demand for security is Israel's main motivation and that it therefore aspires to expand the basis of its existence, to alter boundaries and, above all, to hold on to some strategic strongholds.

Israel is proud of and confident in its army and sometimes tends to disparage Arab force, organizational ability and fighting power, but beneath the calm surface there simmers apprehensions stemming from the same basic quantitative imbalance between the two sides, which impells Arabs to believe in their eventual victory. Israel cannot overcome this imbalance except through constant efforts to strengthen itself, and it is well aware that it cannot achieve security until peace prevails and the threats to its existence vanish; hence its profound desire for peace.

Because of their predicament and the imbalance between them and the Arabs, the Israelis are convinced of the moral validity of their demands to change the borders, and claim that the extremist stand of the Arabs provides the justification for the strategic strongholds it is demanding.

It is true that after the Six-Day War there were manifestations of Israeli expansionist aspirations in the name of Zionist objectives, and historical ties and national myths were cited in their support. But these were apparently subordinate to the desire for security, which is not easily admitted since it contradicts the Israeli image of self-confidence and pride. The brandishing of nationalist slogans and historical rights is also aimed at arousing the national vitality which is needed for security purposes, in the light of the dangers lurking from outside.

The desire for security as a prime motive was augmented, among part of the Israeli public, by the belief that in the light of the Arab revanchism Israel was obliged neither to gratify the Arab states by withdrawal nor to go out of its way to appease them. It was also feared that even a complete withdrawal to the former lines would fail to placate them and that such a move would only be exploited to renew the onslaught. Furthermore, it seems that the appeal for nonwithdrawal in the name of historical rights has been abetted or at least facilitated by the apprehension that a pullback would prove ineffective.

Israel is in the grip of a terrible dilemma. There can be no peace in the foreseeable future without withdrawal; on the other hand withdrawal, especially complete withdrawal, may increase the probability of war. Even if Israel should win such a war, it would cost dearly in human life.

Israelis are now more aware than before the Six-Day War of the suffering of the Palestinians as a result of the Zionist enterprise, but they regard this suffering as an unavoidable evil. Many Israelis tend to admit that Israel bears responsibility and guilt as the cause of the dispute, since the Jews came to settle lands on which Arabs already lived, and not vice versa. But if Israel bears the primary guilt for the dispute, Arab reaction and conduct constitute even greater sins. The balance has been redressed in Israel's favor, justifying a firm stand on its part.

The attitudes of both sides have been affected by a tendency toward greater symmetry. Before the Six-Day War the conflict was pronouncedly asymmetrical and this was reflected by a lack of parallelism between the objectives of the two sides. The extreme objective of eradication of the national entity of the enemy was advocated only by the Arabs. The aims of greater Zionism and territorial expansionism were on the wane in Israel before the Six-Day War and there was readiness to accept the armistice boundaries as permanent borders.

Even before the Six-Day War it was asked whether an asymmetrical dispute could endure for long and whether the unqualified nature of the Arab objective would not render the Israeli aims more extreme. There would seem to be a logical foundation to the hypothesis that if one party to a dispute persists in demanding the whole, while the other side demands only a part, the latter will eventually increase his demands.

This tendency became evident in Israel in the demand for expansion of borders, and an opposite trend would appear to have operated among the Arabs, i.e., the move to relativity in their stand, though this relativity was not free of the previous absolutism, as transpires from the third explanation.

The harsh circumstances of the dispute aroused on the Israeli side a desire to take a more comforting view of the situation. The urge to detract from the fierceness of Arab opposition appears in Israel in both moderate and extreme circles: among the moderates in the view that by a political step, such as withdrawal to even less than the 1967 lines, it is possible to appease the Arabs; among the extremists it takes the form of the conviction that the Arabs will eventually acquiesce in extremist Israeli nationalist demands, and hence of the sanction for intensification of demands.

Prior to the Six-Day War this tendency to unrealistic "subjectivism" was more prominent among the moderate circles. They claimed that the Arabs did not yearn for Israel's destruction, this being merely a figment of the Israeli's imagination and that they could easily be appeased by a series of measures which would remove the main obstacle to peace. For instance, at one time military government and the official policy toward the Arab minority in Israel were depicted as the chief stumbling block in the way of a peaceful settlement, and it was sometimes suggested that Israeli acceptance and absorption of Arab refugees would bring in its wake peace, or that Israel's refraining from retaliatory action could bring about a radical change in the situation. The Arabs did, in fact, condemn Israel for these actions but this was a means of slandering it and not a condition for acceptance of its existence, as believed in moderate circles. However, paradoxical as this may sound, this moderate Israeli view implied a certain contempt for Arab statements, and it was based on the presumptuous belief that it reflected the "true" Arab stand more faithfully than did the Arab leaders themselves.

Detachment from reality and concentration on an inner world are symptoms of the disease known in children as autism, and a corresponding phenomenon would appear to exist in societies as well. In such a case, satisfaction at one's own idealism takes precedence over sober assessment of reality. The Six-Day War, and even more so, the two weeks preceding it, delivered a stunning blow to Israelis, which led to reexamination and greater awareness of the situation which had formerly been ignored. These circles suddenly realized that their refusal to admit the intransigence of the Arab stand reflected detachment from the true facts. Their former views and the period in which they had advocated them now appeared to be a frivolous reverie. The measure of disagreement within Israel was reduced for a time and the gravity of Arab intentions was universally recognized. This was a moment of national truth and autistic tendencies were abandoned. But since the latter had been rooted in ideology and temperament, its abandonment turned out to be merely transient. These circles readopted their autistic approach and once more turned a blind eye and deaf ear to Arab attitudes.

* * *

The Six-Day War altered the nature of the gap between the adversaries. The Arab attitude, which was homogeneous, now became more heterogeneous: the extremists still adhere to their old objective of destroying Israel, while the moderates agree at most to the pre-War borders but not to concessions in the Golan Heights, East Jerusalem, the Jordan Valley or Sinai.

Between the extremists and the moderates lies the center of gravity of the Arab stand, which demands a return to the Partition boundaries as the basis for a settlement, and makes additional demands for the return of the Palestinians. Practically speaking, this stand is still closer to extremist attitudes.

On the Israeli side, the focus is on non-withdrawal to the old borders and the demand for significant boundary alterations. Moderate elements in Israel tend to agree to the previous borders or something approximating them. The fact that moderates, who in both camps are located on the fringes, have come closer to one another, is of limited practical significance, since the centers of gravity are still far apart.

Only those Israelis intoxicated with their own grandeur can seriously believe that Israel can help the moderate Arab elements to prevail and become the determining factor in the Arab camp. Paradoxically enough, it is more likely that continuation of the present situation will impel moderate Arabs to adopt more extreme attitudes, rallying to the focal point of the Arab stance.

It is, of course, also possible that some of the Arab extremists will take up a stand closer to the center, perhaps for tactical reasons. It is the disparity between the two centers that has prolonged the dispute and frustrated hopes of resolving it. It seems to me that, in the light of the events of the past and of the asymmetry inherent in the dispute, there is justification for the demand that the Arabs take the first step to bridge the gap and display greater understanding of Israeli sensitivity.

14

A Dream of Israel

As in a dream, I see Israel emerging from the crucible of the Yom Kippur War cleansed of dregs and impurities, healed of complacency and smugness, balanced in its judgment and of lucid vision, with its feet planted in the soil of reality, sober yet idealistic, calm, firm and united by the bonds of common destiny.

An Israel for which the War of the Day of Atonement will be a Day of Judgment—of views, illusions, concepts, ideologies, and customs.

An Israel squarely facing its problems without embellishment, and mature enough to overcome psychological urges to adorn reality, and thus cultivate delusions. An Israel which finds that strength which leads to firmness and wisdom. An Israel which realizes the full intensity of its rejection by the Arabs, and understands that for Arab nationalism to reconcile itself to Israel's existence is so radical a change in outlook, and so complete a transmutation of values, that it is almost comparable to asking Zionism to abandon the idea of Jewish statehood.

An Israel which realizes that the moderates among the Arabs, even though they may not wish for its destruction as a political entity, do not agree to more than a mutilated and emaciated Israel; not so much because of viciousness but because Israel's reduction to such a state is the inevitable consequence of their demands, which they consider just and legitimate. The Soviet attitude is similar.

An Israel aware that its enemies do not look forward to its sudden collapse as an *event*, but rather hope for its decline and demise as a *process*, with UN resolutions serving as an instrument to achieve it.

An Israel conscious of the fact that its enemies have endeavored to present their objectives to the world as being limited, and have convinced many, while Israeli spokesmen have aided them in doing so by expounding to the world the view that Arab attitudes have changed after the Six-Day War and a new mood prevails among them. Today, Israel needs to concentrate its diplomatic efforts on exposing Arab attitudes for what they are and on making their implications understood. Thus, Israel has to negate its own previous argumentations.

An Israel that comprehends that it is facing a protracted struggle, yet nevertheless understands that however bitter the conflict may be, it is not eternal. Situations may arise which will impell the Arabs to adopt a different attitude. However, an Israel that knows that there is no sense in proclaiming the imminent end of the conflict long before this event is actually in sight. A driver is right in sounding his horn when he approaches a crossing; but there is no point in blowing the horn far from the intersection, and especially to sound it all along the road, on the assumption that blowing the horn will bring the crossing closer by the magic of a "self-fulfilling prophecy." He who prophesies peace before its time may bring war.

An Israel reasonable and open-minded enough to listen to explanations of the severity of Arab attitudes to it without boggling, without dismissing such an analysis as "pessimism," and without seeking relief by burying its head in the sand, and as a result, indulging in the delusion that an armed showdown between Israel and the Arabs is out of the question.

An Israel that is capable of taking a comprehensive view

of the problems faced by the Arabs and the agonies which the conflict presents to them as well. An Israel that does not wave away their statements of aim and, when they act accordingly, does not seek refuge in claiming that they practiced deception and dulled its vigilance.

An Israel that is proud of its strength and its achievements, yet is not inebriated by greatness and remains conscious of its limitations. An Israel that sizes up correctly its position in the international arena—and its predicaments—and knows that its international standing is not to be taken lightly, that endeavors to make its policies appear to others reasonable and logical rather than egotistical and covetous; and presents the policies of our adversaries in a negative light.

An Israel that recognizes that what its situation calls for is not heroism alone but also wise council and sagacity; and which will therefore give serious consideration not only to long-term aspirations and final goals, but also to ways and means, tactics and maneuvers.

An Israel that knows that the plodding, onward march calls for an analysis of past errors; and therefore is ready for a soul-searching self-examination. An Israel in which alongside the accounts of heroic deeds, books will be written presenting the balance sheet of the nation in which researchers will set forth the beliefs and views of the past, recalling what leaders, writers and commentators had to say, and spell out what proved correct and what proved imaginary and misleading.

An Israel that recognizes that political conduct is influenced by the public mood, which in turn is shaped by leaders and opinion-molders. An Israel in which opinion-makers feel that they speak for the record and that a man's standing is not established by statements that momentarily gratify the public, thereby relying on its short memory, but by the lasting significance of these statements. Only thus can a sense of a responsibility be developed, with opportunism and frivolity rendered reprehensible rather than useful. Of course everyone is free to change his mind and review his opinions, but he will do it frankly, pointing out the changes for all to see. Otherwise everybody will eventually return to his old views as these stem not so much from rational considerations as from personal psychology. The division into doves and hawks was not always relevant on the Israeli scene, but "chameleonism" must cease to be a condition for gaining prominence.

An Israel strong, confident, prepared for self-criticism, ready to admit errors and draw lessons from them. There has been, however, one basic misjudgement which I dare point to even at this stage. Since the Six-Day War, Israel has believed—erroneously—that what was on the agenda was a political settlement and that both sides were only jockeying for positions to improve the terms. In actual fact, what was on the agenda, in these recent years, was a competition, each side attempting to blame the other for the absence of a settlement. The Arabs understood it, while in Israel both government and opposition circles shared in this error. The anticipation of a settlement prevented Israelis from presenting Arab attitudes in all their starkness. At the same time, it enabled the Arabs to castigate Israel. Thus, a warped picture of the situation gained currency and many observers came to believe that the war broke out because Israel, in its stubborness and intransigence, had left the Arabs no other choice. Arab propaganda was aided by Israel: on the one hand, by Israeli extremists whose declared position gave Israel a bad name abroad; on the other hand, by those Israeli intellectuals who criticized their own government for its "intransigence." Without help from Israel, Arab propaganda would not have appeared persuasive. Criticism is vital for us and critics are praiseworthy, but they should also be aware of how their words, albeit spoken with good intentions, can be manipulated against Israel.

Israeli moderates were not wrong in presenting moderate aims. They erred in believing that such aims were acceptable to the Arabs. Their criticism of Israel, for not adopting their own policies, made it appear as if Israel was preventing a settlement and peace; and in this they slandered.

Israeli extremists were not wrong in hoping that Arab intransigence might assist them in promoting their aims. They were wrong in proclaiming their extreme objectives because this allowed our enemies to exploit their statements to show Israel in a negative light.

An Israel which understands that the "dignity" which the Arabs gained from their achievements in the war will not only give them satisfaction and release from frustrations, but is equally an incentive for them to make a greater effort and to try again. The reversal of their military fortunes in the second phase of the war is doubly painful to them precisely because it followed so high an initial elation. Renewed reverses may increase Arab hostility. It is rash to conclude that this time the Arabs have become convinced that peace with Israel is inevitable.

An Israel which understands that secure borders are important and that the arguments of those who negated their value were not sound. It is true that ultimate security lies only in peace, but only if it is a peace which spells the end of the conflict, not a mere lull between wars. Israel needs to recognize that such arguments are disingenuous as long as there are no indications that the gap between the Israeli and Arab positions could be bridged and that peace became a practical possibility. Peace is the ultimate ideal solution. The ultimate solution for the prevention of earthquakes may be to "eradicate" them. But until this can be done, we would do well to build our houses so that they can withstand such tremors. Thus, if we cannot ensure lasting peace, let us see to it that we are strong—and strength includes defensible borders.

the force (or, rather, anti-Israel motivation) which had spurred the Arabs to action—to the buildup of military capability—and had inspired in them the daring to activate their forces and initiate hostilities.

That the threat of war existed was noted, if at all, by rote but underlying it was the unconscious conviction that war would not break out, and it was this belief which determined patterns of behavior, obscured vision and served as the background for the surprise.

3. This self-congratulatory approach, according to which all danger had passed, was not confined to the ideological sphere but spilled over the social sphere of "bourgeoisification"—the headlong rush to improve living standards, the general attitude of "every man for himself," frequent strikes, and economic scandals. This insidious mood reached the army as well, apparently affecting military readiness and blunting the creativity and keeness of Israeli military thinking.

4. The claim that everything would have gone off smoothly if military intelligence had given sufficient warning appears to be an attempt to understate the problem. There may be some truth in the bitter evaluation of several military experts that had larger reinforcements been despatched to the southern front and employed in a similar fashion to the armor already located there, Israel's losses would have been even greater. Who knows?

Our doctrine of armor warfare was flawed. Do we really need to be reminded by a Syrian ex-officer (Hithan al-Ayoubi, in a survey in *Shuʾūn Filastiniyya*) that the Army monthly *Maʿarakhot* itself published an article two years ago analyzing the shift in the balance between the tank and anti-tank weaponry? He expressed surprise at Israel's failure to take note of this analysis.

5. Historically speaking, it is ironic to note that our complacent mood was nurtured by both extreme and

moderate elements, hawks and doves. The extremists were convinced of Israel's overpowering deterrent force and believed that the Arabs would eventually come to terms with the expansion of its borders and with its possession of the lands conquered in 1967. These circles were aware of Arab hostility but underestimated the motivation for action inherent in it.

The moderates, who denounced the government and demanded a moderate political policy, "initiative" for a settlement, and a proclamation of readiness for withdrawal and concessions, tended to substantiate their analysis by arguing that there was growing willingness in the Arab countries to arrive at a settlement with Israel, that "new winds" were blowing there, that the Arabs had abandoned the idea of war, and that Israel had nothing to fear because Arab disunity precluded cooperation between Arab states.

Paradoxically enough, the implication of their statements was that even the occupation of Arab territories, which they themselves condemned, was tolerable to the Arabs. They also advocated the theory that the Arab leaders were not serious in their pronouncements that they intended to go to war, and by disseminating this theory they unwittingly fostered the complacent mood.

There is now a degree of hypocrisy in the stand of the former moralizers who once contributed to the general mood by denying the possibility of war and claiming that peace was within reach, and who now condemn the government for its unpreparedness and unreadiness for war.

The delay in issuing a warning and in mobilizing forces was a human miscalculation which may be understandable, particularly in the light of the events of May 1973.[1] Those who now raise an outcry cannot be sure that they themselves would have acted differently. The grave aspect is the erroneous conception, and this was the result of prolonged misjudgment rather than of a single decision taken under pressure. And both the government and the opposition were equally in error.

6. In short, the foundations of the present crisis are our shattered national illusions and concepts, and our predicament is spiritual to the same degree as it is political. It is convenient for Israelis to define it as a political crisis and to suggest that there are technical means of remedying it, through altering procedures and through reorganization (changing the electoral system or replacing the leadership). Such changes may prove useful but this is not the crux of the matter. They are merely instruments, whereas the focus should be the content—the effort to develop a national conception, to conduct a national stocktaking in the light of the newly exposed reality.

7. In the face of the present predicament of our politicians, the intellectuals cannot proclaim their own innocence and hurl accusations at the political parties and their leaders. Unlike the ancient prophets, today's Israeli intellectuals did not denounce the people for their detachment from reality, for steeping themselves in illusions. It may be stated in their defense that where Israel's security situation was concerned, we were all led astray by the smug statements of politicans and military men ("Our situation has never been so good," "No war is to be anticipated," "The Suez Canal is the best anti-tank ditch in the world") but this cannot exonerate us.

If the main flaw is moral and derives from the mode of life of the leadership, then those denoted "intellectuals," the writers of articles and commentators should search their own hearts and examine whether they themselves acted with intellectual integrity and avoided opportunism and superficiality.

8. It is painful to realize that the moral stocktaking by the Arabs after the Six-Day War was more profound and incisive than any manifestations of soul-searching by the Israelis after the 1973 War, even though the Arabs also

published a considerable amount of trivia. I am not conducting this comparison in order to offer the Arabs as a shining example but merely to establish the facts.

After the 1948 War the Arabs tended to focus the blame on individuals (Farouk, Abdullah), but in 1967 they went beyond this primitive stage of individual incrimination and sought the flaws in basic social and national phenomena. We, however, are still bogged down in that stage and are deluding ourselves into thinking that negligence was displayed by only a few individuals and that the blame ends there, so that we can indulge in a collective exercise of exculpation.

This attitude diverts attention from the search for the more fundamental factors responsible for the omissions of the "guilty" parties. Obviously, those office-holders who were found negligent should most certainly bear the consequences, but we cannot content ourselves with this step.

It is the task of the Agranat Commission,[2] as a judicial committee, to determine who was to blame, but it seems to me that there is urgent need to analyze the conceptions underlying the errors in evaluation and in our national behavior and to seek their origins. The main task now facing the Knesset (Israel Parliament) Foreign Affairs and Security Committee is to make a national reckoning and to assess the conceptual errors, examine their development and formulate new national conceptions appropriate to Israel's situation.

The members of this Committee may find it gratifying to hear intelligence officers and senior government officials divulge "secrets" to them, but they should realize that this renders their task passive and confines it to mere querying and requests for additional information. What is needed today is initiative and activity on their part; they should become the focal point of reassessment of the general national situation with all its implications and should formulate the new political program.

9. The Arabs have devoted immeasurably greater thought to the problems of the conflict with Israel than have the Israelis. The more serious Arab attitude, as reflected in the post-1967 reckoning, derives from the extensive Arab literature on the dispute, which Israelis, including orientalists, have tended to underestimate. Thus the prevalent view was that the Arabs tend to be irrational, and the fact that they finally planned and carried out an attack in rational fashion came as a great surprise.

The Knesset Foreign Affairs and Security Committee should also take on the urgent task of promoting research on the Arab-Israel dispute at the universities, which could aid Intelligence research.

10. The Arab-Israel dispute, which holds out so many challenges to Israel, should have become a key factor in our educational network, providing the stimulus for excellence and model conduct. A nation like Israel, finding itself in such grim conditions, must develop its inherent good qualities and abilities, and bringing this about should be the task of our educational authorities. Instruction in schools in the history of the conflict could help disseminate information on Israel's existential circumstances and thus prepare our young people for their destiny and the ordeals they may one day undergo.

Study of the dispute and fair discussion of the Arab grievances and claims could help bolster our spirit and our firm stand. If the youth were prepared in our schools in this fashion we would not now be witnessing certain manifestations of disheartenment.

There are undoubtedly many teachers who have considered this problem seriously but in general the negligence of many years has contributed to the alienation of a part of our young generation from the problems of the state, the dispute and their own destiny.

This educational omission is no less serious than the

military omissions and causes long-term harm since it cannot be overcome in a short time and by administrative means. Where is the textbook according to which the history of the dispute is taught? What instructions have been given to our teachers on this vital issue? Is it really enough to preach the need for peace in schools without engaging in discussion of the dispute?

In fact, the educational network would seem to have become a negative factor since it nurtured hopes which could not be realized and aroused frustration and depression. Again it seems to me that the Knesset Committee for Education and Culture should study the educational problems deriving from the situation and urge the Ministry of Education to do its duty in this sphere. National rehabilitation should commence in the schools.

11. In order to act wisely in this dispute, and to be able to conduct negotiations with the Arabs, we must understand their standpoint. They have devoted considerable thought to formulating their stance, systematizing their ideology and explaining it to the outside world. The more moderate elements among them now favor the "theory of stages" but the stages have changed since this theory was first propounded by Bourguiba (and his predecessors).

The first step in this plan is to force Israel by military and political means to contract to the pre-1967 borders, and thus undermine her image as a success story. This, they hope, will weaken the ties of Diaspora Jewry to Israel, detract from their preparedness to immigrate and to invest money in the country, and cause internal dissension in Israel itself. It should be noted that the Arabs have long anticipated the crisis now taking place in Israel, and have analyzed and described it.

The second step toward Israel's annihilation is social, to be brought about by internal developments in Israel. These are to be the outcome of the impact of the first stage and of the return of Palestinians who once resided in Israel's territories to receive their lands. The Jews now living on these lands will be obliged to evacuate them (including Lydda, Ramleh, Beersheba, etc.) and this will create chaos which will lead to emigration and the gradual eradication of Israel.

Thus the Arabs and the Palestinians are able to claim that they do not intend to destroy Israel, since, according to this viewpoint, they will not destroy it by blood and fire; it will rather disintegrate and the united democratic Palestinian state will be established on its ruins.

This theory is not conclusive, and need not constitute an obstacle to negotiations, but it is important to recognize it in order to formulate our stand and plan our tactical moves, and to exploit it in propaganda and in negotiations.

12. It is very possible that Sadat truly yearns to liberate Egypt from the bondage of the dispute and to arrive at a settlement with Israel in order to devote his attention to improving his country's internal economic situation. But it would be a mistake to halt here without taking into account the fact that he is laboring under two main constraints: firstly, Egypt's claims that it cannot continue the negotiations without the Syrians; secondly, the settlement of the Palestinian problem.

These compulsions could reverse the situation and force Sadat to change direction and readopt a militant stand, although he is fearful of taking such a step since renewed hostilities could wipe out his achievements of October 1973. The Syrians have emphasized that they will never agree to a settlement without Israel's withdrawal from all of the Golan Heights, and they have shown no indications of being ready to content themselves with less.

I have never encountered the commonly bruited Israeli phrase "territorial compromise" in Arabic nor is it evident as an Arab trend. We will be faced with a very serious problem concerning the key question of the Golan Heights—

though this evaluation does not detract from the complexity of the issues of the West Bank and Jerusalem. But the demand that the Golan, or part of it, should remain in Israeli hands has been voiced even by those known in Israel as moderates.

13. It in no way follows from the assessment that the Arab stand against Israel is hostile and intransigent that our policy too should be rigid. It is wise, both politically and militarily speaking, to avoid repaying the enemy in his own coin and to employ against him methods differing from his own.

We should adopt flexible methods and stratagems and display readiness for concessions, even if this is merely a tactical ploy. The main stumbling block in Israel between 1967 and 1973 has been that our thoughts were concentrated on a settlement rather than on tactics, while the Arabs have behaved in exactly opposite fashion and have discussed extensively the question of political stratagems.

We should adopt a moderate, flexible stand of compromise, and endeavor to make it evident to all that it is our rivals who adhere to unreasonable and intractable attitudes. Zionism succeeded in this in the past, winning its achievements by agreeing to the various partition plans (which were certainly far from ideal). However, in recent years we have abandoned flexibility because every tactical step and proclamation of readiness for concessions takes on ideological significance.

We certainly have historical links to Judea and Samaria, but I believe that realistic considerations should make it clear to us that we cannot maintain the present borders and refuse to withdraw or refuse to abandon settlements.

We should avoid gloomy thoughts and refrain from claiming that the abandoning of a new settlement spells a national disaster. By inflating our hopes we only court a rebuff and future disappointment, and prepare a trap for ourselves. I am not trying to present a particular ideological stance but am merely offering my own assessment of the situation. The viewpoint that we must adhere to the present borders is optimistic in that it assumes that we are politically able to do so. But it is pessimistic in that it implies that the alternative is catastrophe.

On some issues it is necessary to demonstrate readiness to risk the continuation of the conflict and to adopt a resolute stand. Such a stand may strengthen our bargaining position in the negotiations. But it is sometimes also necessary to take the risk of making concessions. Furthermore, in order to be resolute on one question we should be lenient on others. We should recall that the international arena is one of frustration. There is no country in the world that gets everything it wants. Corresponding to the balance of power between nations is a kind of "balance of frustration," influenced by the former but not inevitably reflecting it. Our frustration will be the less if we avoid aspiring to objectives which are beyond our grasp. We must assess our situation and our possibilities without becoming intoxicated by ideologies, aspirations and dreams, and we should always endeavor to view reality in its true dimensions.

14. Our awareness of the need to display readiness for compromise and concession should not derive from the illusion that Arab hostility and malicious intent are on the wane, nor from an attitude of self-deception (like that of several political columnists who claim that concessions entail no risk), but should rather be fostered *despite* our knowledge of the threat involved. We must endeavor to exploit our maneuverability, which is considerable. There are common denominators to the Arab stand but it is not monolithic, but rather consists of several standpoints which contain contradictions and conflicts: between Jordanians and Palestinians, between various Arab states, between different Palestinian circles. We should exploit these differences as well as the rulers' fear of the radicalization of their

societies if the conflict continues. I shall not enumerate all the possibilities and will content myself with one example which is of elemental significance.

15. Israel's proclaimed attitude of unwillingness to enter into negotiations with the Palestine Liberation Organization seems to me misguided. The PLO has been recognized by close to 100 states and we must avoid burying our heads in the sand when faced with this fact. Nor would PLO participation in negotiations inevitably constitute Israeli recognition of this organization as the sole representative of the Palestinians.

The argument that we cannot negotiate with the PLO as long as it advocates the destruction of Israel is basically a reasonable one. But the PLO has succeeded in creating the vague impression throughout the world that it has changed its stance, and now recognizes Israel and agrees to co-existence.

One of the subterfuges it employs calls for a PLO spokesman to make an announcement in this spirit, which is promptly denied as unauthorized by a second spokesman. Another stratagem is to proclaim that they agree to make peace with us, but that such a peace settlement "is not the end of the conflict." The world does not understand these tactics. Furthermore, the Palestinians have benefited from the fact that they are able to cite in their support statements made by Israelis who have testified that these organizations have changed their views and are now ready for peace.

This is not the sole instance in which Israelis act to the detriment of their own interests, and Arab propaganda has, to some extent, based itself on statements made by Israelis; in fact, the best Arab propagandists are Israelis. This too is a worthy subject for the perusal of the Knesset Foreign Affairs Committee.

I believe that it would be wise to proclaim our consent in principle to conduct discussions with the Palestinians, headed by the PLO, while voicing the demand that the written settlement specify that it marks the end of the dispute (what kind of peace agreement would it be if the dispute continued to exist?) and be regarded as signifying recognition of coexistence with Israel.

Such a specific statement would violate the principles of the PLO as contained in its covenant and its persistent rejection of Security Council Resolution 242. If it agrees to accept these qualifications and conditions, this is all to the good since it will mean that a settlement is possible, even though we may have to purchase it by concessions. If it refuses to accept these conditions, as I believe it will, we will gain thereby.

An attitude of readiness to negotiate with the Palestinians would facilitate the adoption of a more accommodating position by the Egyptians. It could prove important vis-à-vis Jordan we well, since the possibility of negotiating with the PLO would provide us with greater maneuverability against Jordan, which has never before had to fear rivals.

16. Furthermore, when the Geneva talks are resumed, we should even demand that discussion of Palestinian demands precede negotiations with the Arab states, possibly in contradiction to the intention to postpone the "solution of the Palestinian problem" to the very end, after reaching an agreement with the Arab states.

We must be wary not to be drawn into a creeping process of making concessions, lest we find that, after having satisfied the Arab states, we are yet confronted with far-reaching Palestinian demands. We must claim that we cannot agree to concessions before we know the final limits of the demands. Thus we can demonstrate the extremity and absurdity of the Arab demands. We should not permit the definition of "Palestinian rights" to be the subject of bartering during the negotiations, but must demand that they be defined at the beginning of the discussions or even earlier.

17. The discrepancy between our position and that of the Arabs is perhaps so great as to preclude any true agreement. In the face of the extreme Arab demands, and in the light of the views of Israelis, including moderates, on the maximum limits for concessions, it would be an almost unbelievable miracle if we succeeded in bridging the gap in a final settlement of peace.

Those Israelis who claim that peace would now prevail if we had only taken their advice, are deluding themselves and others. A flexible sophisticated approach will help us to stand firm in the face of the difficulties which still lie ahead.

Notes

1 The concentration of Arab troops along the borders in early May 1973 was correctly evaluated by Israel Intelligence as not being indicative of an immediate threat of war.
2 The Agranat Commission (named after its chairman, Shimon Agranat, third president of Israel's Supreme Court) was appointed in November 1973 to inquire into the shortcomings of Israel's preparations and conduct of the war. The other members of the Commission were a Supreme Court judge, the State Comptroller and two former chiefs of staff.

16

Israel in the Face of Present Arab Policy

Basic to the molding of Israel's policy are the Arab positions summarized below.

The Arabs tend to divide into two phases the process of attaining their objectives. For Israel's withrawal to the 1949 Armistice lines, Egypt and Jordan would probably agree to *cease belligerency* (Syria is less willing on this point), while true *peace* would remain conditional on the settlement of the Palestinian problem, i.e., the fulfillment of the Palestinians' demands. The practical implication of these demands is the liquidation of Israel and the establishment in its place of an allegedly democratic Palestinian state. The idea of liquidating Israel has surfaced, even though the actual verb "to liquidate" is now rarely used explicity. Its meaning, however, is implied in the demand for the restoration of the "rights" of the Palestinians.

Arab policy of reaching their objective by stages is consistent with another recent trend—that of separating ideology from political and diplomatic tactics. The rejection of coexistence with Israel is enshrined in the ideology, whereas the actual tactics adopted are aimed at realizing this ideology without proclaiming it vocally. This represents an achievement of the Arab political leadership, and is apparently the result of Arab analysis of the conflict's history. Thus, Arab spokesmen tend to refrain from public discussion of the long-range goals, and to concentrate on the more immediate stages which, they consider, would inevitably lead to the accomplishment of the more distant goals.

Arab leftist writers go into detailed theoretical discussion of the distinction between ideology and tactics. It is an irony of history that this should be an indirect contribution by Lenin to Arab nationalist thought, right-wing as well as leftist. The articulation of this approach is found in the writings of Arab Communists, calling for concentration at this stage on the realization of "the right of the Palestinian nation to return to its homeland and determine its fate in it."

In a speech at the National Congress of his party, in November 1971, Khalid Bakdash, Secretary General of the Syrian Communist Party, stated that the expression of the demand for Israel's annihilation in its different verbal forms, such as "the liberation of Palestine," "liberation of the usurped homeland," or "elimination of the Zionist institutions" was "a slogan which is incorrect, unrealistic, incongruous with our class, harmful to our cause and to the Arab nations." He also stated that:

> The solution to the Palestine problem lies in the struggle for the right of the Arab nation to return to its homeland and to achieve self-determination there. At present this slogan is satisfactory. Determining the final, detailed character of the Palestine problem is difficult. The important point is to set a slogan and stimulate a movement for its sake, which will elicit maximal response internally and externally at the same time. . . . It is difficult to delineate the forms of reality which the right to self-determination will assume, or the actual stages of its development (*Problems of the Dissension in the Syrian Communist Party,* Dār Ibn Khaldūn, Beirut, September 1972, pp. 200, 217).

Thus, when the Palestinians, or a majority of them, return to the country (many having been born outside), and the

Jews are forced to restore their former property, new conditions will develop, in which will lie the Arab solution to the problem.

The Arabs have learned a lesson: focusing on ideological objectives is injurious. The October war taught other lessons of a mixed nature. It may be inferred from statements by Arabs that many of them, under the impact of the war, have realized the impossibility of a military solution to the dispute, because of Israel's power; but they also conclude that Israel cannot defeat them thanks to their own strength and the intervention of the Great Powers. On the other hand, confidence in an eventual Arab victory has increased, leading to a certain degree of moderation and flexibility as regards interim steps. The internal weaknesses of Israel, long analyzed by Arab writers, have been confirmed. The image of an invincible Israel has faded. The Arabs have been relieved of their misgivings about a flaw in their make-up, personal and collective, which seemed to thwart a coordinated military effort on their part. Their faith in themselves and their ability to cooperate has increased; in Arab states there is a growing recognition of their own stature in the international system, almost to the point of their aspiring to the role of a "sixth big power." At the same time, the attitude most common in Arab writings is not euphoric, but rather a sober realization that the basic problems of the Arab societies remain unchanged, despite the successes of the Yom Kippur War. The radicals fear that the military achievements (such as they were) which occurred under the existing Arab establishments will obstruct the course of the long-awaited revolution. Center and conservative circles fear radicalization in Arab societies as a result of internal difficulties and the continuation of the Arab-Israel conflict.

In short, generally speaking, the Arab states may be ready for some kind of settlement with an *emaciated* Israel, assuming or hoping that the reduction in size will weaken it.

Israel will suffer shocks and dissension, the Palestinians will continue their fight, and the eventual end will come, whether as a result of all these factors combined with the change in Israel's population balance after the return of the Palestinians, or, if necessary, supplemented by a military blow, the discussion of which at present would be, from their point of view, damaging.

Throughout the course of events the Arab position has evinced a considerable degree of consistency, combined with a trend toward *moderation* in the *presentation* of the Arab case, but *not* necessarily in its contents. Arab behavior in the conflict has been rather *rational ;* they have adjusted to situations they could not change, and thus postponed the implementation of their ultimate objective. In this manner they have escaped the cognitive dissonance between their ideology in the conflict, which focused on the idea of liquidating Israel, and their inability to carry it out. However, it should be pointed out that their ideology, excluding some of its wild offshoots, was relatively rational. They both thought and acted rationally. This fact makes it difficult to isolate any possible political arrangement from the entrenchment of ideology in the Arab stance.

Israel's Policy

In the face of the Arab challenge two political approaches emerge in Israel. I shall polarize them for the sake of presentation (despite the risk of oversimplification). They are less dichotomous and their differences more relative than their respective adherents will concede.

1. *The first position,* more ideologically based, conceives of only *limited withdrawal ;* in political jargon this attitude is termed "hawkish." Its proponents are alive to the internal perils which would beset an emaciated Israel, and more so to the dangers to its very existence from without were it

indeed to make major withdrawal. Therefore, proponents of limited withdrawal advocate that a line of consolidation be delineated, from which no further withdrawal be made regardless of circumstances. In all versions of this concept the line runs at a considerable distance from the pre-1967 armistice lines.

2. *The second position* is more pragmatic. Called by some "dovish," it recognizes the need for *more considerable withdrawal,* even approaching the pre-1967 lines. It cherishes the hope that in return for such concessions a permanent settlement with the Arab states may be achieved, and that the support and aid of the United States could be enlisted to underpin such a settlement.

Let us examine the basic assumptions of these two views.

The *first position* underrates the significance of Israel's international problem if it sticks to the present borders. Some of its proponents believe in the possibility of mobilizing support for their position among those US circles inclined to a stronger stance toward the USSR. They are pessimistic with regard to the possibility of reconciling the Arabs to Israel's existence, and optimistic about the chances of Israel's survival within the present, more defensible borders. Inspiration for this position is derived from national, Zionist and religious values, and from the great incentive of believing that there is no other choice.

The *second position* underrates the vehemence of the Arab position and its persistence, and is thus more willing to make concessions and to withdraw. It is more pessimistic about the effect of international isolation on Israel's capacity to resist, and optimistic about the chances of bringing the Arabs to a settlement under pressure of the interests which will emerge in the course of the negotiations and the influence of international powers.

The *weakness of the first position* is that it allows a narrower range of political maneuver and tactics, since any tactical posture or withdrawal are seen as tantamount to a sacrilegious desecration of Zionist ideology. Moreover, it tends to view withdrawal as catastrophe, thus rendering more disastrous the result of withdrawal if this should eventually become necessary.

The *weakness of the second position* is in the illusions it harbors about the Arab position, and its lack of appreciation of the importance of those national values cherished by the holders of the first position, branding them as "myths." Adherents of this position tend to disregard the fact that they may eventually be in greater need of these values (or myths), in order to survive within the shrunken borders which they are ready to accept, and the internal shocks which may ensue from their realization. Even an Israeli existentialist approach needs Zionism, and even Judaism.

I believe that what Israel needs is a policy which combines both positions—the national ideological strength and recognition of the gravity of the Arab challenge inherent in the first view together with the pragmatism and flexibility of the second. At first sight this combination may seem contradictory, since recognition of the intransigence of the Arab position allegedly necessitates a rigid stance on Israel's part and a refusal to withdraw (as if flexibility on its part were dependent on a similar flexibility from the other side).

The required combination in fact implies a considerable degree of political wisdom and maneuverability which assumes, on the one hand, a recognition of the grave dangers to us in the Arab position, and, on the other hand, the ability to avoid giving every concession and tactical step an ideological significance. This solution is complex, and cannot be briefly described in detail, since its pragmatic nature requires the concrete treatment of each problem as it arises.

Furthermore, I believe that after a hard diplomatic struggle and a withdrawal, Israel will have to stand put at some line and consolidate. But a willingness to compromise and make concessions should precede this stage, and will facilitate consolidation along whatever lines are accepted. In other words, we may finally have to adopt the policy of "limited withdrawal," and it is that which will predominate, but it should be attained by a more pragmatic approach. A stance of refusing to make concessions down the line may be damaging; concessions on secondary—though important—matters of borders will facilitate the adoption of a firm stand on the basic question of national survival. Although these concessions will worsen our security situation, we shall need them both for internal purposes—for the sake of national unity, to refute the doubters who may maintain that "Israel did not try" to meet the Arabs half-way, and for external purposes—to ensure support and aid.

Trying ordeals may await us in the future. Let us hope that the fools' paradise in which we lived before the Yom Kippur War has died with its victims. One of the chief illusions of this pre-war complacency has beed shattered, namely that Israel was no longer struggling for its existence, whether because of its tremendous military strength or because the Arab position had mellowed. I believe circumstances will undermine a second illusion, which is popular today since it fulfills a psychological need—that flexibility and initiative in the previous period could have led to a peace settlement with our neighbors, despite their rejection of a partial settlement, let alone peace, with Israel. Such a belief constitutes an obstacle to a firm upright stance on our side. Drawing far-reaching conclusions from the disengagement agreements would be a mistake, since in both cases Syria and Egypt were anxious to reach an agreement which would nullify the Israel Defense Forces' achievements in the wars of 1967 and 1973. Israel had no practical alternative but to agree. However, the Geneva negotiations, should they resume, may stall soon enough, since Egypt and

Syria will demand considerable withdrawals, including the abandonment of all the Golan settlements and its evacuation by Israel. The tragic fact will be revealed that the gap which has in the past, as well as at present, thwarted a settlement, does not lie solely between the positions of the extremists on each side, but rather between those regarded as moderates in their own camps.

The Arab separation between ideology and tactics is not only proof of political wisdom, but also makes it possible for them to hold negotiations with us. This was impossible when their position obligated them to link every step *explicitly* with the final goal of our liquidation; at present, they are able to agree to a temporary accommodation. We must act so that such an accommodation, by force of the facts which will develop from it, and the US financial, technical and other inducements to the Arabs, combined with pressures on them, will limit their latitude of action and frustrate their continuation of the conflict. It is precisely this eventuality which they fear, and discuss, and which was the chief subject of debate at the 12th Palestinian National Council, held in June 1974. The practical resolution of these matters will form the basis of the ongoing political struggle between Israel and the Arabs, and perhaps of any peace in the distant future.

17
The Debate at the Twelfth Palestinian National Council, June 1974

Following the Six-Day War the Palestine Liberation Organization (PLO) and its affiliates rejected a political solution to the Arab-Israel conflict, and the establishment of a Palestinian state limited to the West Bank. In the wake of the Yom Kippur War of October 1973 and the initiation of agreements between Israel and Egypt (and later Syria) on the disengagement of forces these organizations were confronted with the problem of what should be their stance toward the Geneva negotiations.

Two basic schools of thought emerged, one taking a positive view of participation in the negotiations, and the other a negative view. The question was a public and political one, and the debate and controversy received wide coverage in periodicals, inter alia in the form of a revealing symposium between the heads of the fedayeen organizations.

What follows is a summary of the arguments raised by both sides, some of it adhering closely to the original material and some being additional supplementary matter. Familiarity with these arguments and an understanding of the concerns of the Palestinian organizations and their tactics are necessary elements in our response and in the formulation of our policy, since such a policy must in part attempt to counter certain of the trends implicit in the PLO's stance.

Argumentation of those Favoring Participation in the Geneva Conference

1. The PLO's refusal to participate in the Geneva negotiations will leave the field clear to Jordan as the sole Arab claimant to the West Bank as well as to the Gaza Strip, areas which may pass under its sovereignty if a settlement is in fact reached. Jordan will use force to liquidate the fedayeen presence in these areas, as it has done on the eastern bank of the River Jordan, and Lebanon will be their last resort; Lebanon, too, in the wake of a settlement, might tighten its control and prevent the fedayeen from acting against Israel. In the absence of military action against Israel the fedayeens' *raison d'être* will cease, as eventually will the organizations themselves. Taking measures to prevent the West Bank from falling into Jordanian hands is therefore a vital imperative for the fedayeen and the PLO.

2. By its refusal to participate in negotiations the Palestinian position reverts to its traditional intransigence. The history of the Palestinian movement teaches that extremist positions courted misfortune, as proposals which at first had been rejected subsequently became keenly sought objectives. Negotiations would facilitate consolidation of the gains of the Yom Kippur War, whereas failure to exploit them would constitute a major default. Should the Israel Defense Forces withdraw from some areas, the Palestinians would take their share in the resultant profits. Revolutionary wisdom commands that no achievement, however small and problematic, be turned down, as long as it involves a weakening of the adversary and strengthening of the revolutionary's position. The objective is to be attained in stages, the first of which is the establishment of a "national authority" in every area from which Israel withdraws, provided no commitment be given, or circumstances develop, to prevent continuation of the struggle toward the final ob-

jective—Israel's destruction and the establishment of a Palestinian state. Thus, it is considered worthwhile making some effort for even limited gains within this longer-term perspective.

3. Israel will undoubtedly demand a settlement which will safeguard its security, and involve an Arab commitment to end the conflict. This should not cause undue worry. The continued struggle against Israel will be nurtured by the facts of reality, such as the resultant change in the balance of power, rather than by any formal settlements. The blow to Israel's status entailed by a withdrawal to the 1967 lines, and even more so to the Israelis' self-confidence, will be such as to shake its very foundations. Israel's image as a success story will be shattered, and as a result Jews will cease to immigrate to the country and invest their money there. Signs of this development have already become evident in Israel's present situation. The country's expansion during the 1967 war has become a hindrance to it; in the words of the Arab saying, "When God wishes an ant to die, he causes her to sprout wings." The wings which Israel sprouted during the Six-Day War will lead to its downfall. Israel's relinquishment of the far-flung boundaries to which it has grown accustomed will undermine the Israeli population's confidence of a secure future. Furthermore, even if Israel does withdraw to the 1967 lines, the Arabs will still be able to claim that the Palestinian issue is not yet settled; they will be able to maintain their demand that Israel withdraw to the boundaries of the 1947 Palestine partition resolution and that all the Palestinians formerly residing within the area be allowed to return and receive their property. Thus, a settlement will not terminate the conflict.

4. The tenuous hold of the PLO on the West Bank has hitherto been a point of weakness. The inhabitants of the West Bank undoubtedly rejoiced at the achievements of the fedayeen and wished them luck, but in the PLO's concept

of war against Israel to the bitter end it is implied that the inhabitants of the West Bank will remain under Israel's rule until the final victory is attained. The West Bank's inhabitants have found it difficult to reconcile themselves to this idea. Thus, the only other possibility open to them has been to hope that the West Bank would revert to Jordan and thus relieve them of Israeli rule. Jordan therefore has many adherents among West Bank residents. Moreover, pejorative PLO allusions to a Palestinian state on the West Bank, such as "statelet," "Falestinistan" or "the emaciated entity" *(al-kiān al-hazīl)* imply contempt toward its residents. Accepting Palestinian authority on the West Bank would close the gap between the PLO and West Bank residents; such a policy would attract the population toward the PLO, which would come to be regarded as the people's representative. (As far as the PLO is concerned, practical expression of this trend is found in the appointment of four persons, deported from the West Bank, to the PLO Executive Committee, which was reconstituted at the 12th Palestinian National Council (June 1–9, 1974). This step also indicated to West Bank leaders that a political future is reserved for PLO supporters alone.)

5. It is important that the Palestinians be integrated into the mainstream of Arab nationalism, as represented by Egypt, even if they are forced to pay for it by going to Geneva. They must not refuse Egypt's entreaties for a positive response concerning participation in the negotiations. Even though differences of opinion may exist between the Palestinians and the Egyptians as to the most suitable method, there is unanimity with regard to the final objective, as has been asserted more than once by Egyptian leaders. Adoption of a separate political line by the Palestinians would only weaken them as well as the entire Arab front. Such a trend must be rejected, unless there is absolutely no other alternative and it becomes clear that the Arab states have in fact

TWELFTH PALESTINIAN NATIONAL COUNCIL   273

betrayed the Palestinian cause. This is not the case at present.

6. The Palestinians and the other Arabs should have no fear at all of expressing their readiness to reach a settlement with Israel. Such a settlement, in actual fact, is impossible, since Israel will not agree to withdraw to the pre-1967 boundaries, will not concede the Golan Heights and will not relinquish its rule over Jerusalem, or at least not over the newly constructed Jewish quarters. Egypt and Syria have committed themselves definitely never to agree to any territorial concessions. Resolution 242 will support them, as will the world powers which have promised that they, too, would make withdrawal demands of Israel. Moreover, the Arab condition for a settlement also includes realization of "the legitimate rights of the Palestinians," i.e., fulfillment of UN resolutions: reversion to the 1947 partition boundaries, and permission for every Palestinian who lived in the area of the present Israel to return and receive his property, in accordance with the UN Assembly Resolution of December 11, 1948. Fulfillment of this resolution involves the eviction of Jewish residents from cities and large areas of Israel, so that a large homeless Jewish population would be created. This would bring about the economic, social and political collapse of Israel, without necessitating any acts of violence on the part of the Arabs. The UN resolutions are the instrument by which Israel will be annihilated, and the Arabs should not spoil their chances by rejecting Resolution 242 and demanding Israel's obliteration in the crudest terms. The Arab's greatest mistake was to call bluntly for Israel's destruction. Instead of being directly stated, their objective should become the *by-product* of attaining the more palatable aim of "the restoration of Palestinian rights" according to UN resolutions.

In short, Israel cannot possibly fulfill the demands of the Arabs, including the UN resolutions, even if it is governed by the whitest of those calling themselves doves. Since even the doves in Israel cannot agree to the Arab requirements, including the implementation of UN resolutions, they are nothing but hawks, unaware of their own hawkishness. However, the Israeli internal controversy itself, and the illusion cherished by the doves that a settlement could be reached on their terms, benefit the Arabs, since they serve to aggravate internal tension in Israel and give to it a reputation for extremism and recalcitrance. Eventually the negotiations will come to an explosive end, and the "immobility" which developed in Israel before 1973, and for which the Israelis are now reproaching themselves, will reappear. It is desirable, however, for the negotiations to break off due to Israel's intransigence. A Palestinian refusal to go to Geneva will prejudice Palestinian interests. The Palestinians must attempt to appear reasonable in their demands, anxious to attain a righteous settlement, based on the UN resolutions, and to realize their rights. It would be best not to specify now what these rights are, and to reveal them only when the time is ripe.

7. The Arab side can create difficulties for Israel by requiring an end to Jewish immigration, since it is this which creates Israel's need for expansion. Such a demand will be based on the grounds that it safeguards the security of the Arab states and constitutes a proof of Israel's non-expansionist intentions. In order to compound Israel's difficulties, its agreement to Arab demands must be couched in terms which contradict the Zionist ideal and the very foundations of Israel's existence. Israel will refuse this, and thus facilitate continuation of the Arab struggle.

8. The Palestinian National Council need not formulate an unequivocal resolution favoring participation at Geneva. The PLO has yet to be formally invited to the talks, and any decision on the matter would be premature. Moreover, such a resolution may splinter the organizations and lead to internal strife. It is thus preferable to use a formula

which on the one hand does not seal off the possibility of participation at Geneva, while being on the other hand ambiguous enough to gain the approval of all factions. Opponents of participation at Geneva may be placated by the addition of a clause to the effect that before accepting an invitation to participate in the negotiations, a new Palestinian National Council will be convened.

9. It is true that Resolution 242 refers to the Palestinians as refugees rather than as a people with national rights. It is true that Resolution 242 provides a basis for Jordan's claim that the West Bank should revert to its rule. The problem is merely a legal one, however, and the situation can be rectified by the demand for recognition of the corporate national rights of the Palestinians.

10. The Soviet position recognizes Israel, while adhering to the demand for fulfillment of the UN resolutions including Israel's return to the 1947 partition boundaries. (This position has apparently been made clear to the organizations, through their contacts with Soviet officials.) Although this position contradicts the Palestinian standpoint of obliterating Israel's very existence, for the moment it facilitates a considerable amount of joint action, until Israel's withdrawal to the 1947 boundaries is achieved. As long as this demand is not met, even though Israel should revert to the 1967 boundary lines, there are sufficient grounds for the refusal to recognize Israel and become reconciled to its existence. Even if the USSR were to recognize an Israel within the 1947 proposed borders, the Kremlin cannot ensure the viability of so truncated a state.

Argumentation of Those Rejecting Participation in the Geneva Conference

1. The Geneva negotiations will be based on Resolution 242 of the Security Council. It is true that an amendment to

the resolution to refer to the Palestinians as a nation rather than as refugees will be an achievement, but the actual passing of such an amendment is far from certain. Resolution 242 also constitutes a legal basis for Jordan's claim to the West Bank. Israel and Jordan will therefore jointly oppose any change which would have an adverse effect on both.

2. Resolution 242, although it does not refer to peace or recognition, states that belligerency must cease, and Israel will demand that physical and legal arrangements be made, as well as guarantees, demilitarization and supervisory measures. Even if the Palestinians are given authority over the West Bank, they will either be forced or unwillingly ensnared into a commitment in the course of the negotiations, according to which they will cease their military struggle against Israel. Any talk of continuing to wage war using a Palestinian state on the West Bank as a base can only be self-deception.

3. Participation in the Geneva Conference and agreement to a political settlement, even a temporary one, is a denial of all the resolutions adopted by no less than the ten recent Palestinian National Councils (nine regular sessions and one extraordinary session), and makes a mockery of the Arab ideology in the conflict. The very act of deviation and change in the Arab position, and the willingness to agree to a small Palestinian state will invalidate the national Palestinian vision of a Palestinian state throughout the area west of the River Jordan. This inconsistency will undermine popular faith in the PLO's course of action. It should be borne in mind that a proposal for a political settlement was made in the past, and the PLO and the fedayeen organizations did not then hesitate to reject it flatly. The results of the October 1973 War do not justify such a change at all.

4. A Palestinian state on the West Bank would provide a solution for the local population, since they would be free of the Israeli presence. However, it provides no solution

whatsoever to the real Palestinian problem, since the masses of Palestinians abroad will not be able to settle there. A chasm will open between the two sections of the Palestinian people, those leading a peaceful and normal existence on the West Bank, and Palestinian refugees abroad, the only ones who embody the Palestinian problem in all its gravity. The solution to the Palestinian problem can only be the establishment of a Palestinian state throughout the area west of the Jordan, especially after Jewish withdrawal from all Arab land (including premises built on that land). The returning Palestinians will then come into a rich inheritance, in compensation for their suffering. The establishment of a Palestinian state on the West Bank, on the other hand, will make possible the claim that the Palestinian demands have been fulfilled, and the Palestinian masses abroad will be condemned to eternal exile; the Palestinian struggle would thus come to grief.

5. The PLO can exist only in an atmosphere of continued warfare between Arabs and Jews. Any political arrangement between the Arab states and Israel, which might be supported by the Palestinians, contradicts this prerequisite, and would deprive the confrontation of its urgency. Even a settlement which is considered as a tactical step may become firmly rooted and achieve permanency.

6. A Palestinian state on the West Bank will be caught between Israel and Jordan. Its existence will be enmeshed in a contradiction, since, while it will have been established with the aim of undermining both Israel and Jordan, it will depend on the goodwill of both these countries for the right of its citizens to cross through Jordan to the Arab countries and to pass through Israel to the Gaza Strip. A Palestinian state being landlocked cannot be viable without these two outlets, and the granting of these rights will enable Jordan and Israel to exert pressure on it. Jordan, in particular, will be able to threaten to cut off the Palestinian state from the

Palestinian population still in Jordan, and thence from the Palestinian communities scattered throughout the Arab countries.

Such a situation of dependency on Jordan and Israel would condemn the state to the service of two masters, a satellite obsequious toward both. Geographical reality therefore dooms such a state to misery; certainly it would be in no position to serve as a base for a campaign to defeat either Jordan or Israel. This is a vicious circle from which it would not be able to extricate itself. Practically, as well as legally, the notion that a Palestinian state on the West Bank may be a base to continue the struggle against Israel may prove an illusion. The existence of such a state in the face of the pressure exerted by both neighbors is questionable. Internal problems and disputes within the Palestinian state would facilitate the intervention of these neighbors, to the point of annexation; this is especially true of Jordan. Internal malaise of the Palestinian state may even impel its citizens to request annexation by Jordan.

7. The idea of agreeing to a settlement with Israel (and Jordan) with the intention of later undermining their existence is self-contradictory, since it is presented solely as a tactical step aimed at the attainment of an opposite strategic goal—peace with Israel in order to wage war against it; acceptance of its existence in order to later repudiate it. Tactics are valid only if they are congruent with the strategy they are meant to serve; in this case there is a contradiction, and therefore the entire program is flawed from the outset.

8. The Palestinians should not fear a settlement which the Arab states may reach behind their backs with Israel, thanks to the pressure and inducements of the United States. They should not even fear a confrontation with Egypt, despite its present prestige, which has risen due to the achievements of the 1973 war. The Palestinians are not

alone, and can find aid and support in countries such as Iraq and Libya. Furthermore, PLO threats of personal vengeance against deviants carry considerable weight and influence. The Palestinians are more powerful than they believe, and can change the trend favoring an agreement with Israel, even if this trend is supported by the Arab states. Moreover, deviant states which participate in a settlement with Israel will only hasten their own internal revolutionary processes. No regime will be able to withstand internal resentment at such treason, and the Palestinians will find aid and allies among the opposition within these states.

9. There is no need to fear that after a political settlement, which will place the West Bank under Jordanian rule, the existence and struggle of the Palestinian organizations will die away. Salvation will come through the Arab social revolution, and efforts must be made to achieve this. This is especially true of Jordan, where the regime should be overthrown. A social revolution is bound to come throughout the Arab world, and it will hand over both Jordan and the West Bank to the Palestinian organizations, facilitating the development of the struggle against Israel into an all-Arab war of national liberation. The successes of the regular Arab armies do not render less valid the central idea enshrined in the National Covenant that the struggle against Israel should develop into a protracted people's war.

Resolutions of the Twelfth Session of the Palestinian National Council

Over and above the differences of opinion, the leaders of the Palestinian organizations were aware that the opening of a rift between them would be catastrophic for all. They were conscious of the need to act with restraint and seek the way to an agreement, since all concede that the final objective is the obliteration of Israel and establishment of the Arab Palestinian state in its place. After prolonged discussions, the Council, which convened in Cairo on June 1–9, 1974, adopted a resolution which approved the summary of a compromise earlier achieved between the leaders of the organizations. This summary is a masterpiece of wizardry, a dish to please everyone.

It includes agreement on principle to participate in the Geneva negotiations, while stating that any settlement reached must provide the possibility of continuing the struggle against Israel (and Jordan). It rejects Resolution 242 on the ground that it does not refer to the Palestinians as a nation; this gives the impression that Resolution 242 only suffers from a slight blemish which should be corrected, while in fact the 12th Council rejects all other sections of Resolution 242 as well, such as cessation of belligerency, and recognition of the sovereignty and right of the states to live within secure boundaries. Moreover, the Council's resolution pledges allegiance to the Palestinian Covenant and the "Political Program of the PLO," approved by the 11th Council (January 1973); these two documents vehemently reject any political settlement, including Resolution 242. The Council's resolution also implies agreement to establish "national authority" in any area from which Israel withdraws, so that it may serve as a base for the continuing struggle. On the other hand, a challenge is posed to the Jordanian regime, and the intention to topple it is clearly stressed.

Vague moderacy and explicit extremism are kaleidoscopicly interlinked throughout the Council's resolution. The contents of the resolution are rather a public relations stratagem, meant for internal as well as external consumption. The Council has thereby attained its objective, since any factor, internal or external, Arab or foreign, can find a phrase to suit it in the resolution, and disregard the remainder.

Palestine National Council: Political Program

The following is the text of the PLO Phased Political program (BBC translation):

Proceeding from the Palestinian National Covenant and the PLO's Political Program which was approved during the 11th session held from January 3–12, 1973, believing in the impossibility of the establishment of a durable and just peace in the area without the restoration to our Palestinian people of all their national rights, foremost of which is their right to return to and determine their fate on all their national soil, and in the light of the study of the political circumstances which arose during the period between the Council's previous and current sessions, the Council decides the following:

1. The assertion of the PLO position regarding Resolution 242 is that it obliterates the patriotic *(wataniyah)* and national *(qawmiyah)* rights of our people and deals with our people's cause as a refugee problem. Therefore, dealing with this resolution on this basis is rejected at any level of Arab and international dealings including the Geneva Conference.

2. The PLO will struggle by every means, the foremost of which is armed struggle, to liberate Palestinian land and to establish the people's national, independent and fighting authority on every part of Palestinian land to be liberated. This requires making more changes in the balance of power in favor of our people and their struggle.

3. The PLO will struggle against any plan for the establishment of a Palestinian entity the price of which is recognition [of Israel], conciliation [with it], secure borders, renunciation of the national right, and our people's deprivation

of their right to return and their right to determine their fate on their national soil.

4. Any liberation step that is achieved constitutes a step for continuing [the efforts] to achieve the PLO strategy for the establishment of the Palestinian democratic state that is stipulated in the resolutions of the previous National Councils.

5. The PLO will struggle with the Jordanian national forces for the establishment of a Jordanian-Palestinian national front whose aim is the establishment of a national democratic government in Jordan—a government that will cohere with the Palestinian Entity to be established as a result of the struggle.

6. The PLO will strive to establish a unity of struggle between the two peoples and among all the Arab liberation movement forces that agree on this program.

7. In the light of this program the PLO will struggle to strengthen national unity and to elevate it to a level that will enable it to carry out its duties and its patriotic and national tasks.

8. The Palestinian national authority, after its establishment, will struggle for the unity of the confrontation states for the sake of completing the liberation of all Palestinian soil and as a step on the path of comprehensive Arab unity.

9. The PLO will struggle to strengthen its solidarity with the socialist countries and the world forces of liberation and progress to foil all the Zionist, reactionary and imperialist schemes.

10. In the light of this program, the Revolutionary Command will work out the tactics that serve and lead to the achievement of these aims.

A recommendation has been added to the political program. The recommendation stipulates that the Executive Committee implement this program. Should a fateful situation connected with the future of the Palestinian people arise, the Council will be called to hold a special session to decide on it. ("Voice of Palestine," Cairo, June 8, 1974, quoted from BBC Monitoring Service, June 11, 1974, ME/4622/A/2.)

In a dispatch datelined Cairo, June 8, the INA (1310 gmt June 8, 1974) said: "The Palestine National Council has decided to commit the PLO to call the Council for an extraordinary meeting should a matter of destiny concerning the Palestinian people's future arise. This decision has been added to the ten points submitted by the Executive Committee at the request of the Palestinian forces which reject a settlement. This means the Executive Committee will be unable to participate in the Geneva Conference or to negotiate without going back to the Council." (BBC Monitoring Service, June 11, 1974, ME/4622/A/5.)

List of Palestinian National Councils (or Assemblies)

National Congress and First National Council*—Jerusalem, May 28–June 2, 1964

Second Council (Assembly)—Cairo, May 31–June 4, 1965

Third Council (Assembly)—Gaza, May 20–24, 1966

Fourth Council (Assembly)—Cairo, July 10–17, 1968

Fifth Council (Assembly)—Cairo, February 1–4, 1969

Sixth Council (Assembly)—Cairo, September 1–6, 1969

Seventh Council (Assembly)—Cairo, May 30–June 4, 1970

Emergency Council (Assembly)—Amman, August 27–28, 1970

Eighth Council (Assembly)—Cairo, February 28–March 5, 1971

Ninth Council (Assembly)—Cairo, July 7–13, 1971

Popular Congress and Tenth Council (Assembly)—Cairo, April 6–12, 1972

Eleventh Council (Assembly)—Cairo, January 3–12, 1973

Twelfth Council (Assembly)—Cairo, June 1–8, 1974

* The full title is the First Session of the Palestinian National Council.